Atul Apte

# Java Connector Architecture

## Building Custom Connectors and Adapters

201 West 103rd Street, Indianapolis, Indiana 46290

# Java Connector Architecture
# Building Custom Connectors and Adapters

International Standard Book Number: 0-672-32310-9

Library of Congress Catalog Card Number: 2001094798

Printed in the United States of America

First Printing: April 2002

05   04   03   02        4   3   2   1

## Trademarks

All terms mentioned in this book that are known to be trademarks or service marks have been appropriately capitalized. Sams Publishing cannot attest to the accuracy of this information. Use of a term in this book should not be regarded as affecting the validity of any trademark or service mark.

## Warning and Disclaimer

Every effort has been made to make this book as complete and as accurate as possible, but no warranty or fitness is implied. The information provided is on an "as is" basis.

**Associate Publisher**
Michael Stephens

**Acquisitions Editor**
Carol Ackerman

**Development Editor**
Tiffany Taylor

**Managing Editor**
Charlotte Clapp

**Project Editor**
George E. Nedeff

**Copy Editor**
Nancy Sixsmith

**Indexer**
Chris Barrick

**Proofreader**
Melissa Lynch
Suzanne Thomas

**Technical Editors**
Andrew Yang
Jan Haderka
Raj Rao

**Team Coordinator**
Lynne Williams

**Interior Designer**
Anne Jones

**Cover Designer**
Aren Howell

# Contents at a Glance

# Table of Contents

# About the Author

**Atul Apte** is the President and CEO of iConexio Technologies Inc., a leading application integration framework and tools company based in Ontario, Canada. He has more than 16 years experience in designing and developing real-time distributed systems and enterprise application integration. He continues to strengthen his programming skills in C, C++, and Java—especially with wireless technologies—as well as identify and analyze application integration related design patterns. Since 1999, he has dedicated his career to advancing adapter technology and creating an awareness of its benefits to e-Business.

He is the co-author of another book on EAI, *Integrating Your e-Business Enterprise*, and has authored many published articles and white papers on the topic of adapters and application integration. He currently resides in Georgetown, Ontario, Canada.

# Dedication

*I dedicate this book to my parents Aai and Baba.*

# Acknowledgments

"Without involvement, there is no commitment. Mark it down, asterisk it, circle it, underline it. No involvement, no commitment."

*—Stephen Covey*

This book was possible due the involvement and commitment of many individuals. Personally, it has been wonderful communicating my experiences as an adapter developer in the form of this book. Successful software development requires great teamwork and a collective sense of purpose. Similar attributes are required for publishing a book. After having gone through that process, one develops a lot more respect for every new book that one sees in the bookstore.

I want to thank Michael Stephens of Sams Publishing for believing in the concept and objectives of authoring a book on adapter development. A big thanks is also in order for Carol Ackerman, who will make a great project manager on any software development project. Her management skills kept the momentum going, ensuring constant progress in writing the book.

I want to thank the technical editors of this book Andrew Yang, Jan Haderka, and Raj Rao, who volunteered their time for reviewing my chapters and providing me with valuable feedback. In many ways, it is a humbling experience when others give their time to read what one writes.

Thanks to Lyn Morrison of TogetherSoft for her assistance in getting the license for Together® ControlCenter© tool, which was very useful for developing the example resource adapter.

Last, but not the least by any stretch of imagination, I want to thank members of the CONNECTOR-INTEREST community. Their support and enthusiasm gave me the motivation necessary to complete this book.

# Tell Us What You Think!

As the reader of this book, *you* are our most important critic and commentator. We value your opinion and want to know what we're doing right, what we could do better, what areas you'd like to see us publish in, and any other words of wisdom you're willing to pass our way.

As an Associate Publisher for Sams Publishing, I welcome your comments. You can fax, e-mail, or write me directly to let me know what you did or didn't like about this book—as well as what we can do to make our books stronger.

*Please note that I cannot help you with technical problems related to the topic of this book, and that due to the high volume of mail I receive, I might not be able to reply to every message.*

When you write, please be sure to include this book's title and author as well as your name and phone or fax number. I will carefully review your comments and share them with the author and editors who worked on the book.

Fax:      317-581-4770

E-mail:   feedback@samspublishing.com

Mail:     Michael Stephens
          Associate Publisher
          Sams Publishing
          201 West 103rd Street
          Indianapolis, IN 46290 USA

# Introduction

"One writes only half the book; the other half is with the reader."

—Joseph Conrad, English Novelist

Welcome to *Java Connector Architecture*. It is indeed a privilege to write this book and get an opportunity to share with you my experience with adapters in general, and the Java adapter standard known as Java Connector Architecture in particular. The value of this book depends on its use and your participation in implementing the ideas and concepts and improving the technology and techniques discussed in this book. The target audience includes hardcore developers tasked with the onerous job of integrating applications, architects managing the bigger picture and defining the target architectures, teams evaluating adapters available in the market, and project managers managing the integration project.

The technology of adapters is not well-known. It is not a subject that has a lot of discussion, controversy, or even hype about it. For a change, this technology is rooted deep in the realities of application integration. This is mainly because it is an enabling technology—largely invisible, yet doing the hard work of providing physical connectivity to applications, integrating functions, and exchanging data. The renewed trend of componentization of applications and the increasing need for integration of platforms, applications, and business processes have resulted in a stronger focus on adapters. The need for adapters is generally derived at a design stage of an application development project or is hidden as an integral part of an integration project. This book presents some additions to traditional development methodologies with the intention of providing better tools for project managers to use in planning, estimating, and monitoring projects that need adapters.

In its simplest form, an adapter is a software component connecting two applications and facilitating data exchange and/or functional integration between them. The more complex adapters are capable of maintaining state across different data exchange sessions, can participate in distributed transactions, and support different execution contexts. However, the lack of a common definition for an adapter makes it very difficult to understand, explain, and evaluate the technology.

The central theme and objective of this book is to provide a holistic view of adapter technology, with specific focus on Java 2 Enterprise Edition (J2EE) and Java Connector Architecture (JCA). As such, I have tried to cover most of the related important topics, including a logical architecture for adapters independent of any industry standard or proprietary technology, a development methodology highlighting the challenges in managing adapter development, and an actual adapter implementation using J2EE and JCA standards. The J2EE standard is very comprehensive in its scope, and because this book is more about adapters and JCA, I have included only an overview that highlights the important architectural concepts. I have also included an overview of the Enterprise JavaBeans (EJB) specification to give readers an idea of the component architecture supported by J2EE.

## How This Book Is Organized

To facilitate an easy selection of relevant chapters, the book is divided into six parts, as follows:

Level I is suitable for all readers, and contains an overview of J2EE technology as well as the EJB specifications. This part also has chapters describing the adapter technology in detail, including the role of an adapter in different contexts (for example, EAI, B2B, and Web services).

Level II contains chapters defining the Adapter Reference Model. This model is the logical architecture of an adapter, and is useful for building a robust framework for implementation in different contexts. This section is likely to be of specific interest to architects and experienced developers, although the contents are useful to all developers.

Level III is targeted toward project managers assigned with the task of managing application integration projects in general and adapter development in particular. The additions to development methodology and a list of known pitfalls should facilitate better management of such projects. Various scenarios, including customizing adapters, developing proprietary adapters, and evaluating off-the-shelf adapters are presented, with key milestones highlighted in each scenario.

Level IV gets into the details of implementing adapters using Java technology in general and the J2EE and JCA specifications in particular. The chapters in this section take a step-by-step approach to building a JCA connector using the adapter development methodology described in the previous section. The example connector in this book is an ASCII JCA connector, which can be configured to read ASCII files of various formats and transform them into XML documents. The full source code of the ASCII file connector is included in Chapter 17.

Level V covers many topics on the current technology trends affecting adapter architectures. It also presents the results of a gap analysis between the logical adapter reference model and the JCA 1.0 specifications. It is important to know the differences because it points to the areas where JCA needs further attention and also provides guidelines on how to build adapters on other platforms such as IBM MQSeries, BEA Tuxedo transaction engine, Integration brokers, and so on. This section will most likely be more interesting to architects.

Level VI is composed of appendixes, including a comprehensive glossary of terms used in this book and a set of references for more reading on the subject of adapters and related technologies. It also has a listing of all the source code of the ASCII File Resource Adapter (see Chapter 17).

To facilitate focused and faster reading, I have defined the following three reading tracks—each customized to suit the particular interests of a specific type of reader:

1. Developer track:

    - Level I (Chapters 1, 2, 3)

    - Level II (Chapters 4, 5, 6)

    - Level IV (Chapters 10, 11, 12, 13, 14)

    - Level VI (Chapter 17, Appendixes A, B)

2. Architect track:

    - Level I (Chapters 1, 2, 3)

    - Level II (Chapters 4, 5, 6)

    - Level IV (Chapters 10, 13, 14)

    - Level V (Chapters 15, 16)

    - Level VI (Chapter 17)

3. Project manager track:

    - Level I (Chapter 1)

    - Level III (Chapters 7, 8, 9)

    - Level IV (Chapter 14)

    - Level V (Chapters 15, 16)

You can indeed choose to read all chapters in the sequence in which they appear in the book. The chapters are grouped into sections and ordered to enable you to understand the general concept of an adapter, get an overview of the Java standards applicable to adapters, analyze the adapter reference model, build a Java connector, and prepare for some of the future trends affecting adapter technologies.

## Summary

I sincerely hope that this book helps all readers to better understand the importance of adapters in the world of application integration in general. In today's technology-driven world, integration of business systems is fundamental to any technology projects, especially those related to e-Business. There is a general misconception that adapters are required only for B2B-type projects. The reality is that applications need integration to support all e-Business objectives—not just B2B initiatives. Thus, the publication of the J2EE: JCA specification is very significant as it marks the beginning of the trend to standardize adapter infrastructure and simplify adapter development. I welcome your comments, as I believe that's the best way to improve this book and in the process benefit all readers.

**1**

# Introduction to Adapter Technology

"I am interested in what happens to people when they must adapt to a new world."

—Jean Renoir, Film Director

W e, the humble folks in the world of IT, have to adapt to new technologies constantly. Adapter technology is one such technology we need to confront as part of any e-Business projects and initiatives. Although it is not really new, it is getting a lot of attention for the first time. This chapter presents the concept of an adapter and the different integration scenarios in which adapters are required.

It is quite common to think of e-Business within the constraints of either Web-enabling existing applications or automating supply chains using business-to-business (B2B) software. Although these are valid components of any e-Business initiative, the more difficult scenarios are related to enterprise application integration (EAI) or integrating internal systems. Without integration of end-to-end business processes, e-Business can be only partially successful at best. However, integration is not easy.

Even the best-planned integration efforts sometimes fail, mainly due to the large scope of the problem and the time required for completing the project. The more successful integration projects are based on iterative and incremental automation of business processes beginning with the process with the greatest impact on business. Another important success factor is the selection of component-based technology and frameworks. The technology platform enabling the integration and automation should allow customers to add components and functionality as the scope of the project increases. Adapters are special classes of integration components. They connect the actual enterprise applications with a target environment that may include enterprise applications, middleware, databases, or external gateways.

## Understanding Adapters

The term *adapter* may not be familiar unless you were involved in EAI and system integration projects in the last couple of years. Generally, new terms—especially those related to software concepts—are not supported by a single definition. This is true with adapters as well; however, the concept of an adapter has existed for quite a long time. The term *adapter* has been in use in the computer hardware and other industries to mean a device that enables connection of two incompatible devices.

In order to not complicate and confuse the definition and concept of adapters any further, this book will use a very specific new term: *Application Integration Adapter (AIA)*. In its simplest form, an AIA is a software component that connects two incompatible business applications with the specific purpose of facilitating information exchange.

Information exchange can happen in various different contexts. Some exchanges can happen between databases, whereas others are part of a business transaction. Hence, the definition of an AIA needs to be generic enough to include the different techniques of application integration, yet specific enough to set the right functional scope. This is not easy, and could well be the reason why no single definition exists for AIA.

## History and Evolution of Adapters

Unlike most software innovations, adapter technology was born in the corporate IT shops. The need to connect two business applications has existed for a long time, and generally was driven by the requirement to exchange data between applications on different platforms (operating systems). The typical solution to this problem involved downloading data from an application database and uploading it to another application's database. As the number of applications grew, the relatively straightforward task of moving data between two applications became much more complex. Differences in the data models, architecture, and executing environments (platforms, databases, and so on) added to the complexity.

Proprietary solutions for integration were developed and deployed. The proprietary solutions were mainly in the form of standalone applications or scripts that were scheduled to execute as background processes. These applications and scripts could be regarded as the first-generation adapters. There were no standards or design patterns to follow when developing these first-generation adapters. One common problem was keeping the proprietary solutions upgraded with the various dependencies on operating systems, database products, programming languages, and applications.

As computing environments became more distributed, integrating applications became more difficult—especially between the older generation of applications and the new, more modularized applications. The complexity grew with the Internet revolution when it became a fundamental requirement that all applications be integrated to support the self-service, automated world of e-Business.

Corporate IT departments encountered a common and never-ending problem with homegrown first-generation adapters: It was very difficult to keep track of the changes in various business applications as well as the underlying platforms. Adapter development was not a one-time task. It required a sustained, budgeted effort to keep the applications integrated. Changes in enterprise applications and upgrades to operating systems and databases resulted in upgrades to the homegrown scripts and adapters. Hence, it was a very attractive proposal for corporate users when EAI software vendors began bundling some adapters as part of the EAI platform. This action shifted the burden of keeping the adapters up-to-date to the EAI vendors and, in some cases, package software vendors.

## Adapter Contexts

Most of us are familiar with the concept of exchanging data between two or more applications. Database administrators have been exporting (downloading) and importing (uploading) data between different databases for a long time. This process seems to work well most of the time. Errors sometimes occur during the download and upload tasks, mostly due to bad data or incompatible data models. But for the most part, these errors are handled by massaging the bad data or forcing the data upload by relaxing some of the data integrity rules.

This offline data synchronization method is outdated and not suited to the dynamics of e-Business. In the context of e-Business transactions, real-time or (more appropriately) near-real-time data synchronization is one of the fundamental requirements. This can be achieved only by integrating applications to enable e-Business transactions and manage data exchange. The different application models and the inconsistent points of integration make the task of application integration harder to solve.

Adapters play an important part in three basic contexts or integration patterns. There can be numerous variations of these patterns, but understanding the basic patterns will give you a better perspective of any specific variations, which are not covered in this book. The three basic contexts we'll explore further are the following:

- Data synchronization

- Online services

- Process automation

## Data Synchronization

The main objective of the data synchronization pattern is to ensure the data integrity of all applications participating in a business process. Applications are responsible for maintaining the data integrity of their own databases. The application transactions and the business rules encapsulated in them achieve this data integrity within the context of the individual applications. However, maintaining data integrity across applications without further human intervention is a task easier said than done. For successful automation of business processes, it is important for applications that were not designed to synchronize their databases with other application transactions to be integrated.

The primary role of adapters in this context is to provide a mechanism for opening the application transactions to the outside world. For every application transaction, the action (add, update, delete), the actual data, and the metadata should be made available to all other applications in the business process. The objective of doing this is to enable all other applications to replicate the specific application transaction (action, data, metadata) in their specific application environments.

One of the major challenges of maintaining data integrity across applications is the different data models that are encapsulated by the applications. A single data object, such as a customer object, is invariably implemented as different customer data models—each designed to suit the specific application. Ensuring that any change in one customer data model is replicated appropriately in all applications' customer data models requires a common superset definition of the customer data object. Defining such a data model is now possible with XML; however, the task is not simple.

Chapter 7, "Adapter Development Methodology and Best Practices," outlines a process that could be used in building such superdata models. Adapters capable of enabling data synchronization must have a common definition of data objects in need of synchronization. Invariably, adapter development begins with the creation of the required superdata structures, and implements them using a platform-independent, extendible data description language such as XML.

### Persistent and Transient Data Synchronization

Another important aspect of data synchronization is the difference between *persistent* and *transient* mechanisms. The frequency of data updates and the type of action sometimes drive the choice between the two mechanisms involved in the synchronization process. For example, if the data synchronization is about adding a new data object or deleting the data object, a persistent mechanism is preferable. It enables the adapter to ensure that the data synchronization is achieved when the target application is available. However, if the action is an update action, the number of updates is very high, and the target application maintains only the latest updates, a transient mechanism may be enough. Obviously, persistent data synchronization has overhead, so a careful analysis of the actual integration scenario is always beneficial.

### Rollback Mechanism

Management of distributed transactions is an ongoing challenge of distributed computing. When you're integrating transaction-enabled applications with non-transaction enabled applications, this problem is amplified further. One particular problem is managing transaction rollbacks. If an integration scenario is replicating an application transaction in two other applications or is extending an application transaction by incorporating two more applications into the scenario, a rollback of the entire distributed transaction is indeed hard to guarantee. Hence, the rollback requirements as well as the impact of the inability to support transaction rollback need to be identified very carefully.

Typically, a transaction-processing monitor (TPM) is required to maintain the state of individual application transactions in the context of a bigger distributed enterprise transaction. An adapter rarely performs the job of a TPM; a better option is to develop the adapters with interfaces to the TPM as an option.

## Online Services

The online service context is useful for exposing application functions in the form of easily accessible services. Service-based application architecture has been in use for some time, especially when using object-oriented techniques for developing applications. The emergence of e-Commerce has put a further demand on applications to expose application services and make them accessible to Web applications. Recent technology trends such as Web services and XML are a serious attempt to expose internal corporate applications and external B2B applications as a set of available services accessible over the Internet or an intranet.

Application functions encapsulate business rules and business logic automated by the application. However, these functions are typically available only to the direct users of the application. In a process-centric business world, it is increasingly important for applications to be able to collaborate with each other and access the collective services to automate respective business processes. But collaboration between applications (both old and new) is not an easy task. The concept of a Web service is supposed to make the job of searching for appropriate services and invoking the selected services much easier.

Microsoft's .NET platform enables Web services by supporting SOAP-based service access. Similarly, SUN and other vendors have defined their own service platforms. Adapters have an important part in the Web service domain. If a Web service is about advertising business services on the Internet and making the service accessible to its users, adapters do the job of fulfilling the services by linking internal application functions to the Web service. This architecture and collaboration between Web service and adapters is consistent with the business-modeling view in which business services are outward-facing business process (customer service, and so on), and internal support processes are modeled as business applications.

Generally, there are two types of services: a service that is part of an application and runs in the same address space (embedded), and a remote service accessible by an API or a message-based interface.

### Embedded (In-Process) Service

An *embedded service* is generally used when performance is of paramount importance. Being in the same address space as the application removes any overhead of communication, session management, and so on. However, change management of an embedded service is more difficult. Any change to a service needs to be replicated in all applications where it is embedded.

More stable services, such as security services, are good candidates to be made part of an application. Note that the security service itself may have to access remote databases and communicate with other remote services. But they can invoke the security service much more quickly. A common scenario could be an embedded service communicating with a remote adapter to fulfill its service functions.

### Remote (Out-of-Process) Service

A remote service, on the other hand, is the more common approach for implementing shared services. The current trend of SOAP-based Web services is an example of remote services. Storing service information in a central registry or repository enables finding the location of a remote service. Directory servers such as LDAP are ideal for storing physical location information of services, such as the port number or the message queue name, machine names, and so on. But a central repository is just part of the puzzle. Depending on the scale of the distributed computing environment, a federated name space for a hierarchy of business services may be required. The Universal Description, Discovery, and Integration (UDDI) specification brings together the necessary technologies for supporting distributed business services.

## Process Automation

Process automation comes in various flavors; some are focused on internal workflow automation, whereas others are focused on automating supply-and-demand chains. Regardless of the technology, a major objective of process automation is to close the paradigm gap between business models and technology-based applications. The end game is to have a bidirectional tracing capability between business concepts and technology. It is argued that this would help change management and also facilitate faster technology implementations.

The reality, however, is not as simple or easy as the concept. For business process automation to really work, there has to be a mechanism of connecting both old and new applications to the business processes and other business models. Collaborative tools are making it easier to construct these connections. But for the integration to be really cost-effective and have a serious impact on the bottom line, applications and other collaboration tools must be more tightly integrated. Adapters can fill that gap by providing an event/trigger-handling mechanism as well as maintaining the appropriate state of related business events.

### Event Adapters

Process automation tools are generally event-based, managing the state of a process. Events are related to the current state of a process, and can either initiate a change in the state or communicate the internal state to other processes and their environment. When integrating application to a process automation tool, one of the basic requirements is for the application to process events. Unless an application has a built-in event-handling mechanism, it is difficult to modify the application to include this new functionality. Event-handling capabilities usually require support from an event model in the application framework. Before adapters, the only option was a major rewrite of the application—which is obviously not easily justified.

Event adapters essentially wrap the target application and extend its functionality to include event handling and processing capability. The adapter can map inbound events to specific application actions. This event-action mapping enhances the success of process automation, as well as ensuring execution of proper application functions related to the process events. Many times, a process expects an application to generate events, indicating the completion of an application function, either successfully or unsuccessfully. Event adapters provide this capability whereby application functions and their status can be mapped to process events to be generated and posted by the adapter on the applications behalf. Together, the event-processing and event-generation features of event adapters are critical for integrating applications with business process automation tools.

## Definition of Application Integration Adapter

It is always a good idea to have two types of definition: a logical definition that is free of any constraints imposed by the implementation details and a physical definition that clearly states the physical attributes. The logical definition of an adapter is derived from the concepts discussed in this chapter, whereas the physical definition is derived from the JCA specification.

### Logical Definition

The logical definition of an Application Integration Adapter is as follows: a software component enabling the adapted application to participate and function in one or more integration patterns without significant changes to the application. The primary integration patterns include

- Data synchronization

- Online services

- Process automation

This definition can be extended to include other integration patterns as they evolve. These three patterns are generic and cover most of the e-Business technologies, including mobile computing, e-Commerce, Web services, business process automation, supply chain automation, data integrity, and business intelligence.

Note that the logical definition is not bound by any architecture. This is intentional; our goal is to define the concept of an adapter, regardless of the implementation and its inherent architecture.

## Physical Definition

The physical definition of adapter depends on the technical environment and the specific vendor's adapter architecture. In the context of J2EE, an adapter is known as a *resource adapter*, and is expected to comply with the JCA specification. A reference implementation of the JCA is available for download from the SUN Java Web site, available at `http://java.sun/com/j2ee/connector`. At the time of this writing, the compliance or certification aspect of JCA was still being formalized. As such, a complete definition of a resource adapter is hard to state. Nonetheless, the minimum definition of a resource adapter can be a J2EE component that is compliant with the JCA specification.

Similar definitions can be found in other contexts, such as MQSeries Adapter Offering for MQSeries adapters and other proprietary adapter platforms. However, this book is focused on JCA, and therefore doesn't include physical definitions of adapters in other contexts.

Chapter 7 defines a logical architecture of an adapter. The benefit of the logical definition combined with the logical architecture described in Chapter 4 is that customers can compare adapters from different vendors based on different technologies using a common adapter definition. Not surprisingly, vendors tend to define adapters in physical terms that are more suitable to describe their technology.

## Application Models

To identify the role of adapters in any of the contexts of application integration, we need to understand the different integration scenarios, sometimes referred to as *integration patterns* or *integration use cases*. Regardless of the term used to define the specific integration scenario, the role of the adapter depends on some basic parameters, which are explained in this section. We begin by identifying the most common application architectures or models that you will come across when solving the integration problem. The application models enable you to identify the appropriate points of integration and the challenges in designing the adapters.

The term *points of integration* means the mechanism of accessing application data and services or functions. Some application models are more open and have multiple mechanisms or points of integration. Others are more closed in their architecture, limiting the number of choices for defining points of integration.

## Application Components

Every application has three types of components at the highest level of abstraction: the user interface component, the business logic component, and the database component. Each of these components can be hosted in a different environment, or all of them can be hosted on a single computer. The combination of hosting these components and the technology needed to tie them together is captured in an application model.

## Host-Based Application Model

In a host-based application, all components of the application are hosted on a single computer. A desktop application is an example of a host-based application. The user interface, business logic, and database are on a single desktop. These applications can be multiuser, but they support only one user at a time. Contrary to the general thinking, quite a few small desktop applications are still used, especially where remote site automation is required.

The term *host-based* is generally used in the context of mainframe applications. These applications are truly multiuser and multitasking systems. In the case of IBM mainframes, the user interface is rendered to the end-user on a dumb terminal. Connecting the terminal to the application is a powerful data stream capable of translating user input and display attributes back and forth. Sometimes, dumb terminals are replaced by desktop systems with a terminal emulator.

One obvious problem with host-based applications is the non-availability of points of integration. All components of the application are tightly integrated with each other, with little room for enabling integration in different contexts. A very common solution to integrating mainframe applications is using the data streams to simulate user interaction. The role of a human user is played by an adapter, which navigates the screens, and performs business functions and database updates. Although many sophisticated integration tools have been built using similar techniques, it is not considered an ideal integration solution.

The other end of the application is the database, and integrating mainframe applications by developing adapters for the mainframe database is sometimes preferred. The choice of adapters and the point of integration depend on the integration scenario. If the scenario demands the use of business logic encapsulated in the mainframe application, you have little choice but to use terminal-emulation techniques. Either way, the benefits of integrating the application with the rest of the application outweigh the technical limitations most of the time. Figure 1.1 is a representation of a host-based model.

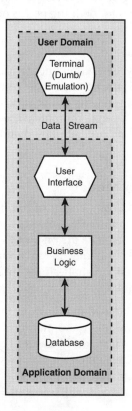

*FIGURE 1.1*   Host-based application model.

## Client-Server Application Model

Most client-server applications are data-centric, meaning the emphasis is more on data integrity and building strong data models. Not surprisingly, database vendors led the client-server application era. In this application model, the user interface component and the business logic component are hosted by a desktop, and the database is hosted on a separate server. Databases are expected to handle the load of multiple users, each with a desktop connected to the same LAN as the database. The middleware connecting the client components (user interface and business logic) to the server component (database) is generally an ODBC-compliant driver.

As the client-server application model has matured, the database technologies have become very powerful; they can support huge numbers of transactions and large numbers of users. However, integrating a classic client-server application with other applications is still not easy.

Probably the easiest solution is to build an adapter encapsulating access to the database server. However, doing so will still exclude the business logic encapsulated by the client components. Also, no data streams are available to emulate the user interactions. In some respects, exposing the business logic of client-server applications is more difficult than mainframe applications. The one exception is when the client components use desktop components, such as ActiveX and COM components. In these scenarios, it is quite possible to build an adapter to access the COM components and get access to applications' functions. However, these components are single-user most of the time, and proper analysis is required before deploying the adapters in a multiuser integration scenario. Figure 1.2 represents a server application model.

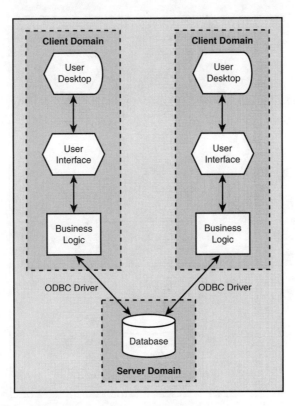

*FIGURE 1.2*   Client-server application model.

## Thin-Client Application Model

As client-server applications were deployed in high data volume and dynamic business environments, a few problems began to crop up. One of them was change management. With hundreds of users connected to the LAN and accessing one central database, any change in the data models or an upgrade to the database software was very hard to manage. Users expected to get notification of the downtime, and IT staff had to precisely manage the upgrades. Even more difficult was upgrading the client components. Making simultaneous upgrades to all the client desktops was a very time-consuming job. Backward compatibility of the databases and their data models was vital.

The thin-client application model was designed to solve some of these problems. The idea was to move more of the business logic from the client to the database. This also had the desired effect on performance. The amount of data moving between the client and server dropped as the business logic that processed the information was moved to the server. From an adapter perspective, the thin-client application model is better because encapsulating the database can expose more business functions, as shown in Figure 1.3.

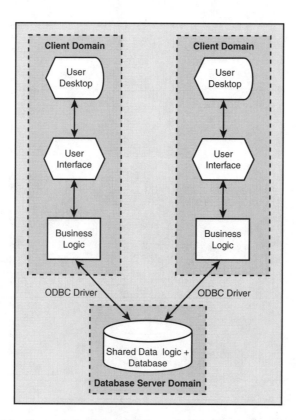

*FIGURE 1.3*    Thin-client application model.

## Three-Tier Application Model

The real breakthrough came with the three-tier application model. The business logic component could now be hosted on a separate server. The user interface components or client components became thinner and more specialized. The middle tier of the application tier hosted the business logic or business services. These services interacted with the database tier and maintained database integrity. On some occasions, the user interface components still accessed the database directly using ODBC, especially when querying large volumes of data. But for most of the transaction-type activities, the business services hosted on the application server were the point of access.

The same point of access is ideal as the point of integration for an adapter to encapsulate. Many times, the application server also includes a transaction management platform or a messaging and queuing platform. Either way, the capability of the adapter to enable three-tier applications to participate in online service and data synchronization scenarios is greater, as shown in Figure 1.4.

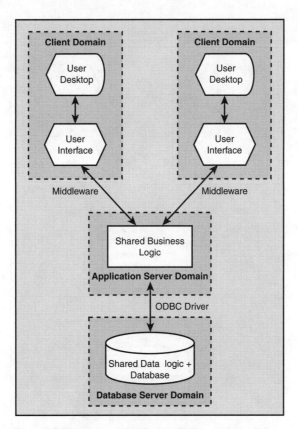

*FIGURE 1.4*   Three-tier application model.

## Web Application Model

Although the Web application model is fairly new, it is important to understand it because in most integration scenarios the objective is to integrate a Web application with legacy applications. The Web application model is truly distributed, and is a good example of an N-tier application model. An *N-tier application model* is a highly component-based environment capable of collaboration between components. It is by far the most ideal for sharing and reuse of business services and data. At the same time, it is more complex to manage. A sophisticated application hosting platform, such as a J2EE-compliant application server, is a basic requirement for these applications.

The need for adapters in this kind of an environment usually involves one-way integration of legacy applications with Web applications. The JCA specification is a good example of how to integrate non-Web applications with Web applications. However, in some instances, a much larger legacy application, such as an ERP system, may need to access a Web application and use its services. Adapters play an important role in integrating Web applications with older applications and systems. Figure 1.5 shows a Web application model.

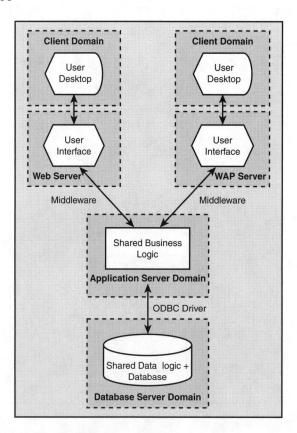

*FIGURE 1.5*    Web application model.

Various other application models have been developed for proprietary environments, for other application domains such as embedded systems, and so on. You can define your niche application models using similar techniques.

## Points of Integration

Now that you know the different application models, the next step is to identify the available points of integration in each model, as required in the different contexts. Some application models may not have a clear point of integration.

A *point of integration* is an entry point into an application, providing its users the capability to access some application functions or facilitate information (data) exchange. In some applications, a point of integration can be a set of APIs or the capability of the application to process messages. Stored procedures or other forms of dedicated interface tables also qualify as points of integration. Thus, a point of integration is a publicly available interface of the application. This interface can be part of the database, a function API, or even a desktop component such as an ActiveX or COM component. Some of the points of integration available in each of the application models are identified in the previous sections of this chapter.

In a host-based application model, data synchronization is possible only at the database level, unless the application is modified or extended to include an API. A very simple point of integration in a database is an *interface table*: a special database table or data structure with no dependencies with any other tables and structures. It is a freestanding space capable of staging external data. Special procedures or programs can be developed to then read the data from the interface tables and populate the more complicated production database tables and data structures. This is a common technique used in integrating and synchronizing data between legacy and other applications.

In a client-server application, the scenario is not much different, but there is a middleware (ODBC) between the client and database. This provides developers an option of tapping into ODBC transactions to capture the different database actions, and replicate or duplicate them by distributing information on the action and the actual data to other applications. Potential exists for a significant performance hit if the integration is not designed properly.

In a thin-client server application, similar techniques can be used. The availability of shared database logic in the form of stored procedures, and so on adds to the available points of integration. However, new programs will have to be developed to access these stored procedures, and such programs sometimes can be quite complex. Developers need to study stored procedures in detail to know which database tables are updated and under which business rules. Only then can a stored procedure be safely considered as a point of integration. One reason for being cautious about exposing stored procedures is that they need to be designed for multiple user access ensuring proper database/table/row locks, and so on.

A three-tier application model is more likely to have business function API and business services accessible by messages. These points of integration are ideal for enabling online services. An adapter can encapsulate services on the middle-tier, and make them generally available to different applications. Three-tier applications also have a stronger middleware component as part of their architecture. A transaction monitor such as BEA Tuxedo is an ideal platform for hosting transactional online services. Other transaction engines, such as Software AG EntireX, perform similar functions and enable integration with mainframe applications.

Remember the impact on the backend database when you're developing adapters wrapping the business services of a three-tier application. Although three-tier applications are designed to be multiuser, the number of users in a Web environment and their usage patterns are very different. Thus, if the objective of developing an online service-enabling adapter is to make the business services of a three-tier application available in a self-service environment on the Web, careful analysis of the impact on the database, middleware, and hosting environment in general should be conducted.

## Summary

The objective of this chapter was to introduce the concept of an adapter and identify some of the difficulties of developing adapters. Developing adapters for applications with different architecture models requires a deeper understanding of the underlying limitations of the application platform as well as the available points of integration. Localizing the integration logic in the form of an adapter makes change management easier. Changes to application functionality or upgrades to platforms can be encapsulated by the adapter. Also, by developing adapters enabling three different contexts—data synchronization, online services, and process automation—you enhance the encapsulated application and further extend its usefulness. This chapter should serve as background as you read the remainder of the book.

# 2

# Overview of J2EE

"It is of interest to note that while some dolphins are reported to have learned English, up to fifty words used in correct context, no human being has been reported to have learned dolphinese."

—Carl Sagan

This chapter is a brief introduction to J2EE, and is intended as background for the rest of the book. The actual J2EE specifications are quite extensive, and many books are dedicated to the topic of J2EE programming. Because this book is about adapters and the Java Connector Architecture (JCA), this overview focuses on topics and concepts useful for adapters.

## Introduction to J2EE

J2EE is an acronym for Java 2 Enterprise Edition, which is a platform for developing and deploying distributed, component-based enterprise applications. Another version of Java, known as the *standard edition*, is not based on a distributed architecture, and is useful for developing smaller standalone applications. J2EE is based on the J2SE, which is the foundation of all Java applications. Version 1.3 of J2EE includes a new specification called Java Connector Architecture, which supports application integration adapters (resource adapters) as components, or modules of a J2EE application or the J2EE environment (server) in general.

To many readers, J2EE is perhaps synonymous with an application server. However, there is a common misunderstanding that J2EE is only an application server standard. The J2EE specification is not bound to any specific application server implementation. The specifications are a set of services that enable components to collaborate and interact with each other in the context of distributed business applications. Any enterprise-class application platform can choose to support and implement the J2EE specifications. This would give the platform capability to host Java components in the form of Enterprise Java Beans (EJBs), Java Server Pages (JSP), and resource adapters.

For example, an enterprise database server could implement the J2EE specifications, giving its users a tighter integration between Java components and the database. A Web server could do the same and provide a better platform for Web applications. Many such products are available in the market today, including the leading Java application environments such as IBM WebSphere, which includes not just the J2EE-compliant server but also MQSeries and other application development tools from IBM. Another leading application server, BEA WebLogic, also includes the Tuxedo transaction engine and other tools in addition to the J2EE-compliant application server. However, most of them have been branded as application servers and support the new generation of Web applications. Even IDE vendors such as Inprise (Borland) supply J2EE-compliant application servers as part of their products. It is quite obvious that J2EE-compliant servers have become the platform of choice for enterprise applications, especially in the non-Microsoft technology domain.

The intention of this chapter is to provide a high-level overview of the J2EE technology and its important components. Two of the most important components from adapter perspective are the component model (EJB) and the JCA specification. These two technologies are covered in more detail in separate chapters in this book. Chapter 3, "Overview of EJB," presents an overview of the EJB specifications; and Chapter 10, "Overview of JCA," presents a detailed overview of JCA specifications.

## J2EE Specification

At the time of writing this book, the latest publicly available version of the J2EE specification was 1.3.1. Every version of the specification defines the roles and responsibilities of the various stakeholders, including vendors who sell J2EE-compliant servers and tools, as well as developers who build business applications and components. The capability to support the different stakeholders as part of the specification results in better design and quality of the applications. Each role has a specific responsibility, and the tasks of these roles usually overlap in software development, making it difficult to develop, deploy, and maintain applications.

The J2EE specifications enable software developers to focus on developing business components, server vendors to focus on developing platform-specific or platform-independent servers, application assemblers to assemble different components and package them as a business application, and deployers to configure the application and deploy it on the J2EE application servers. This clear delineation of tasks and roles helps in faster development, lower costs due to increased reuse, and better deployment due to the flexible configurations in the production environment.

The specification itself is a big document, and you don't need to read all of it. For example, JCA resource adapter developers can build resource adapters after understanding the JCA specifications and possibly the EJB specifications. The J2EE architecture makes it easier to pick and choose parts of the specifications that are relevant, and still build high-quality Java applications and components.

## J2EE Architecture

The J2EE architecture is based on the client-server model in an n-tier environment. The client-server application model has been popular with application developers for many years. The platforms supporting this model have changed many times, from the classic two-tier environment to the more prevalent n-tier environments. One notable difference with J2EE is that its architecture supports different client types as well as different servers. Using the J2EE platform, a business application can distribute its various components over different servers running on different operating systems and different hardware platforms. This distribution model gives developers, system administrators, and users the flexibility to choose the best of breed technologies to support their business applications.

There are four basic tiers of a J2EE application, and each tier is responsible for supporting specific features of an application:

- Client tier—Hosts end user components, and deals with presentation and user preference management.

- Web tier—Responsible for hosting Web components such as HTML pages, Java server pages, XML documents, and so on that are required for a Web-based client.

- Business tier—Responsible for hosting business components that encapsulate business rules, business logic, and business functions.

- Enterprise Information System (EIS) tier—Responsible for hosting information management components such as databases or legacy applications.

### Server Configurations

Although there are four tiers, each tier does not need its own server or hardware platform. It is quite possible for more then one tier to be managed by a single server.

A typical server configuration of a J2EE application consists of two servers: an application server and a database server. The application server hosts the Web tier and business tier, whereas the database server hosts EIS applications and databases. Some vendors also host middleware as part of the application servers. For example, the IBM WebSphere server includes MQSeries, which is a JMS-compliant messaging engine; BEA Web Logic supports Tuxedo, which is a transaction monitor.

For large installations, there can be a server farm with application servers running different tiers distributed over the network. The important thing to remember is that J2EE provides users with the flexibility to choose different configurations to host the servers. Providing this flexibility is the responsibility of J2EE containers and the J2EE architecture overall.

## Containers

Developing multitiered distributed applications is not an easy task. In addition to the usual system-level interfaces, a distributed application needs to manage the coordination of distributed components—transactions that involve the distributed components and other overheads associated with distributed computing in general. The cost of flexibility is more complex in dealing with different platforms and services. Distributed platforms such as CORBA provide a host of services and API to make the task of developing distributed applications easier.

Whereas CORBA supports multiple programming languages in addition to multiple platforms, the J2EE specifications focus only on the Java programming language. With J2EE applications, there is no need for an Interface Definition Language (IDL) such as the CORBA IDL, which is independent of programming languages. This may simplify the J2EE model a little, but the complexities of dealing with multiple platforms remain. This is resolved by J2EE containers—one for each different type of component. The job of a container is to provide system services to components and hide platform details ensuring that the components will work on any platform supported by the container. A *container* is the hosting environment of J2EE components, which are configured to work on specific containers during the deployment phase of an application.

Some of the examples of container services include security services, which grant or restrict access to system services. Note that this feature is provided by the container, and hence the component can be configured differently without requiring changes to the component code. Similarly, transactions can be defined to include methods of components and their relationships, making the task of transaction management easier. Such features are referred to as *container-managed features*. So, there are container-managed transactions and component-managed transactions. It is obvious that allowing the container to define and manage the transaction lets the component developer focus on business logic instead of coding transaction demarcations.

This architecture of container-managed services opens up real possibilities of component reuse. Component providers can build domain-specific components without tight coupling to any specific platform or server. Figure 2.1 shows the J2EE architecture and the relationships between servers, application tiers, containers, and components hosted by the containers. The diagram shows only some of the common interactions between the components. One important aspect to note is that the JCA resource adapters do not have a special container. JCA resource adapters, which are extensions of the application server, enable other components (such as session beans and message-driven beans) to communicate with the EIS.

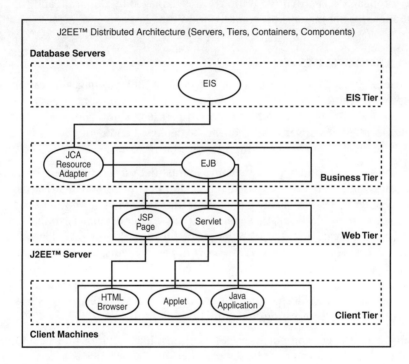

**FIGURE 2.1**  J2EE architecture.

### Types of Containers

There are three types of J2EE containers supported by the application server: business component containers or Enterprise Java Beans (EJB) containers; Web containers that manage Web components, such as servlets and JSP pages; and client containers, such as the application client containers (for managing Java applications) and applet containers (for managing Web browsers and plug-ins that support Java applets).

Each container provides services that host specific components and also provide the component with access to system interfaces. For example, the EJB container provides a container-managed transaction service. This service enables EJB component developers to leave the transaction code out of the business component. The component developer declares the type of transaction support required in the deployment descriptor, and the deployer maps this to the appropriate transaction service. The EJB container manages the transaction on behalf of the EJB component. This makes the J2EE application much smaller and simpler. If the component developer chooses to embed transaction management code in the EJB component, then the deployment descriptor can declare that the transaction is managed by the bean, and the container will not manage the transaction in that case.

## J2EE Components

Because J2EE is a component-based architecture, a J2EE business application is composed of more then one type of component. Each component has a specific role and responsibility that are useful in supporting the business application. A *component* is a self-contained software unit that can be deployed and configured in different environments to support the business applications' requirements.

Application clients and applets are components that run on the client or users' machines. *Applets* are browser-based application client components that require an applet container that is usually a plug-in in the Web browser. Another example of an application client is a Java GUI application. These clients (applets and GUI applications) communicate with the Web tier or the business tier directly, depending on the type of client. For applets and HTML browser-based clients, the Web tier provides components such as Java Server Pages (JSP pages) and Java servlets, which receive requests from the Web clients and send responses back to the clients. Servlets and JSP pages can communicate with business components of EJBs, such as session beans and entity beans, to access business functions and services.

Of all these different component types, it is most likely that business components in the form of session beans will be the real users of JCA resource adapters. It is likely that a standalone Java application (based on the standard edition of Java) can communicate with a JCA resource adapter, but in most cases, J2EE application components will interact with resource adapters.

## J2EE Reference Implementation

The reference implementation is a non-commercial implementation of the J2EE specification available for free to be used for education, demonstration, and prototyping projects. You can download this implementation from the Web site `http://java.sun.com/j2ee/download.html#sdk`. The J2EE SDK includes a binary version of the

J2EE reference implementation in addition to other development tools and documents. The SDK supports multiple platforms, including Solaris, Windows NT, Windows 2000, and Linux. The same URL also contains sample JCA resource adapter code and binary files. The reference implementation defines a baseline of functionality that should remain constant across implementations by different vendors. The SDK includes a J2EE compatibility test suite that helps in testing the vendors' J2EE products for compliance with the J2EE specifications. This does not mean that vendor implementations will be identical, but ensures that the behavior is consistent, as defined by the specifications.

Another interesting use of the reference implementation is in quality assurance of the applications' components, including the resource adapters. For example, if the resource adapter works properly in the reference implementation, it should work equally well in other application servers, assuming that all external dependencies are working properly.

Also part of the SDK are tools such as deployment tools and scripts that help in packaging, deploying, and configuring application components. The reference implementation is packaged with these specific tools:

- J2EE administration tool—A script that enables users to add resources such as JDBC drivers, JMS destinations, JCA resource adapter connection factories, and so on.

- Cleanup tool—Removes all installed applications. It is not recommended that you use this tool unless a server needs to be cleaned up and reinstalled for some reason.

- Deployment tool—Supports both a command line interface and a GUI interface. This tool can be used to package and deploy components and applications.

- Key tool—Creates public and private keys when required. These keys may be needed, depending on the security options selected and configured.

- Packager tool—Useful in packaging components in a command-line mode.

- Realm tool—Primarily for user management (add and remove users, groups, and so on). It can also import public or private keys (digital certificates) generated by the key tool.

- Verifier tool—Checks if the various J2EE archive files are valid and displays the contents of the archive files.

The reference implementation is a complete set of tools, SDK, and runtime servers that enable developers to start developing J2EE applications and components without requiring a third-party application server. However, for large, industry-strength, mission-critical systems, a vendor-supported application server may be a better option.

## Summary

J2EE is a highly sophisticated application development, deployment, and management platform. It supports n-tier application models and component-based application architectures. The intention of the J2EE platform is to provide a platform-independent model, API, and specification capable of hosting application components from many vendors. Although the J2EE platform is not tied to any vendor's specific API, the specifications enable vendors to add their own extensions to the platform. Also, the specifications do not impose implementation guidelines, which enables vendors to be creative in their implementations.

A key design or architecture concept of J2EE is that of containers that implement system services, enabling J2EE developers to focus on business logic encapsulated in application components. Containers host different types of application components, including Web components such as servlets, JSP instances, Java beans, resource adapters, and so on. Each component is managed by a specific container. A container isolates the application components from system-level details, adding to their platform independence and flexibility.

The J2EE environment is one of the most comprehensive and flexible application development, hosting, and management environments. This chapter was a very brief overview of the J2EE environment; understanding the J2EE environment takes time, practice, and experience. JCA is the standard mechanism for extending the J2EE environment's capability to integrate with legacy applications. The remaining chapters in the book focus on JCA adapter development. A J2EE tutorial can be found on the following Web site: `http://java.sun.com/j2ee/tutorial/1_3-fcs/index.html`.

# 3

# Overview of EJB

"Your present circumstances don't determine where you can go; they merely determine where you start."

—Nido Qubein

This chapter is a quick overview of Enterprise Java Beans (EJB) and their role in J2EE-based business applications. Components of an application EJB will be the primary clients of resource adapters, and hence resource adapter developers need to understand the dynamics of EJB. Entire books are focused on EJB programming, and therefore this chapter focuses on how EJB and JCA resource adapters can work together in the context of J2EE applications.

## Introduction to EJB

*Enterprise Java Bean (EJB)* is the component model for developing software components that are managed by the J2EE platform. The EJB specifications that outline the model also define the hosting environment responsible for managing the components (beans) at run time. The primary objective of EJB is to enable business application developers to focus their time developing the business functionality instead of building system functions such as multiuser support, transaction support, and so on. A typical EJB application developer does not need to know the system-level details of how the J2EE platform manages transactions, for example.

The EJB specifications handle the encapsulation and isolation of system interfaces by defining specific roles for EJB developers:

- Enterprise bean provider

- Application assembler

- Deployer

- EJB server provider

- EJB container provider

- System administrator

It is possible that some of these roles will be fulfilled by one entity instead of one entity for each role. For example, the enterprise bean provider and the application assembler could be the same team of programmers; or the EJB server provider and the EJB container provider can be the same vendor. Each role defined in the EJB specification has a set of contracts or interfaces that support the roles' responsibilities.

Notice that although the JCA specifications define specific roles, there is an overlap with the roles defined in the EJB specifications. The application assembler, deployer, and system administrator roles exist in JCA and EJB specifications. An application assembler will assemble the business application by tying together (assembling) relevant EJB components and JCA resource adapters. Hence, it is quite possible that in the context of a business application, an EJB component can call a JCA resource adapter, which in turn can call another EJB, and so on.

## Understanding EJB Roles

Every EJB developer assumes the role of enterprise bean provider, as defined in the EJB specifications. This entails the responsibility for not only developing the specific EJB components or beans, but also packaging them in a Java archive file (.jar) together with the deployment descriptor. Because EJBs are reusable discrete components, they can be supplied by third-party vendors just like resource adapters. Domain experts can develop and sell EJBs that can be used by application assemblers to assemble specific business applications. Figure 3.1 shows the different roles specified in the EJB specifications and the overlap with the roles specified in the JCA specification.

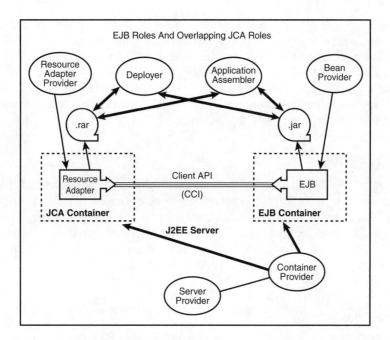

*FIGURE 3.1*    Roles specified in EJB specifications.

An application assembler is responsible for packaging all the necessary EJB jar files and any other jar files, including resource adapter .rar files, into an assembled business application. Note that *assembling* does not mean installing and deploying the application; it means bringing together the various application components necessary for the application, and changing the individual components deployment descriptors as necessary.

The deployer takes the assembled application, and deploys it in a specific run-time operational environment consisting of an EJB server and EJB containers. Although it is not necessary that the EJB server and EJB container be provided by the same vendor, in most cases it is (especially because the current specifications assume that the EJB container provider also supplies the EJB server). Any configurations required by the components are also handled by the deployer, who uses a deployment tool to install all external software that the application components depend on.

The EJB container provider is responsible for supplying a server and container that conform to the EJB 2.0 architecture specifications. The EJB *container* is a hosting environment for EJB instances. The container also has a deployment management tool that enables the deployer to manage J2EE applications.

The system administrator's role is much broader than just maintaining the J2EE environments. A system administrator is also responsible for managing the EIS environment and monitoring the distributed environment. No specific system administration and monitoring contracts are specified in the EJB specifications. Neither are any similar contracts defined in the JCA specifications. Thus, for the most part, the system administration and monitoring function is customized to match the specific enterprise's requirements.

## Types of EJB

The EJB 2.0 specification has several major and important additions and changes. One of the biggest additions has been a new type of bean—a *message-driven bean*. These beans provide the J2EE applications with the capability to be triggered by a messaging engine, and more specifically by the arrival of a specific message. Three types of beans are defined in the EJB specifications: entity beans, session beans, and message-driven beans. Each bean enables a specific set of interactions between the client and the J2EE application.

### Entity Beans

An *entity bean* represents the different data objects of a J2EE application and the relationships between them. Entity beans are a representation of a J2EE application's data, and are independent of the actual persistent storage mechanism. Each entity bean has an abstract schema that describes the structure (fields and relationships as well as the access mechanisms). The fields and their relationships are actually managed by the entity bean container in an implementation-specific way. The deployment descriptor of the entity bean describes the abstract schema that is associated with the physical classes used by the container to store the entity bean fields and relationships.

#### Container-Managed Persistence

In container-managed persistence, the container is responsible for making the right calls to the persistence storage mechanism (RDBMS, XML database, ASCII files, and so on), and ensuring the synchronization between the entity bean and the physical storage. An entity bean is essentially a framework for transforming data stored in external persistence mechanisms into Java objects. The code of a container-managed entity bean does not have any calls to the physical persistence environment. So if the data is actually stored in a relational database, then the entity bean has no JDBC calls to update the database. That is deferred to the entity bean container. The deployer maps the entity bean schema (and its fields) to the RDBMS tables and columns. The deployment tools provided by the container provider generate the necessary classes (drivers), which interact with the RDBMS and transform data to entity beans.

**NOTE**

Deployment tools play a critical role in the installation, configuration, and maintenance of J2EE applications. J2EE users have the choice of using deployment tools from third parties that specialize in deployment management technologies. For example, tools such as TopLink and CocoBase are commonly used for deploying J2EE applications, especially when some of the application servers do not have deployment tools.

This separation of the entity bean from the actual storage mechanism makes the container-managed persistence scheme very flexible. If the entity bean needs to change its underlying persistence mechanism, the deployer can do it without having to change the entity bean code. The individual fields of the entity bean will be remapped to the new persistence mechanism.

Because there are no direct JDBC calls in the entity bean, there has to be a different interface for querying persistence environment for data. EJB QL is the query language used by the entity bean, and is very similar in syntax to SQL. So although the entity beans are independent of the persistence environment, the query language is very much like SQL-based RDBMS queries. It is the deployer's job to map EJB QL to the physical interface, which can be JDBC-based SQL or another persistence-management mechanism depending on the implementation classes generated by the deployment tool.

The benefit of container-managed persistence is the resulting flexibility, but the over-head of working with logical schemas is not always justified—especially if the schema is small or if the persistent storage is expected to remain constant for a long time.

### Bean-Managed Persistence

In this method of accessing persistent data, the entity bean provides an object view of the data. Just as the container-managed persistence mechanism transformed exter-nal data representation into a Java object, a bean-managed persistence mechanism transforms the physical data structure to a Java object. The difference is that the entity bean has code that accesses the persistence environment directly. There is no logical schema involved, and therefore there is no mapping of the entity bean's structure (fields and relationships) to the physical data model.

Bean-managed persistence can be used to reduce the overhead of container-managed persistence, but the price to pay is loss of flexibility.

## Session Beans

A *session bean* is an EJB that manages sessions (or conversations) on behalf of the client (application components or JCA resource adapters). The lifecycle of a session bean is controlled by the client. In some situations, such as server (host of the session bean) errors, the EJB container can terminate a session bean. Therefore, clients of a session bean should be prepared to create a new instance of the session bean if the original instance is terminated by the container.

A typical session is transient, and its state is usually not persistent. An example of a session could be tracking your courier package using a Web-based status query application. If for some reason the Web server dies or the session times out (does not get the response back within a predetermined time interval), then the session terminates and the user is required to start a new session. Most online transactions are session-oriented, with the user initiating a session, performing a set of actions, and then terminating the session. Hence, a session bean generally stores its state in transient variables.

Not all sessions are conversational, and some sessions are unidirectional—with the client invoking some methods or actions as part of the session without expecting any reply. These sessions are called *stateless sessions*; the state management mode of the session bean is described in the deployment descriptor. Conversational sessions are managed by *stateful* session beans. In practice, especially in the context of distributed Web applications, the stateless session beans are used more frequently than stateful session beans.

There can be many session bean instances being managed by the bean container, and it is possible that not all session beans are active at any given moment. Session beans can be active as a result of direct invocation by client components or as part of container-managed transactions. In either case, it is possible that the session bean container may want to swap out inactive session beans to secondary storage temporarily, and swap them back when required. This swapping-out process is known as *passivation*, and the swapping-in process is known as *activation* of session beans.

All session beans must implement the `SessionBean` interface. The bean container invokes the `setSessionContext` method to associate a session bean instance with a context that is maintained by the container. The context instance is usually held by the session bean instance as part of its state. Because the context is valid while the session bean is in existence, it should be held in a transient variable. This is to ensure that when the session bean is swapped out by the container, the context instance is not lost when the session bean is swapped back in.

Some of the events generated by the session bean container, which are associated with specific actions in a session bean, include `ejbRemove`, `ejbPassivate`, and `ejbActivate`. When a session bean receives these notifications, it should release the resource (in the case of `ejbRemove` and `ejbPassivate`) and require the resource (in the case of `ejbActivate`).

Unlike stateful session beans, stateless session beans do not store any reference or state information that associates the bean to a particular client. This makes stateless session beans equivalent in terms of servicing clients. The session bean container can therefore pass along the client's request for a specific stateless bean method to any instance of the stateless bean, as long as it belongs to the right class.

This means if the resource adapter interacts with an asynchronous messaging engine, then a stateless session bean may be better suited as the client. If on the other hand the message engine is a synchronous message platform, or if there is a synchronous service that the resource adapter is interacting with, then a stateful session bean is better suited as a client. Overall session beans (stateful or stateless) will be some of the primary clients of resource adapters.

## Message-Driven Beans

A *message-driven bean* is different from the session bean or the entity bean. Its client is the container that invokes the message-driven bean upon receiving a JMS message. So a client that wants to access the business logic encapsulated in the message-driven bean must send a JMS message to the appropriate JMS destination (queue or a specific topic). The message-driven bean listens for messages on a queue or for a topic. In some ways, a message-driven bean is like a stateless session bean, with the capability of waiting for a JMS message on an asynchronous messaging platform.

Because JMS is a messaging standard not restricted to the J2EE environment, other messaging platforms that are also JMS-compatible, such as IBM MQSeries, can be used to integrate legacy applications. Herein lies a conflict in terms of what is the better mechanism for integrating message-based legacy systems. Would a message-driven bean be the appropriate mechanism for receiving messages from the legacy application, or should that job be left for JCA resource adapters? Note that a JCA resource adapter does not have a message-driven interface in its client component interface (CCI) interface. Thus, in some instances when the legacy application is sending messages to the J2EE application, a message-driven bean could then be a trigger for processing inbound messages. Outbound messages could be generated by a resource adapter.

Figure 3.2 shows a possible design pattern in which message-driven beans and JCA resource adapters work together to support a distributed asynchronous integration scenario involving a message platform-based legacy application and a J2EE application. In the scenario, a session bean that is part of the J2EE application accesses the resource adapter for the legacy system using its CCI interface. The resource adapter creates a JMS message encapsulating the service request, and puts the message into the legacy application's inbound message queue. At this time, the resource adapter has completed its job, and either returns a successful status if the message is written properly to the queue, or throws an exception. The legacy system processes the inbound message when it has time, and encapsulates the response in a message before writing the message to the outbound queue. A message-driven bean is monitoring the outbound queue, and the bean container invokes the message-driven bean as soon as it detects the presence of the response message.

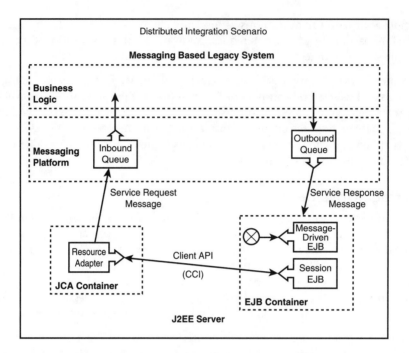

*FIGURE 3.2*   Distributed J2EE integration scenario.

Suppose that the scenario changes a little, and instead of processing the response in an asynchronous way, the J2EE application wants to wait for the response. Then, the JCA resource adapter must monitor the outbound queue and wait for the response message before returning control to the client session bean. A number of similar design patterns involve session beans, message-driven beans, and entity beans, in conjunction with resource adapters, to solve application integration problems and scenarios.

## Client Access

With different types of beans, the client access mechanisms and views need to be formalized to reduce complexity and simplify maintenance. Clients can be instances of EJBs or other Web application components such as JSP, Java applets, and so on. To a client, a session bean is a non-persistent enterprise bean that encapsulates business logic, and an entity bean is an object-oriented (Java) representation of different types of persistent data (RDBMS and others).

Every bean has two interfaces that define the client access mechanisms: home and component interfaces. Together, these interfaces define the clients' view of enterprise beans. The bean container provides the implementation of these interfaces, but the container is transparent to the client.

A client can be either local or remote, and the client views (interfaces) to EJB are different depending on the client's location (local or remote). This means that if the client is local to the EJB, then the interfaces used by the client to access the EJB are different from the interfaces used by a remote client to access the same EJB. The remote client's view is composed of two interfaces: a remote interface and a remote home interface. These remote interfaces can be used by a client that can be running in the same Java Virtual Machine (JVM) or a different JVM on a different machine. The remote client view interfaces remain the same, and are independent of the location of the client. Both the remote and remote home interfaces are Java RMI-based (Remote Method Invocation-based).

If the client and the bean are both hosted in the same JVM, then the remote client view is an overhead that can be removed by a local client view. Similar to the remote client view, the local view is composed of a local interface and a local home interface.

Both the local and remote client views enable entity and session beans' maximum scalability and flexibility. Together with the capabilities of entity (independent of persistence mechanism) and session beans (stateful and stateless) and the client access views (local and remote), EJB form a strong foundation for distributed applications. JCA resource adapters can have EJB clients, or they can interact with EJB to fulfill some of its internal functions.

## Adapters and Beans

The brief outline of some of the capabilities of entity beans, session beans, and message-driven beans in the previous sections is bound to create some doubt in terms of the usefulness of JCA as compared with EJB. The benefits and strengths of JCA are not in its system contracts as much as in the formalization of the client API in the form of the CCI. Future versions of JCA will probably have a more comprehensive client API and stronger support for emerging XML-based protocols and APIs. There is no reason why this cannot be done with EJBs, but the objectives of EJB and JCA are different. EJB is a component model for distributing business logic of the J2EE application in relevant components. JCA is a standard method of accessing legacy systems.

Of the three types of beans, the session bean will tend to be the most likely client of JCA resource adapters. Entity beans map Java objects to persistent data models, and it is unlikely that entity beans will need to access JCA resource adapters. There can be times when an entity bean maps its schema (fields and relationships) to the JCA interface (XML document). The resource adapter can then store the document or data in the legacy system's database.

It is very likely that JCA adapters will interact with entity and session beans, especially those of other J2EE applications. Message-driven beans will be useful in triggering application components upon arrival of JMS messages from external applications. The same mechanism can be used to trigger resource adapters if required. The bottom line is that resource adapters will collaborate with enterprise Java beans and support complex integration patterns.

## Summary

Enterprise Java Beans have become the foundation for developing distributed application components. However, the EJB standard does not include specific contracts for adapters; hence the importance of JCA specifications. Perhaps you can argue that the EJB specifications could have been extended to include adapter-specific contracts. An adapter can be conceptualized as a specialization or a new type of EJB. Just like there is an entity bean, a session bean, and a message bean, there could have been an EIS bean. However, the scope of adapters goes beyond the J2EE environment, and because EJB is a J2EE component model, a separate specification for adapters makes sense.

However, EJBs will be the primary clients of JCA resource adapters, and they will also be the primary J2EE application access points for resource adapters. The relationship between EJBs and resource adapters is bidirectional, and the resulting scenarios can range from simple to complex. The job of the application assembler will be to tie together the relevant EJB components and JCA adapters, and ensure the integrity of the J2EE application.

Perhaps the JCA and EJB specifications will merge at some point, especially because there is an overlap in their roles as well as in their capabilities. The intent of JCA is different from the EJB objectives, which are restricted to J2EE environments. Nonetheless, sometimes a session bean or a message-driven bean can do the job of application integration; and if it's a simpler design pattern, it could be justified.

**4**

# Adapter Reference Model

The test of a good architecture is that it will last. The sound architecture is an enduring pattern.

—Robert Spinrad, 1988

Software architecture is an art similar to software programming. Being recognized as a software architect may be the wish of many programmers, but not every programmer can succeed in becoming an architect. Architecture is as much about the mind set as it is about software engineering and the art of problem solving.

## Role of Software Reference Models

Software reference models are central to any software engineering methodology or technique. A *reference model* is an accurate and complete representation of the internal design (static and dynamic) of a software system. As such, these models are also the primary means of communication with various stakeholders of the system. *Stakeholders* view the system differently, and also use different languages to express requirements and understand the design. An *architect* is a person capable of understanding these different languages and views and able to define a reference model that can be used during and after the development of the target system.

Although there are multiple models of a system, each model has a specific role. The contents of these models are also different, although they all refer to the same system. The now ubiquitous UML techniques include many different system models and views. For large and complex software, it is no doubt beneficial to follow a model-based development process. Software adapters also require models to capture the analysis and design decisions. It is very important that we build reference models to capture the important aspects and artifacts of an adapter, without any outright bias to the supporting technologies and infrastructure.

In general, reference models fill many different roles in adapter development, including the following:

- Communicate (accurately and concisely) system requirements and structure to the stakeholders. This is very important because the stakeholders need to agree on the end result before it's developed. Software development is still a very costly proposition, and the trial-and-error methods frequently prove to be very expensive.

- Define the acceptance criteria, including the identification of certification requirements. A comprehensive test plan is part of a complete reference model.

- Provide a consistent and repeatable design concept to adapter developers. Because part of the challenge faced by adapter developers is the adaptation of different systems, a consistent architecture and design model ensures maintenance is manageable.

- Maintain the integrity of the software system as it proceeds in the development lifecycle. Even with the advances in UML, it is very easy to miss critical aspects of the software system during the transition from one phase of the development lifecycle to the other. Research into development practices and methodologies has repeatedly shown that the cost of fixing problems becomes significantly higher after each subsequent step of the development lifecycle. Needless to say, a reference model goes a long way in reducing the changes of such costly mistakes.

## Choosing Reference Models

A common challenge is deciding which models are critical to adapter development, and which aren't. It is difficult to determine which models are more important than others; however, it is possible to put the models into perspective and select the appropriate models, depending on the type of adapter. As stated earlier in this section, a software system is viewed differently by the different stakeholders. By understanding which model represents the specific views of the stakeholders, architects and developers can decide on the priority of the models. Figure 4.1 shows the different stakeholders and their views of the adapter.

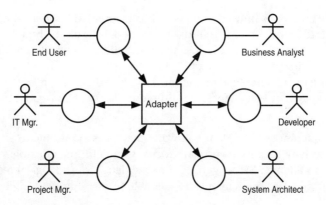

**FIGURE 4.1**    Adapter stakeholders and views.

# Adapter Requirements and Architecture Models

In the ideal scenario, all the stakeholders will get to review the system model match-ing the criteria of their specific view. Modeling tools and techniques, such as UML, support multiple types of models. In this chapter, we focus on two important views: the end user view (requirements model) and the system structure view (architecture model). That is not to say that the other models are not important, but they are more relevant to specific adapters rather than to a generic model. Even the require-ments model is better understood in the context of real requirements, but there are generic requirements that can be modeled and can form the basis of the generic architecture model.

There are two types of architecture models: a logical model and a physical model. A logical model captures the design details and concepts, whereas the physical refer-ence model captures the implementation and deployment details. This chapter is focused on the logical adapter model, and is used in the development of the example resource adapter in Chapter 17, "Source Code for ASCII File J2EE Adapter." The bene-fits of the logical model are that it can be used in different physical environments such as J2EE-compliant application servers, proprietary application servers, messag-ing platform environments (IBM MQSeries), and so on, while preserving the core concepts and design to be implemented by the adapter.

## Logical Models

When does a *logical model* become a *reference model*? It depends largely on the context in which the model is developed and applied. If the logical model is built to solve a specific adapter problem, it cannot be classified as a reference model because its reference context is limited to the specific adapter. To build a generic logical reference model, the requirements that drive the model should be broad in scope and applicable to more than one adapter. You can build adapter reference models for specific categories (classes) or adapters. For example, a reference model for ERP system adapters or a reference model for database adapters can be defined to maintain consistency between adapters for different ERP systems or adapters for different databases.

The logical reference model defined in this chapter is applicable to any type (class) of adapter, especially because its primary focus is on defining a flexible structure (architecture) for an adapter. Before getting into the details of the logical reference model, a list of objectives for the reference model will be useful in defining its scope.

## Objectives of the Logical Adapter Reference Model

The primary objective of the adapter reference model is to define an abstract (generic) design model that is capable of supporting most adapter patterns and behavior. To achieve this objective, the model needs to exhibit several important properties, including the following:

- A flexible component-based architecture supportive of plug-and-play capability

- Clearly defined functional boundaries ensuring no redundant functionality

- Consistently universal applicability

These properties are difficult to maintain in one model. In practice, multiple models are necessary, each capturing different aspects and different dimensions (static/dynamic, logical/physical, transience/persistence) of the adapter. One important objective is to keep the reference model as simple as possible without losing any significant details.

### Assigning Responsibility

Any object-oriented architect and programmer will quickly admit that one of the difficult tasks of object modeling is assigning responsibilities. It takes several iterations of analysis and design before a stable and robust distribution of responsibilities can be achieved. Another equally challenging job is drawing clear functional boundaries. After the boundaries are drawn and components are defined, it is not easy to change them in the future without significantly affecting the system design.

A good place to start understanding the boundaries and responsibilities is by capturing the requirements in a use case model. Figure 4.2 shows the use case model that defines the generic requirements of an adapter. The use case identifies the various actors, use cases, and subsystems (or system boundaries) responsible for managing the use cases.

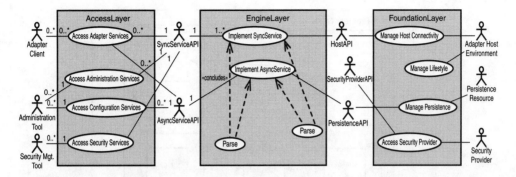

**FIGURE 4.2**   Use case model.

## Reducing Complexity

It is obvious from the use case model that the level of complexity is quite high, and the reference model needs to simplify the associated design. Simplicity is typically achieved by deferring the complications of the constraints of physical environment to another model (physical design model). Another useful architectural paradigm in reducing complexity is the concept of layers or tiers, with the higher layers representing (higher levels of abstraction) design models simpler than the lower (increasingly concrete) layers. Application architectures such as the three-tier model use the layered architecture principle to define functional boundaries. The logical adapter reference model is also based on a layered architecture.

## Defining the Problem Domain

The first step in building the reference model is defining the problem domain. Figure 4.3 shows a block diagram with the major domains and their relationships. The block diagram also shows the role of an adapter and its relationships with other software components and their domains. There are three main domains in any adapter problem model: the adapter domain, the administration domain, and the target domain.

The adapter domain consists of the actual adapter, the adapted application, and the adapter configuration information. Each of these components can be in a different hosting environment or in a single hosting environment. From a logical perspective, all these components are part of a single domain, regardless of the potential cross-platform, distributed physical environment. By deferring the implementation details and focusing on the component responsibilities and relationships, the resulting reference model will be more robust.

The target domain consists of only one component: the target entity. This can be either an application or middleware or a database. Similarly, the administration domain has only the administration tool component.

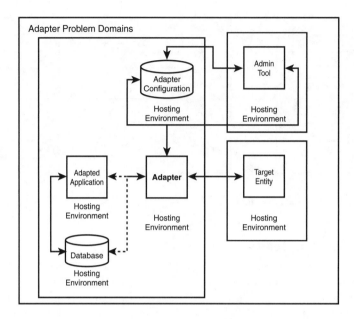

*FIGURE 4.3*   Primary problem domains of adapter analysis.

It is obvious from the block diagram that the adapter is the central piece, with many points of integration and multiple stakeholders—each driving different requirements. In a situation in which requirements are coming from multiple sources, the system design needs to be such that changes driven by one source of requirements does not affect other system components. At the same time, the integrity of all the components in the system needs to be maintained at all times. In a homogenous environment, in which all the system components defined in the block diagram are physically hosted in the same environment, the physical reference model will be much simpler than in a distributed heterogeneous environment. The complexity of the task of modeling the physical environment is the reason why most projects fail to define the physical reference model. Especially under these circumstances, a complete logical reference model becomes even more critical.

## Layered Architecture

The concept of layered architecture is neither new nor very difficult to understand. The seven-layer application architecture model from Open Systems Institution (OSI) is a classic example of a successful layered architecture model. Before using the layer concept for building the adapter reference model, a quick overview of some of the advantages of the layered architecture will be useful.

A *layer* defines a conceptual boundary that isolates a set of software functionality from other layers. Synonymous with the concept of layers is the concept of *tiers*, where layers are stacked on top of each other, with the higher layers defining more generic and abstract concepts than the lower layers. This means the higher layer in the stack defines the most generic concepts, and the lowest layer defines the most concrete concepts. The terms *generic* and *concrete* take different meaning, depending on the context in which the layers are defined. In the context of the OSI application model, the highest layer (layer 7) is the Application layer, and the lowest layer (layer 1) is the Physical layer. In between are different layers, increasing in application-specific functionality (layer 6 is Presentation, layer 5 is Session, and so on).

Figure 4.4 shows the concept of layers and their dependencies in the context of adapters and the adapter reference model defined later in this chapter.

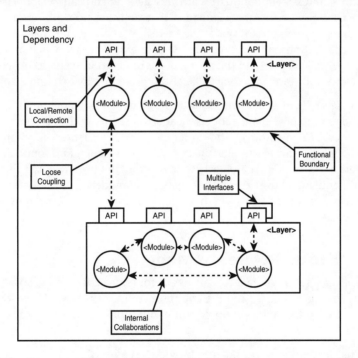

**FIGURE 4.4**  Concept of layers and their dependencies.

A layer encapsulates one or more modules that define the functionality isolated by the layer. Access to the modules is restricted or defined by a set of APIs associated with the layer. The connectivity between the APIs and the modules of a layer can be either local or remote. There can be one or more APIs for any specific module of a layer. Each API defines a specific access mechanism or channel for accessing the layer's functionality. The modules encapsulated by the layer can collaborate between themselves, and may or may not use an internal API. However, when layers are stacked in tiers, interlayer collaborations between modules of different layers are facilitated by APIs. Restricting direct communication between modules of different layers helps maintain the integrity of the individual layers and preserves their functional boundaries, resulting in a more robust architecture.

## Use Case Models

Before getting into the details of the reference model—its structure, dependencies, and responsibilities—an analysis of the generic adapter requirements will be useful for understanding the scope and complexity of the problem domain. Figure 4.2, earlier in the chapter, shows the use case model for an adapter. Notice that the use cases, actors, and system boundaries are very generic and can be applied to most adapters. One more noticeable element is that there are no real users accessing the adapter except other applications and systems. After all, adapters are supposed to integrate applications, and as such the use case model shows which applications interact with the adapter and their role in the integration scenario. Also, the use cases interact with each other via APIs, also represented by external actors.

The use case in Figure 4.2 is generic and can be used as a guideline for building specific adapter requirements models. Real use cases are bound to be more complex, but the basic idea and strategy should remain the same. Three subsystems are identified in the model: the access subsystem, engine subsystem, and foundation subsystem. There are common data objects shared across the use cases, but they appear as part of the individual use cases rather than being modeled as a separate use case. The adapter reference model, however, has a separate layer to encapsulate shared data and services.

## Logical Adapter Reference Model

The *logical adapter reference model* consists of four layers: the access layer, the engine layer, the foundation layer, and the common component layer. These four layers define a solution to the four most common questions involved in software (adapter) modeling:

- What features does the adapter provide to its users?

- How are those features implemented?

- What are the dependencies between the adapter and its hosting environment?

- What information and services are common and shared by the various modules encapsulated by the layers?

Figure 4.5 shows the logical adapter reference model, its different layers, and the major modules (components) of each layer. The layers are stacked in a two-dimensional model, one dimension consisting of the common component layer and its modules, and another dimension consisting of a stack of three functional layers (access layer, engine layer, foundation layer).

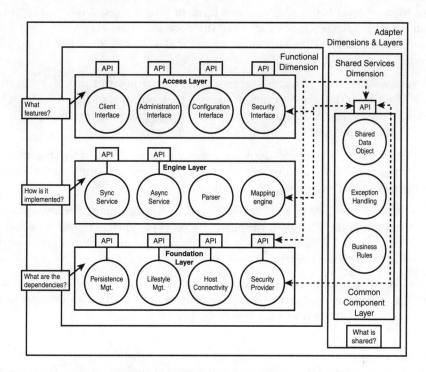

**FIGURE 4.5**   Adapter reference model (dimensions and layers).

The reference model is based on the principle that each model has one or more types of dimensions. A *dimension* is defined as a distinctly different view of a system, sometimes defined by the roles played by set of layers and modules. The two dimensions of the logical adapter reference model provide two views: a functional view of the adapter and a shared service view. The functional view is useful to determine what services and functions the adapter is designed to provide, whereas the shared services dimension helps to determine the dependencies between various layers of the functional dimension. This separation of code into logical groupings (modules, layers, and dimensions) is a very powerful structural pattern capable of supporting mutually different views of the adapter in a cohesive model.

## Functional Dimension

The *functional dimension* of the logical reference model consists of three layers: the access layer, the engine layer, and the foundation layer.

### Access Layer

The topmost layer is the adapter access layer, or simply *access layer*. This layer has four basic modules, each of which is an interface accessible via an API. Each module represents a set of services targeted at a specific stakeholder identified in the use case model:

- *Client interface*—Provides a set of services that represent the actual adapter services. If the adapter is a SAP adapter, then one of the client interfaces can access a specific SAP Business Application Programming Interface (BAPI) or a SAP Intermediate Document (IDOC) document.

- *Administration interface*—Provides adapter services to any external administration tool. Typically, these services include starting and stopping the adapter, tracking the exceptions, and so on.

- *Configuration interface*—Consists of services enabling static and dynamic configuration of the adapter. If the adapter accepts parameters in real-time and can adjust its behavior accordingly, then the configuration interface is an important part of those features.

- *Security interface*—Exposes security services, such as logon and logoff, and provides the capability to accept security credentials from an external security environment such as a single sign-on platform.

### Engine Layer

The next layer below the access layer is the *engine layer*. This layer is the heart of the adapter, and it does most of the work. There are four important modules in this layer: the sync service and async service modules, as well as the parser and mapping engine modules. Generally, this layer provides an API only for the sync and async services. The parser and mapping engine modules are used internally by the sync and async service modules to parse incoming data and map different outgoing data types to one another.

### Foundation Layer

The last layer in the functional layer is the *foundation layer*, which is the layer closest to the hosting environment. In the case of the JCA resource adapter, the foundation layer consists of modules that implement the system contracts defined as part of the JCA specifications. These contracts include transaction and security interfaces. Apart from the hosting environment interfaces, other modules in this layer include the lifecycle management module responsible for state management of the adapter, a persistence management module providing interfaces to the underlying persistence resource (such as an RDBMS database), and a security provider module that interfaces with the external security infrastructure.

The lifecycle management module should support single-cycle adapters and multicycle adapters. Single-cycle adapters are created to process any existing service requests, and after all the services are processed, the adapter is destroyed. Multicycle adapters can be preconfigured to process services multiple times. This can be useful when the data supplied to the service is for more than one invocation of the service. For example, if the service processes purchase orders and the adapter receives data for five POs in a batch, it might be necessary to execute the service five times, with each cycle getting a different part of the received PO data. Multicycle adapters are necessary when interfacing with a batch-oriented application or environment.

### Shared Services Dimension

All the layers in the functional layer (and their APIs and modules) share some common data objects and services. The *shared services dimension* consists of the common component layer. This layer encapsulates shared data objects and services such as the exception handling service, business rules, and other shared data objects.

If there are a lot of common data and services in a particular adapter, then it might be necessary to define two layers: one for shared services and the other for shared data objects. Reusing components is a major benefit of isolating shared objects and services. Another benefit is easy change management because a change in any of the shared objects is reflected throughout the adapter.

With just two dimensions and four layers, the reference model is simple and has the placeholders to define most of the adapter's design without specific physical constants. There are, however, some potentially essential useful modules, such as session management, that have been deliberately left out of the logical model. Session management and transport mechanisms  (such as HTTP, MQSeries, and so on) are usually captured in the physical models, especially if they result in constraints at implementation time.

## Design Considerations

Some design considerations are not captured in the logical reference model but may be important to some specific adapters. Session management is one of the design considerations that must be captured either in the physical reference model or in a more adapter-specific logical reference model. Session management could well be an issue when developing adapters for legacy systems (mainframe applications), and the reference model for these adapters must define the relevant session layer and modules. Some of the design considerations that haven't been specifically identified in the logical reference models are outlined in the following sections.

## Session Management

Most communication protocols require some level of *session* management. Some of the simpler session management requirements can be the use of a session ID when exchanging information or invoking services over an established session or connection.

Typically, a *session* is identified by a connection between a client and a server resource. Sessions are useful for coordinating information and services relevant to a specific transaction. If the underlying protocol does not support session management, the adapter may have to develop a pseudo-session manager to maintain the integrity of the services and information exchanged by the integrated applications.

### Non-persistent Session

Sometimes the sessions are *transient* or *non-persistent*, meaning that if there is any loss of connection due to physical (hardware) or software problems, then the entire session is lost and needs to be restarted. On other occasions, transient sessions are based on business transactions in which the transaction is real-time or time-sensitive. In these situations, if the transaction cannot be completed in a fixed, predetermined time interval, the session is terminated, and a new transaction initiated.

### Persistent Session

On the other hand, some sessions are *persistent*, and keep their state information in a secondary storage. If for some reason the session is disconnected or broken, the session manager (adapter) can restart the session from the last successful point or state. An example of a persistent session is a file transfer across a network, which can be restarted from the point when the file transfer failed due to network problems.

A session management module in the foundation layer or a completely different layer between the engine and foundation layers will be required to manage the sessions, regardless of their type. One of the reasons why it has been left out of the logical reference model is that, more often than not, session management is included in the underlying protocols that manage connections between machines. Hence, unless the adapter is required to actively manage the session, there is no need to include it in the adapter design.

## Applying the Logical Reference Model

One way to test the effectiveness of any reference model is its applicability to specific problem domains. In the case of the logical adapter reference model, its effectiveness can be measured by its applicability to different types of adapters. Another measure of effectiveness is the degree of customization or specialization required to use the logical reference model and develop a physical model. The logical reference model must be relevant to the context. For example, an abstract Java class such as Exception is generic, but only in the context of exception handling, whereas the class Object is really generic. The logical adapter reference model should be analogous to the Exception class to be effective within the adapter context.

## Adapter Types

Many different types of adapters are required to support integration within an enterprise and between enterprises. Some of the most common types of adapters and the way the logical adapter reference model applies to each type are described in the following sections.

### Point-to-Point Integration Adapters

*Point-to-point adapters* are useful when a small number of applications need to be integrated or when all the applications to be integrated are on the same host machine. It is very rare to find the use of integration brokers in these situations because they are add overhead. The logical reference model does not depend on any external brokers for basic data transformation and mapping features.

There is a distinction between external data transformation and internal transformation. External data transformers are required when there are too many different data models to involved in an integration scenario. Also, the real value of external data transformers is when applied to structural transformations as opposed to data type transformations.

The logical reference model includes basic data type transformation capabilities as a distinct module of the engine layer called the mapping engine. The mapping engine module maps one data type to another data type, and handles any conversation between them. It does not change the structure of the data model. In a point-to-point integration scenario, it is fair to assume that the data structure can remain the same, and the target system can parse the specific data structure. This assumption is made on the basis that both the applications know about each other's data models.

### Brokered Integration Adapters

Will the same logical model hold in the case of *brokered adapters*? Integration brokers are used when the scale of integration is large and in a distributed environment. The value of using a broker is that most of the decisions related to transforming the structure of the data models between integrated applications, routing the data objects (messages), filtering unwanted or erroneous messages, and so on are handled by the broker. The adapters (and therefore the applications) have little or no knowledge of the target applications.

Because the logical reference model does not perform any routing or structural transformations, the same model can be used for brokered adapters. Also, the host connectivity and lifecycle modules in the reference model are responsible for managing the connectivity and state of the adapter, depending on the hosting environment. When the host is an integration broker, these modules can delegate most of the lifecycle and state management tasks to the broker, ensuring proper broker-managed integration.

### Conversation Adapters

Some adapters support conversations or interactions between applications. These conversations between applications can take place within the context of one session or across a session. The state of the conversation also needs to be maintained across conversation sessions. The sync service and async service modules in the engine layer can support bidirectional conversations (interactions) in collaboration with the lifecycle management and host connectivity modules in the foundation layer. One benefit of keeping the lifecycle and host connectivity management in the foundation layer is that adapter can support the same service in a sync mode and async mode while reusing the underlying state management and host connections.

An example of a *conversation adapter* is an adapter for an inventory system that exposes services to query inventory information for items and exposes services to move items from the warehouse to the appropriate locations (retail shops, and so on). Typically, the system moving items from the warehouse to the retail shops will first query the current inventory levels among other things before authorizing the movement of items. This is all part of a conversation between the two applications, and the inventory application adapter must support this type of behavior.

### Query Adapters

A *query adapter* supports data queries exclusively. Generally, query adapters enable remote connectivity with enterprise databases, and consolidate the results in an effort to reduce network traffic. The persistence management module in the foundation layer of the logical reference model is instrumental for managing the submission of selection criteria and retrieving the results. If the result size is large, then the async service module can be used to break down the response into multiple units of data. The security provider interface can provide the necessary interfaces to log on to the database or use existing security credentials. Parsing and mapping of data objects may not be necessary in a query-only adapter.

### Broadcast Adapters

A *broadcast adapter* sends or distributes a piece of information or an object to more than one target system simultaneously. The use of the publish-subscribe pattern in supporting this behavior is getting more popular. In this pattern, the external entity interested in being notified about changes or creation of a specific object or piece of information registers with the adapter. When the adapter recognizes the change, it looks in its registration database for a list of clients interested in being notified of the change, and broadcasts the information to them.

The business rules module in the common component layer is useful for keeping the subscriber information. The fact that the host connectivity module can have multiple interfaces may prove to be useful for invoking multiple instances of the host interface to send the information simultaneously to multiple clients. If the adapter chooses to use the operating system features to do the broadcast (or multicast) of the changed objects, then a single interface will be enough. Either way, the business rules module can be used to determine which clients should get the changed information (objects).

### Event Adapters

An *event adapter* is triggered by an external event, as opposed to being invoked by an external entity such as another adapter or an integration broker. Sometimes, the event is actually a timer event that is set off at predefined intervals. The lifecycle management module can be extended to set timers and self-invoke the services exposed by the access layer. In the case of external events, the host connectivity module can be extended to interface with the external event environment and process the events.

There are many other types of adapters that are part of the enterprise integration environment. The reference model described in this chapter may not be applicable to all the adapters, but it is quite capable of supporting most types of adapters.

## Summary

The process of developing adapter models requires skill, experience, and discipline. You cannot underestimate the time required to build robust flexible reference models that will withstand the test of time. However, that is exactly what system architects are expected to do as part of the software development team.

This chapter presented a logical adapter reference model, and also defined some of the physical attributes of the adapter that need to be part of the physical reference models. The logical reference model can be used as the basis of architecture, and specialized for specific adapter types and their physical reference models. Eventually, the use of adapter patterns will make the job of defining reference models (logical and physical) much easier, but this chapter can help developers with a starting point for developing customized, robust, and long-lasting adapter reference models.

# 5

# Role of XML in Adapters

"You cannot change your destination overnight, but you can change your direction overnight."

—Jim Rohn

XML has become part of the vocabulary for any e-Business-related discussion. Over the last couple of years, XML has progressed to become a rich set of specifications that is capable of handling complex data-definition and transformation tasks. XML started as a simple yet powerful tool for defining data structures in a human readable and computer-friendly format. There are misconceptions and occasionally exaggerated expectations about XML and its role in e-Business and especially in application integration. Some people believe XML will replace the need for adapters entirely, and eventually even replace some other integration technologies in use today. Similar opinions were afloat when Windows NT and object databases were first introduced. Windows NT was expected to replace UNIX, and object databases were expected to be preferred for object-oriented applications. Today, UNIX continues to play an important role in enterprise computing, and object-relational frameworks (capable of bridging the gap between business data objects and RDBMS databases) are more popular than object databases.

Some technologists and industry analyst believe XML will replace Electronic Data Interchange (EDI) as we know it. Others predict public exchanges based on open Internet standards such as XML will eliminate private EDI exchanges. That may still happen sometime in the future, but EDI will most likely be still around, although in a different way. The concept of EDI and the business processes it automates will continue to exist. You can think of existing EDI as the legacy version of a new XML and Internet-based EDI. Many technologies available today convert existing EDI documents to XML documents. Eventually, all EDI documents may be in XML format, but XML does not replace EDI. It makes it easier to understand, manage, and deploy EDI solutions and in that sense is a significant innovation.

XML is a very compelling solution for adapters—especially those with data-integration capabilities. However, XML does not replace the vast array of application technologies such as transaction engines, messaging platforms, network and other middleware protocols, programming languages, object brokers, relational databases, and so on. The job of an adapter is to integrate applications across all these technologies, so the notion of XML replacing adapters is probably exaggerated.

This chapter is about understanding XML and its role in adapter development. That role may be enhanced as XML matures and expands and as more features are added to its specifications. Many books and other educational material on XML are available on the Internet and other media. This chapter does not get into the details of XML itself, but focuses on how XML can be used in adapters. The important thing to remember about XML is that its roots are in document definition and document processing. It is a markup language derived from SGML—the same source used for defining HTML, but with a different objective. HTML was tailored for Web browsers, and is thus limited in its capabilities. HTML has a limited set of markups or tags with specific syntax and semantics (meaning) that cannot be changed. XML is a broader, more flexible standard, tailored for Internet-based data exchange. XML is extendable, and specific markup languages such as MathML, WML, and ebXML are proof of its capabilities. The same cannot be achieved by HTML because it does not allow extensions to its set of markups.

You have probably heard about XML or are actively using the technology. Depending on your level of expertise, you may choose to skip this chapter entirely or read only sections that are of specific interest. Appendix B has a list of XML resources that are useful for getting the latest and further information on XML.

## Overview of XML

XML is an acronym for Extensible Markup Language. It is a structure (format) and content description standard for ASCII documents (files), and is recommended by World Wide Web Consortium (W3C). The term *XML document* can be applied to application data, business documents (letters, memos, and so on), and any other computing information and data (configuration information, log files, and so on) that will be exchanged over the Internet. There are no restrictions for using XML in any particular context, platform, or environment. It can be used in a standalone environment, but its real power and capabilities are better appreciated when deployed in a larger-scale, distributed application integration scenario such as ERP, CRM, and B2B integration or supply chain automation. These scenarios involve different platforms, data models, and application transactions; and XML is an ideal solution to define the data exchanged.

XML is a set of specifications much like J2EE. There are specifications for a document model (DOM), specifications for document definitions (DTD), specifications for transforming XML documents (XSL), and so on. Some of these specifications and compliant products have a greater role in the context of adapters then others. XML, XSL-based transformation, XML parsers, DTDs, and schema are some of the topics of greater interest to adapter developers; this chapter focuses on these components and their use.

XML is constantly evolving, and more standards and specifications will be available in the near future, including XQuery—an XML query language for retrieving XML documents from databases. Existing standards are maturing, and the information in this chapter is a snapshot of XML technologies as they evolve.

## XML and HTML Similarities and Differences

Figure 5.1 shows a simple data structure in XML and HTML formats. It is obvious there are some similarities between XML and HTML files, but the differences are significant.

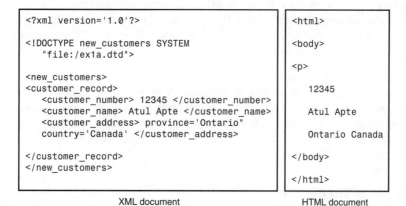

```
<?xml version='1.0'?>

<!DOCTYPE new_customers SYSTEM
    "file:/ex1a.dtd">

<new_customers>
<customer_record>
    <customer_number> 12345 </customer_number>
    <customer_name> Atul Apte </customer_name>
    <customer_address> province='Ontario"
    country='Canada' </customer_address>

</customer_record>
</new_customers>
```

XML document

```
<html>

<body>

<p>

    12345

    Atul Apte

    Ontario Canada

</body>

</html>
```

HTML document

**FIGURE 5.1**   Example XML and HTML files.

The obvious similarities between HTML and XML are that both XML and HTML are ASCII text files. Also, both have the same syntax for defining tags or markups, although the tags that encapsulate the data are different.

However, the differences are not all visible. XML is stricter in applying syntax rules. For example, HTML allows the suffix part of the markups to be missing. In Figure 5.1, the HTML tag <p> (marking the beginning of a paragraph) does not have a corresponding </p> (marking the end of the paragraph). HTML browsers allow processing of HTML documents with such errors. XML is stricter in its enforcement of validation rules. Another difference is that the HTML tags are limited in number and are the same, regardless of the data encapsulated. For example, an HTML paragraph can contain application data as in the example, or any other information and the tag <p> will remain unchanged. However, in the XML document, the tags were more descriptive of the data encapsulated, and these tags will be different, depending on the data. You can still use a single tag to represent all types of data in XML, but that will defeat the purpose of XML, which is to define the structure and the semantics or the meaning of the data.

The data in the Figure 5.1 XML example is easily understood due to the descriptive tags such as <customer_number>, <customer_name>, <customer_address>, and so on. These tags can be replaced by tags that are more relevant to the task. If the XML document is derived from an RDBMS table, the column names for the customer table probably will be different from those in the example. Perhaps <customer_name> will become <c_name>, <customer_address> will become <c_address>, and so on. What is the impact of this on the XML parser? Does the XML parser know that the tag <c_name> is the same as <customer_name>? The XML parser does not know and does not care what the individual tags mean. XML parsers ensure that tags are valid and follow the naming conventions of the XML standard. Understanding the actual meaning of the tags and their data is the responsibility of the application or, in the context of this book, an adapter.

Another important difference between the XML and HTML documents is that HTML tags are designed for presenting documents on different media supporting HTML browsers. Each tag has a specific job related to the task of data or document presentation. These tags cannot be changed to do different things in different contexts the way XML tags can change—depending on the context and the application receiving the XML document.

## Data Management

The following sections explore some of the components of XML, such as XML DTD and XML Schema, which provide more powerful document-validation features than simple checking of the syntax and structural rules. We also discuss the different XML parsers and the document model before identifying some of the roles for the XML components in adapter development. These roles are by no means an exhaustive list of all possible uses of XML, but point to some of the more common XML usage patterns. Other components of XML such as XPath, XLink, and so on are the building blocks for the higher-level XML components. The core piece of all XML components is the XML specification, which defines the format (syntax) and rules (compliance criteria) for XML documents.

To get a better understanding of which XML components fulfill specific requirements of adapters, let's review Figure 5.2, which shows a simplified view of data-management components and data domains applicable to typical business applications.

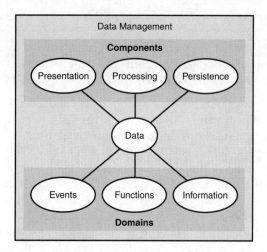

*FIGURE 5.2*    Simplified view of data management.

Almost all data management tasks can be summarized into three types of components: data presentation, data processing, and data persistence. The technology used to support these components and tasks can be simple or complex, depending on the objectives and the context. The data itself can also be classified into three categories: information, events, and functions. Information can include application data, business information, or scientific data, depending on the context. Events represent state changes in objects, and functions include description of business services, and so on.

The data-management components and domain shown in Figure 5.2 are generic and don't cover all aspects of data management. However, they are important to understand where XML technologies fit in this model and derive an appropriate role for XML in adapters.

If you are to accept XML as the foundation for developing data-integration adapters, then you must have access to XML standards and tools to fulfill the responsibilities of data management components. XML also needs to fill the different data domains that exist in different data models.

## Document Type Definitions (DTDs)

Because XML is flexible and can be applied to a broad set of data and document-processing applications, the XML parsers are equally generic in their functionality. An XML parser ensures the XML document is correct in its structure and syntax. But this leads to another problem for applications receiving specific data in XML format: Without a stricter application-specific validation of XML documents, the application will be open to receiving and processing unknown and wrong XML documents. Applications capable of processing XML documents should define specific rules in terms of the structure of the XML document, the set of elements applicable to a specific XML document, the attributes attached to an element, and so on. DTDs enable developers and business analysts to do just that with precision. XML parsers use DTDs to compare the XML document with the specified DTD, and makes a list of places where the XML document differs from the DTD.

Figure 5.3 shows two DTDs for the XML document in Figure 5.1. Using different DTDs, you can define different constraints for the same document used by different applications or adapters. This is one of the benefits of using XML with DTDs. The difference between DTD (A) and DTD (B) is shown in bold. Both DTDs define all the elements and attributes of the XML document. DTA (A) states that the attribute `province` is optional and that the attribute `country` is mandatory. DTA (B) states that both the attributes `province` and `country` are mandatory. The other difference between the two DTDs is in the definition of element `new_customers`. DTD (A) puts the constraint that there will be only one `customer_record` element, whereas DTD (B) allows zero or more `customer_record` elements. The * in (`customer_record*`) indicates the cardinality of `customer_record`.

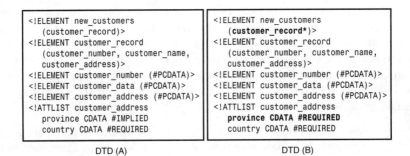

DTD (A)                                    DTD (B)

*FIGURE 5.3*   Examples of DTDs.

Different applications receiving the same XML document can define their own DTDs, which are used by validating parsers to ensure that the XML documents conform to the rules defined in the corresponding DTD. This allows an application-level verification not possible without the features of DTD. DTDs provide many other powerful features, such as support for internal (DTDs embedded in XML documents) and external DTDs, support for externally parsed and externally unparsed data to be included in XML, namespaces, support for different encoding, and so on. (They are not explained in this chapter, but are extremely important for applying XML to adapter development.)

## XML Schema

Although DTDs help with the additional higher-level validation of XML documents, they can't perform data-type validations. DTDs ensure that all the elements and attributes expected in the right structure exist in the XML document. But data validations—for example, if the value of an element is supposed to be a date or the value of an attribute is supposed to be a number between 1 and 10—are not possible. XML Schema is a better mechanism for defining data schemas and ensuring that XML documents have the right data in addition to the right structure.

XML Schema allows the addition of user data types. If you're familiar with C, XML Schema is something like the `typedef` feature that allows programmers to define their own C structures and give them specific names. XML Schema uses two data types: a simple data type and a complex data type. Complex data types are constructed by users, and consist of elements (of other complex data types or simple data types) and attributes. Attributes are always simple data types.

Because XML Schema is still relatively new, support for it in XML tools is not common yet. XML document editors are already supporting XML Schema. This allows XML document managers to incorporate and manage more complex documents then previously possible. It will still be some time before XML Schema is preferred over DTD. As use cases and integration scenarios become more complex, the value of XML Schema will be appreciated. However the next three months will prove to be critical for XML Schema users, especially adapter developers who build data-intensive adapters. If you need stronger type checking of the contents of XML documents, there is no other way except XML Schema. The additional level of checking adds overhead, but if data accuracy and integrity is important, then using DTDs alone is not very helpful. The adapters will have much more validation code without XML Schema.

## XSL-Based Transformation

There are two types of transformations in the context of data integration: *structural transformation*, meaning changing the order or the data and perhaps even its presentation; and *content transformation*, meaning adding, changing, or dropping data elements. Many times, both structural and content transformation are required while exchanging data between two applications. But sometimes, just a structural change or a content change is needed.

XML markup can be very descriptive of the contents, but it needs to be transformed into a presentation-friendly markup for display. XML has two choices for achieving this without changing the code handling XML documents:

- Cascading Stylesheets (CSS)
- XSL Formatting Objects (XSL-FO)

CSS can be used to describe the appearance or particular elements of an XML document. The CSS syntax is not based on XML, and is very different. However, the CSS language is quite small and hence quite easy to implement. One limitation of using CSS is the lack of transformation capabilities, both structural and content related. The CSS syntax works at an element level, and applies presentation rules to the existing markup of the XML document. Using CSS to define the presentation style of the XML document contents results in a more flexible design of adapters, especially those interacting with presentation layer servers such as Web servers, WAP servers, and so on.

Stylesheets are associated with XML documents by using the XML processing instructions. For example, a stylesheet for the XML document in Figure 5.1 could be associated with the XML document using the following processing instruction:

```
<?xml-stylesheet type="text/css" href="ex1.css"?>
```

Many times, the same XML document may need to be displayed on a computer screen, shown on a PDA device, and printed on a regular printer. Instead of generating three versions of the XML document, you can associate three different stylesheets—one for each type of media. Extending the stylesheet processing instruction shown previously, you can add the following three instructions to your XML example document:

```
<?xml-stylesheet type="text/css" href="ex1_screen.css" media="screen"?>
<?xml-stylesheet type="text/css" href="ex1_pda.css" media="handheld"?>
<?xml-stylesheet type="text/css" href="ex1_printer.css" media="print"?>
```

CSS supports many different types of media that are not covered in this chapter. From an adapter perspective, the media types most commonly required are screen, print, and handheld.

Although CSS works with existing XML elements and markup, XSL-FO is an XML application that describes the layout of text on a page. It has a different set of elements representing pages, blocks of text on the pages, graphics, and so on. It is more complex compared to CSS, and you'll rarely have to work with XSL-FO directly. The preferred method of converting XML documents to XSL-FO documents is by using XSLT stylesheets that transform the documents' native XML markup to XSL-FO markup.

# XML Parsers

Two types of XML parsers are available: DOM parsers based on the Document Object Model (DOM), which is recommended by W3C as a language-neutral object model, and SAX parsers.

## DOM Parsers

A *DOM parser* usually accepts an XML document file or a stream or an URI referring to an XML document. After the source XML document is parsed and validated (if the parser supports validation using DTDs or XML Schema), the parser generally exposes an interface capable of traversing the parsed document tree. Each item in the tree is linked to its parent, children, and siblings. Different types of nodes can exist in the tree, such as ELEMENT_NODE, ATTRIBUTE_NODE, TEXT_NODE, CDATA_SECTION_NODE, COMMENT_NODE, and so on.

An important thing to remember is that a DOM-based parser is different from the DOM Node interface that provides an API for traversing the DOM tree. The parser creates a DOM-compatible tree, and the Node interface gives you access to the tree. The Node interface supports get and set operations, and hence is useful for building XML documents as well as reading XML documents.

Because DOM is a hierarchical tree of elements that contain references to other elements, a DOM-based parser requires the entire XML document before it can successfully parse and validate the document. The overhead of maintaining a separate DOM tree for each XML document is also very resource-intensive. This can be an issue for large XML documents if the frequency of receiving XML documents is usually very high, or if there is no requirement to wait for the entire document before commencing to parse the document.

## SAX Parser

*Simple API for XML (SAX)* is usually an event-based API for parsing XML documents. *Event-based* means the API enables you to capture and process the parsing events generated by a SAX parser. Events are generated when the parser encounters start and end tags, processing instructions, and character data. This is helpful to programs that can begin processing XML documents in pieces. Perhaps the XML document has two purchase orders, and the program (or in our case, the adapter) can begin processing the first purchase order without waiting for the second purchase order to be parsed. The SAX parser provides flexibility in how the program processes the XML document. The choice to process after the entire document is parsed or only part of the document is parsed is a design time or run-time decision of the program.

On the down side, SAX-based parsers cannot be used to traverse the document tree, and add new elements or attributes to existing elements. Hence, a common design pattern used by adapter developers is to use the DOM interface to create XML documents and SAX-based parsers to read or parse XML documents. The decision about which parser is suitable for the adapter is partly driven by the integration scenario, the type and size of the XML document, and the capability of the adapted application to process data contained in the XML document either in pieces or as a whole.

Having reviewed the XML components, let's put things in perspective and analyze how much of the data management requirements XML supports. It is evident from Figure 5.4 that XML is able to handle most of the tasks of general data management except for persistence-related functions and any specific support for event definitions. It can handle most adapter-related data-integration scenarios, including data presentation and data validation. XML also provides greater flexibility then other proprietary document definition and parsing technology.

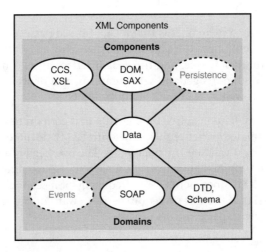

**FIGURE 5.4**    Components of XML.

## Using XML in Adapters

Adapters interface with applications, and process both inbound and outbound data. Inbound data (from the external world to the application) and outbound data will most likely be XML in the relatively near term. The transition to XML-based documents is a gradual process, and during the transition period other proprietary and less-flexible standards will be in use for achieving data integration.

For new adapters or in situations where adapters are being upgraded, a better strategy is to replace proprietary and less-flexible open standards with XML-based documents. Migrating from proprietary document formats to XML is easier because the decision control is inside the organization. With open standards such as EDI, HL7, and so on, organizations must wait for the standards to be XML-compliant, which can take months or years.

Assuming that the application is suitable for XML-based data integration, part of the job of an adapter is to transform the internal application data into outbound XML documents and parse inbound XML documents before updating the native application data. The scenario in Figure 5.5 shows the various XML components and their role in adapters.

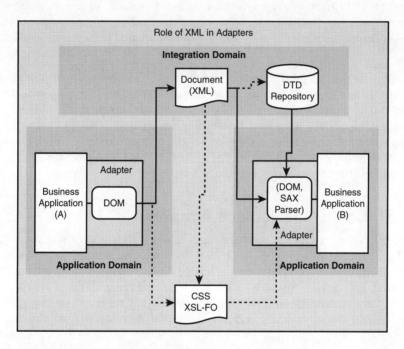

**FIGURE 5.5**   Role of XML in adapters.

The example is a simple integration scenario in which Business Application A is producing XML documents containing different types of data contents to be processed by Business Application B. Application A uses the DOM interface to create the XML document and, depending on the type, to associate a DTD (document definition) or a CSS (stylesheet). Application B uses a DOM parser to parse the XML document and validate it with the associated DTD, or uses a SAX parser to process XML documents with associated CSS before presenting the data.

Using XML as the cross application document format eliminates issues with platform incompatibility and differences between application data models. The benefits of using XML are appreciated when DTD and CSS documents can be changed without necessarily changing code. XML documents can be managed by external XML editors. This is useful in fixing problems in XML documents, DTD, and Schema. As adapter developers continue to use XML, design patterns will evolve, and adapter development will become that much easier.

XML is extensible, and it has proven that by the presence of numerous XML-based protocols and specialized markup languages. One of the most talked-about XML-based protocols is Simple Object Access Protocol (SOAP). We will explore SOAP in more detail in Chapter 6, "Introduction to Web Services." Adapter developers will have to spend time learning these protocols because they are inherently platform independent and capable of supporting a more dynamic form of application integration.

The ultimate metrics for the success of XML will be the existence or non-existence of proprietary and legacy document structures and protocols. EDI is likely to live a much longer life than anticipated, but B2B exchanges are primarily based on XML standards. So, an adapter may still need to interface with non-XML documents, especially in the B2B context, because more then one organization is involved. A quicker transition from proprietary documents to XML is most likely to happen behind a firewall in intranet-based applications.

## Why XML Will Not Replace Adapters

Some people believe that as software vendors adopt XML and its components, the need for adapters will gradually disappear. Indeed, XML simplifies the design and deployment of certain components of the adapter. Probably one reason for thinking that adapters will be replaced by XML is the different definitions of an adapter. No doubt, some classes of adapters—especially those that are heavy on proprietary document models—may become much thinner in their technology footprint. However, adapters do much more than document transformation. We have seen ample evidence of it in our adapter reference model. XML doesn't handle all the design considerations outlined in the adapter reference model. Adapters do the job of connecting with the target application, encapsulating the business rules and integration logic necessary to manage the points of integration, and interface with the middleware and protocols necessary to achieve integration. XML does not do any of this, and it is not intended for it.

For XML to replace even a subset of the adapters, all applications, legacy and new, will have to be converted to use XML as their only data model, and to use one standard transport or protocol to exchange all XML documents. That is not likely to happen anytime soon, given that software and hardware vendors are constantly innovating their technologies. The need for application integration is generated by the existence of different protocols, data models, platforms, and so on. XML is a very important tool for adapter developers because it helps standardize solutions to cross-platform data exchange and management issues, but it does not replace the need for adapters.

## Summary

XML is a powerful standard capable of introducing greater flexibility in adapter design. Data expressed in ASCII files using XML standards and vocabulary is easy to read, process, change, and is platform-independent. All these qualities make XML ideal for defining data integration and exchanging data documents across applications and platforms.

Adapters need a common document model, enabling collaboration between adapters. Today, XML is the most suitable technology for the common document model. Software vendors—including IBM, SUN, and Microsoft—have expressed strong commitment to XML. Not surprisingly, XML is the common thread across platforms, and is an ideal base for adapters.

However, XML covers only a small part of the overall adapter design. Adapters are required to convert data from native application format to XML, and vice versa. Adapters also interface with appropriate protocols to transport the XML documents among other things. The XML set of specifications and standards continues to grow, and adapter developers will save a lot of time by adopting XML as the common data model for integration.

# 6

# Introduction to Web Services

**IN THIS CHAPTER**

- Benefits of Web Services

- Application Services (A Conceptual Model)

- Simple Object Access Protocol (SOAP)

- Universal Description, Discovery, and Integration (UDDI)

- Web Services' Impact on Resource Adapters

"I was taught that the way of progress was neither swift nor easy."

—Madame Marie Curie

In Chapter 5, "Role of XML in Adapters," you saw the role of XML in adapters; but the role of XML is increasing from the perspective of integration in general. One such extension of XML in application integration is Web Services. We discuss Web services in a separate chapter because of their potentially disruptive impact on JCA resource adapters.

Web Services are said to be the next generation of application integration technology, with the potential to radically change e-Business. The concept of Web Services is capturing the mindset of many technology companies and developers. The potential of Internet-based Web Services is huge, but only recently have there been advancements in the technology and platform required to support the concept. The biggest push for Web Services is from Microsoft and its vision for the .NET platform.

This chapter takes a closer look at some important components of Web Services, and discusses their impact on adapter development in general and on JCA resource adapters in particular. If all the hype about Web Services is true, should we even bother to build resource adapters? Yes. Adapters and Web Services are complementary technologies, although they overlap in some areas.

## Benefits of Web Services

The primary benefit of Web Services is that they are designed to work across platforms and programming models (programming languages and paradigms). In some ways, the goals of Web Services are similar to those of CORBA, which also integrates applications across platforms and programming languages. The difference is that CORBA depends on an Interface Definition Language (IDL), whereas Web Services depend on Simple Object Access Protocol (SOAP), which is an XML-based protocol. Another difference is that SOAP is simpler than CORBA IDL, which requires binding with different programming languages at compile time. SOAP, on the other hand, is a late-binding technology, meaning that the application calling a SOAP service does not care which language the service was implemented in. If the same service were implemented in CORBA, it would need an Interface Definition Language (IDL) compiler to map the implementation to CORBA IDL.

Another benefit of Web Services is their acceptance by major vendors—including Microsoft, IBM, SUN, and others. I believe one of the reasons is that vendors are free to define their proprietary technologies (such as programming languages, databases, and so on) without requiring a design-time connectivity to any specific programming language or platform. As long as the Web Service can parse SOAP (XML) messages (documents), it doesn't matter which platform the service is developed and implemented on. Web Services are more flexible than CORBA and other technologies because they're built on top of SOAP, which is derived from XML.

However, the Web Service infrastructure is still very lightweight compared to CORBA, which has a complete array of services to support distributed applications. Perhaps the relative simplicity and small footprint of SOAP-based Web Services is the reason why more developers are attracted to them. JCA Resource Adapter developers must understand the role of Web Services, and how to integrate and collaborate between Web Services and resource adapters. Although product vendors sing the praises of one technology over another, the reality is that both the JCA and SOAP technologies enable developers to build more complete integration solutions.

This chapter is an overview of the Web Service concepts and the potential scenarios in which resource adapters and Web Services can work together. SOAP; Universal Description, Discovery, and Integration (UDDI); and Web Services Description Language (WSDL) are some of the fundamental technologies enabling Web Services. Thus, no overview of Web Services can be complete without a basic understanding of these technologies. Before getting into the details of SOAP and UDDI, a conceptual model of an application service is useful for understanding its role in application integration.

# Application Services (A Conceptual Model)

The concept of application services is not new by any standard. Service-oriented application architectures have been in use for many years, especially in relation to application integration. Figure 6.1 shows a conceptual model of an application service, as well as the roles and components of Web Services. The primary objective of an application service is to make specific functions accessible by external applications. Not all functions and services are integration-oriented. Some services are standalone, and their scope is restricted to one applications. Other services involve more than one application, and are more complex by definition.

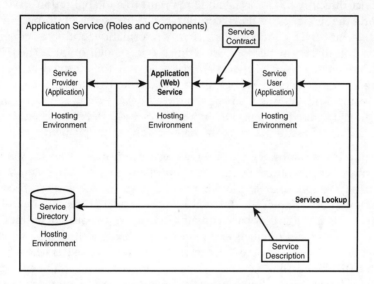

**FIGURE 6.1**    Application services (roles and components).

An application has more than one role in the context of application services. The application that provides a service is known as the *service provider*, and the application(s) that uses the service is known as the *service user*. Any application can be a service provider and a service user at the same time. As a service provider, an application publishes details of each service it provides. These service details are also sometimes referred to as *service contracts*. A service contract defines the prerequisites of using the service; the expected results of successful execution of the service; and any post-service actions, including acknowledgements and exception handling. Together, these parameters define the quality of service and obligations of both the provider and user.

### Service Directory

As a service user, an application needs to know which application provides the necessary service. This is usually accomplished by searching for service definitions in a service directory. The *service directory* stores service contracts and information about service providers (location, availability, and so on). Some of the services can be synchronous, and others can be asynchronous. Invoking a synchronous service results in a dialogue between the service provider and the service user; whereas invoking a asynchronous service results in an acknowledgement, followed by the service user retrieving the results at a future time.

The service directory has a special and important role in application services. A directory stores the service definitions (contracts) as well as service information (physical location of the server, configuration, security information, and so on) in one central location. This makes the task of discovering services much simpler. The UDDI and WSDL components of Web Services are fast becoming the accepted standards for defining and implementing service directories. Before UDDI, Lightweight Directory Access Protocol (LDAP) was the preferred directory server and access mechanisms. LDAP can still be used to store the service contracts; however, access to LDAP servers have to be UDDI-based for a more standards-compliant implementation.

Service directories can be generic or serve specific industries. They are something like the yellow pages in a phone book: Some yellow pages contain the names of all businesses in a geographical area, and other yellow pages are focused on specific industries or professions. One of the differences between a UDDI repository and the yellow pages is that a yellow page contains information about the business and a description of its main products and services. A UDDI repository stores more detailed information about how to access the services provided, as well as where they are located. UDDI also defines more than one data type, which capture different details of the Web Service—including information about the service provider, the location of the Web Service, and technical details such as the port numbers required to access the service.

## Simple Object Access Protocol (SOAP)

This section on SOAP provides an overview of its objectives, capabilities, and potential uses. You should read the entire SOAP specification (the latest version is 1.2, available at `http://www.w3.org`) to understand it before designing Web Services.

SOAP includes a specific definition of an XML document, which can be used to exchange structured and typed information. SOAP is a stateless, one-way XML message exchange mechanism; applications or adapters can extend it to support more complex integration scenarios, including conversations (request response), multicast, and so on. SOAP does not define the routing, transformation, message delivery, and so on. It depends on the underlying transport infrastructure to deliver those characteristics. In short, SOAP is a message definition standard or specification.

What makes this standard powerful is that it's based on XML, which is platform-independent. In addition, the SOAP specification includes definitions of which actions should take place when a SOAP message is received by a SOAP server (also known as a *SOAP processor*). These actions are described in the SOAP processing model.

An example of a SOAP message for a purchase order with three items is as follows:

```
<?xml version='1.' ?>
<env:Envelope xmlns:env=http://www.w3.org/2001/12/soap-envelope>
<env:Header>
  <po:purchaseorder xmlns=:po="http://book.example.com/purchaseorder"
   env:actor=http://www.w3.org/2001/12/soap-envelope/actor/next
   env:mustUnderstand="true">
    <po:Number>12345</po:Number>
  </po:purchaseorder>
</env:Header>
<env:Body>
  <itm:itemList xmlns:itm=http://book.example.com/items>
    <itm:itemType>Book</itm:itemType>
    <itm:name>Integrating Your E-Business Enterprise</itm:name>
    <itm:copies>one</itm:copies>
    <itm:itemType>Book</itm:itemType>
    <itm:name>XML In A Nutshell</itm:name>
    <itm:copies>two</itm:copies>
    <itm:itemType>Book</itm:itemType>
    <itm:name>Patterns In Java</itm:name>
    <itm:copies>one</itm:copies>
  </itm:itemList>
</env:Body>
</env:Envelope>
```

A SOAP message is actually an XML document with a specific structure (tags) and a name space to avoid any confusion in processing the SOAP tags from similar tags defined in the header or the body. The header is an optional part of the message and is usually extended by SOAP applications. Tags in the header section generally have their own application-specific name spaces. The body is a mandatory part of the SOAP message. Without a body, there is nothing to process. The SOAP message structure is very simple and small.

## SOAP Processing Model

A SOAP message can be sent from the sender to the receiver without any intermediate steps (a point-to-point SOAP message exchange), or can involve several processing nodes (SOAP processors). Each SOAP processor can assume different roles for processing specific SOAP messages. When there are one or more SOAP processor nodes between the sender and receiver, the header section of the SOAP message can carry and convey important information to ensure that the processing nodes handle the SOAP message appropriately.

SOAP defines an attribute called `actor`, whose value indicates the role a processor is expected to assume when processing the SOAP message. Three possible roles can be indicated by the `actor`: `none`, `next`, and `anonymous`.

The concept of an envelope suggests that the SOAP structure is an outer shell of the real message or data. This is true, and the actual data can be grouped in one or more application-specific header blocks and body blocks. As a result, a SOAP message may include information that is not intended for the actual processing by the target application. For example, if an ERP system such as SAP generates an EDI message wrapped as a SOAP message that is targeted at an external supplier's system, then the SOAP message may have information about the EDI gateway responsible for transporting the SOAP message to a SOAP server in the supplier environment. This EDI gateway information may be processed by an intermediate SOAP processor, which will ensure that the message has been properly received over the network before forwarding it to the SOAP-enabled application or Web Service.

The attribute `actor` identifies the target processor's role for individual blocks of data in the header section. Each data block in the header can be targeted at different SOAP processors, who may assume different roles as defined by the `actor` attribute of each block. The body section does not have any `actor` attributes, ensuring that the final target SOAP processor must process the body section per the defined name space.

There is obviously much more to SOAP than we can cover in this chapter. However, the basic structure of a SOAP message and some of its capabilities in terms of supporting multistep processing of messages are important to the concept of Internet-enabled Web Services.

# Universal Description, Discovery, and Integration (UDDI)

A central piece of any online service infrastructure is a directory that stores the definition of all available services, enabling users to query the availability of the services before interacting with the specific service implementations. UDDI (http://www.uddi.org) is a platform-independent method of describing services, discovering service providers (businesses), and integrating with the services over the

Internet. UDDI enables users to publish their services and business information, which is stored in a central repository. UDDI is based on SOAP; its data structure provides a framework for describing the service contracts and business information.

## UDDI Data Types

The UDDI data structures are defined using XML Schema. There are four basic data types:

- `businessEntity`
- `businessService`
- `bindingTemplate`
- `tModel`

What do these four data structures represent? Referring to Figure 6.1, the `businessService` data type represents the service description, and `tModel` represents the service contract (or at least part of it). The `businessEntity` data type is useful for getting more details on the service provider (company)—for example, when more than one service provider is capable of providing the same or similar services. You may have a preference for one service provider over others. The `bindingTemplate` data type provides information on the location of the service. In some respects, the `bindingTemplate` provides a more technical version of the service description than is provided by `businessService` data type. Together, these two data types help describe the service. Together, the four data types form the registration information in a UDDI repository. The `businessEntity` data type is mandatory, and every Web Service is required to provide information about the service provider. Other data types are optional.

## WSDL

UDDI also specifies an API for publishing and searching for UDDI entries. The API is divided into publishing API functions and inquiry API functions. These APIs enable businesses to maintain their business and service information, and also search for appropriate Web Services.

Although UDDI builds on top of SOAP and XML, the data types are still quite generic, and it is possible to define more specific service definition vocabularies and specifications. WSDL is one such example of a general-purpose service description language. WSDL complements UDDI, and provides a uniform mechanism for describing abstract service interfaces and specific protocol bindings that support the service. You can use SOAP and UDDI for implementing Web Services, but you will have to develop a proprietary implementation similar to WSDL.

The combination of SOAP, UDDI, and WSDL provide the necessary infrastructure for Web Services without actually depending on any specific platform, protocol, or data models. All these technologies prove that XML has real potential in integrating cross-platform applications built with different programming languages. Doing so is not easy, and requires you to learn many new technologies, but the end result of integrating the applications is worth the effort.

# Web Services' Impact on Resource Adapters

The impact of Web Services on adapters is still undefined. Which of the two is better than the other depends on the integration scenario, the supporting infrastructure, and the available tools. A more immediate impact will be in categorizing and decomposing the integration logic into Web Services and/or resource adapters.

When should you develop a Web Service, and when should you develop a resource adapter? Can a Web Service do what a resource adapter does (provide EIS connectivity to J2EE applications)? Most likely yes, mainly due to the JCA-specific contracts defined in the J2EE environment. A Web Service will have to implement the JCA contracts in addition to receiving SOAP messages and publishing its service contracts to a UDDI registry.

However, SUN is approaching Web Service support in a different context (portal servers), and is using the iPlanet directory servers and iPlanet portal servers as part of the SUN ONE Web Service platform. This does create some confusion about whether J2EE is a valid platform for Web Services. However, SUN's Web strategy is rapidly evolving, and a more stable and feature-rich platform for Web Services from a Java and J2EE perspective will emerge soon.

Technically, not much prevents a Java developer from implementing a Web Service as a JCA resource adapter. Its usefulness will be determined by what role it plays in the context of J2EE applications. J2EE is an application platform, and its components are mostly designed as part of a J2EE application. External (service-oriented) access to the J2EE application is thought to be more of a portal server job. But Web Services can be developed on a J2EE platform as message-driven Enterprise JavaBeans (EJBs). The possibilities are many, but the real issue is where and how Web Services fit in the Java application context.

## Adapters and Web Services Working Together

As complementary technologies, adapters and Web Services can work together to implement complex integration scenarios. Adapters can take on the role of data synchronization, whereas Web Services will enable application functions to interact with each other. A Web Service may need to integrate with other applications to fulfill its service contract. Furthermore, the drivers of data synchronization and Web

Services are also different. Web Services generally will be initiated by a user request/event, whereas data synchronization is generally initiated by state changes in data objects.

A user event can be a purchase order or an online bill payment, for example. User events can also be generated by applications such as a customer service application requiring an account status check from the accounting system. Web Services are an ideal mechanism for implementing a universally accessible application function (service). On the other hand, a state change in a data object can be something like the addition of a new customer record in the customer service application or an update to the customer's billing address. These state changes trigger an adapter to add the new customer record or update the customer record in all other applications that keep their own copies of customer data. Data synchronization is one of the primary objectives of resource adapters.

But adapters do more than data synchronization, and many times they support distributed transactions. This is the area in which there is potential for an overlap between Web Services and adapters. It may be better to define an implementation strategy in terms of when to use an adapter and when to use a Web Service. Figure 6.2 shows a potential scenario in which a Web Service and a resource adapter coexist.

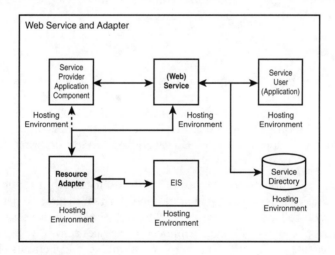

**FIGURE 6.2**   Web Service and adapter coexisting.

The role of the Web Service is to expose the functionality of the J2EE application to non-J2EE clients such as .NET applications and other clients. In doing so, the Web Service may have to integrate with other instances of EIS in the company, or the J2EE application itself may have to integrate with other EISs. In both these scenarios, a resource adapter is required. In this implementation strategy, Web Services become the interface between the company and its customers, partners, and suppliers; whereas the resource adapters become integration components tying up different EISs inside the company. This is just one potential implementation pattern in which Web Services and resource adapters can coexist.

Another potential integration pattern in which Web Services and resource adapters are required to collaborate is in business process integration. Applications that are part of a specific business process will have to expose the required processes (functions), and Web Services are ideal for that purpose. When the applications need to integrate with other EISs to fulfill their part in the business process, they will use resource adapters.

When a SOAP-based Web Service needs to call a resource adapter, the actual call is made by a SOAP server (SOAP node). The SOAP server will have to be hosted in a J2EE environment, and be capable of calling the CCI-compliant interfaces of the resource adapter. J2EE does not support SOAP as part of the specification; neither does it support XML. It is left to the application server vendors to provide the additional SOAP server functionality in their application servers. An alternative to a SOAP container in the J2EE environment is being defined as part of J2EE 1.4 Java API for XML Messaging (JAXM) and Java API for XML-based RPC (JAX-RPC); this alternative will help in building custom SOAP containers and developing components that do the work of SOAP nodes (SOAP processors).

## Summary

The hype surrounding Web Services makes it very hard to ignore this emerging technology. Experienced software developers should study the details of Web Services, and differentiate between the hype and practical uses of Web Services. Already, some of the EAI vendors are downplaying the potential effectiveness of Web Services and their role in application integration. However, Web Services do bring some simplicity to integration solutions.

By using an integration protocol based on XML and focusing on application services instead of data, Web Services enable more sophisticated integration patterns. Interapplication collaborations are easier with Web Services. It is possible that in the near future, applications will invoke application services across the Internet, both inside and outside the firewall. This may sound similar to EDI and its objectives in integrating intercompany processes. However, EDI is a point-to-point data exchange solution, and Web Services are more dynamic service-based application-collaboration solutions.

Web Services pose a challenge to the long-term effectiveness of Java Connector Architecture. SUN had to announce its support for Web Services due to industry pressure, and the roadmap for JCA may have to change as a result. But every challenge is an opportunity, and perhaps the emergence of Web Services will give JCA a more focused objective and role in application integration. After all, JCA is a standard only in the realm of J2EE application servers; and although J2EE is the primary platform for Internet applications today, it will likely face stiff competition from .NET initiatives.

Only time will tell how Web Services influence the evolution of J2EE in general and JCA in particular. In the meantime, Web Services and resource adapters can and will coexist to solve the application-integration problem.

# 7

# Adapter Development Methodology and Best Practices

"Even if you are on the right track, you'll get run over if you just sit there."

—*Will Rogers, American humorist*

Business today is heavily dependent on interactions and networking with customers, partners, suppliers, and employees. This dependency on integration of business processes and resources drives the need for integrated business applications. The days of developing standalone applications are long gone, and today none of the applications can satisfy users' requirements for information and transaction processing without interfacing with other applications. Almost all software development projects can be categorized as one of the following:

- Developing a new business application using emerging technologies, leading edge software paradigms, new platforms, and tools.

- Upgrading existing systems by adding new functions to exchange data and functions with other applications. New functions typically include Web enabling legacy applications and adding integration capabilities.

- Deploying a third-party package or upgrading an existing third-party package. Typically, deploying third-party packages involves data migration issues, customization issues, and integration with existing business applications.

- Research projects and other initiatives that experiment with new technologies such as wireless networking and wireless applications can work in an isolated environment or with limited integration with existing systems.

- Composite applications are a new category of applications that integrate isolated applications as a coherent system capable of supporting e-Business requirements—typically, Web Services.

In each of these scenarios, the need to integrate business applications is driven not just by the technical requirements; it is mainly the business requirements that drive the software development projects. Application integration has become part of mainstream software development, and it is essential to include integration as a primary objective when planning and managing software projects.

Do we need a new methodology for handling the inclusion of integration requirements and adapter development? Not unless software development is managed without a methodology in the first place. This chapter is not about introducing a new methodology, but customizing existing methodologies for adapter development. Many significant differences exist between standard application development and software development involving adapters or integration. The following sections identify the most important aspects of adapter development, and present how to apply known methodologies and techniques to overcome some of the unique challenges.

## Understanding Integration Project Objectives

Most adapter-related projects are initiated as part of other mainstream development projects. Sometimes, an adapter requirement is identified during system integration. In many instances, adapter requirements come from IT staff who handle data integrity issues rather than application users. The reason for this is that most end-users assume that application integration is a normal feature of software. I have seen numerous occasions when end-users were surprised when their applications were not able to share data with other applications without major modifications. In these situations, IT staff are usually commissioned to come up with a short-term solution in the form of shell scripts and other manual processes. The problem is that over time there are too many short-term solutions. Although sometimes time constraints demand patchy solutions and manual application integration procedures, the long-term solution is a proper EAI platform and adapters. This chapter should be useful for project managers who have identified a need for adapters or who are undertaking software development projects.

As an example project, let's consider the Web enabling of a customer service application. The application is currently used by internal customer service staff. These users are trained in-house to handle specific customer situations and exceptions, and to customize business processes to meet the customer needs. However, with the customer interacting directly with the application, most of the work done by the customer service staff will now be the responsibility of the customer. Some of the major differences of Internet-based applications supporting e-Business initiatives and the legacy applications are the end-users and their roles. Web-enabling external business services and internal business processes require the end-users to take more responsibilities than before.

Business processes that were handled manually by the customer service staff now need to be automated by the application and its infrastructure. It is not surprising to see Web enabling of one application requiring significant modifications to other business applications. The need to understand the end-to-end business processes and their impact on all the applications participating in those business processes is fundamental to any e-Business project. As a result, every e-Business project becomes an integration project with varying degrees of complexities.

For many legacy systems developed to work in isolation, integration is a new phenomenon. Adding integration capabilities to existing applications requires careful planning and sustained development. A good design principle is to isolate and localize the integration capabilities of each business application in a separate component that is directly associated with the application. These components are known by different terms: adapters, connectors, components, and so on. The separation of core application functionality and integration logic enables software developers to evolve the business application and the adapter with minimum dependency. Figure 7.1 shows an integration-ready application. The architecture includes an additional integration tier; this tier supports the different types of integration components.

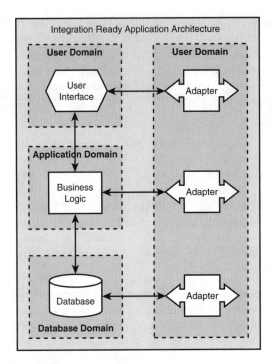

*FIGURE 7.1*   Integration-ready applications.

## Managing Integration Teams

There are two basic models for managing integration requirements and supporting software development projects: enterprise integration teams and business model-driven integration. Both models have their own challenges and key success factors. The choice depends on the corporate culture, the number of project teams, and the experience of project management staff.

### Enterprise Integration Teams

Usually, the enterprise integration team is a separate team or department with dedicated staff to support it. These teams work at an enterprise level, and are liaisons with departmental and other distributed development project teams. The integration team is tasked with designing the integration infrastructure, setting standards, and working with the other project team leaders who implement the various integration strategies and components.

Enterprise integration teams need to have a broader view of the corporate IT function and the corporate business goals. The challenges faced by these teams include getting support from other project teams in implementing enterprise-level integration requirements. It is not unusual for department project teams to feel burdened with extra work by the enterprise teams. There is often conflict between the short-term goals of department project teams and the long-term goals of enterprise integration teams that result in tension; integration often suffers as a result. Enterprise integration teams rarely succeed without continued support from senior management. Figure 7.2 shows the critical role of project managers in enterprise integration teams. These project managers not only manage specific integration projects but also are responsible for coordinating integration analysis across department project teams.

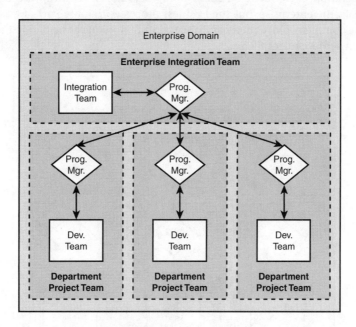

*FIGURE 7.2*   Centralized integration team.

## Business-Model-Driven Integration

Another model used in some corporate environments is to define integration requirements based on the business models. When using this model, the business users or business analysts define the overall business integration objectives, and publish a roadmap. Project teams responsible for implementing the roadmap resolve application integration issues by using the common development process. Individual project teams are completely responsible for adhering to corporate standards in their development projects. Project managers collaborate to schedule, estimate, and plan for integration-related enhancements and developments.

This model works well when the number of project teams is small (between one and five), and when the business models are well-defined and documented. For larger numbers of project teams, a central integration team is required to define the standards and ensure compliance across the enterprise. Also, the business models often are not accurate or even complete. The fast-changing business environment makes it hard to define the business requirements and build a stable business model. As a result, frequent changes to integration requirements bog down the project teams affecting the delivery of software.

Figure 7.3 shows the importance of a complete business model when it drives enterprise integration. A complete business model does not have to capture all business processes in the enterprise, but the business processes that are part of the model should be complete. Only then can integration requirements be derived for implementation across project teams.

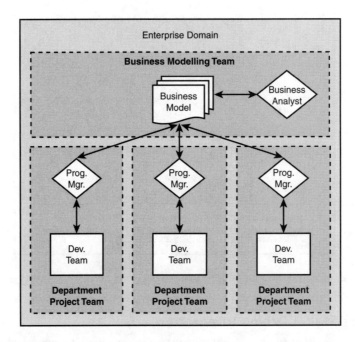

**FIGURE 7.3**   Business-model-driven integration teams.

## Advantages and Disadvantages

Both models have their advantages and disadvantages when applied to project-managing strategies. Isolating integration as a separate project enables the integration project teams to focus on developing the integration solutions more quickly.

However, the practical value of the integration solution can only be realized when deployed in conjunction with business applications that are developed by different project teams. Many times, the integration solutions developed by dedicated integration project teams are technically good, but they are developed in isolation without full understanding of the complete requirements. The usual causality in these scenarios is the technology, which takes the blame for failed integration projects.

On the other hand, empowering individual project teams with the necessary integration standards and tools doesn't automatically guarantee cooperation between project teams. Many times, the management objectives of individual project teams are focused on departmental issues rather then understanding enterprise objectives. Unless a stable business model is defined, project teams are constantly grappling with changing integration requirements.

Software integration is a cross-functional requirement and cannot be solved by isolating the integration teams; nor can it be solved by allowing individual project teams to function in isolation. One approach that yields better results is training the development teams on integration tools and development methodologies that make integration part of the process. Project managers need to change their project management techniques and processes to include closer cooperation from other project managers, technical leads, business analysts, and integration experts. It is very important that every project team has a technical lead (or an architect, depending on the size of the project) who is a member of an integration team composed of technical and business experts.

In very large global organizations where integration issues are not only technical but also geographical, a central integration council with participants from all geographical regions is useful in determining the challenges of integration. In smaller organizations, integration teams tend to be formed on a more informal basis, with representation from each project team as required for specific time-bound integration projects. Regardless of the type of team and the methods used to form them, participation from all involved application teams and availability of integration experts is critical.

The integration experts need to ensure that all software development activities adhere to common enterprise integration standards, tools, and architecture. We will explore the role of adapters in integration projects more in the following sections.

## Role of Adapters in Integration Project

Adapters are endpoints of any integration solution, so they interact directly with the business applications. The role of adapters is defined by the type of integration scenarios. In the case of data integration scenarios, adapters are responsible for extracting data from the business applications database, and updating the application database with external data and actions. When the integration scenario is about workflow automation, adapters must enable applications to generate events representing application transaction and state changes in the database. Adapters also need to handle external events and triggers, which may require the application to take specific actions. In the scenario of Web services, adapters expose application functions to the Web and invoke appropriate application function, depending on the service request. It is usually a good practice to identify adapters with the business application it integrates instead of the integration platform it requires to achieve the integration. In other words, it is very important to understand that adapters are extensions of the business applications and not of the integration platform or infrastructure.

Project managers need to make a conscious decision to include application adapters in any type of integration scenario. If the existing adapter does not provide the functionality required for the integration scenario, the adapter must be upgraded. Following this practice ensures that all integration logic is located in one place (in the adapter), making future upgrades and maintenance in general easier. Without adapters, applications will have to be significantly changed.

Adapters do the actual connections with application resources (such as databases and middleware); and manage application transactions, security, exceptions, and so on. In an ideal integration scenario, all participating applications will have an adapter defining and managing the integration capability of the associated application. Adapters define the point of integration for an application, and hence project managers can build and share development metrics based on a known set of artifacts. The section "Estimating Adapter Development" provides some high-level guidelines on how to build adapter development and maintenance metrics.

## Adapter Analysis

As with any other software development project, analysis is very important for adapter development and maintenance. Understanding the complete integration scenario is fundamental to any adapter analysis methodology or technique. Knowing the objectives of the integration scenario is useful in determining the specific role of the adapters.

Where should a software analyst begin when developing adapters? The analysis is a four-step process, beginning with the business objectives and ending with an analysis model—complete with integration use cases, analysis of application architectures, data models, and API. Following is a series of individual steps and tasks that can be used as a guideline for adapter analysis in general:

1. Understanding the business objective.

   - Integrate applications to eliminate duplicate data entry and ensuring data integrity.

   - Enable Web-based, service-oriented access to application functions. The services can be used by customers, partners, and internal staff.

   - Enhance applications to support workflow and process automation.

   - Document the business objectives that are driving the integration requirements. It will be useful in calculating the ROI as well as justifying future integration requirements.

2. Analyze the end-to-end integration scenario.

   - Identify all the applications participating in the integration scenario.

   - If applicable, identify master or controlling applications. Typically, these applications manage master databases and provide unique services.

   - In a peer-to-peer integration model, identify the initiator of integration scenarios. If the initiators are different, based on business rules, a table stating the association between business rules and which application is the initiator when the business rule is asserted.

   - Identify the mismatch between individual data models of all participating applications. This information will be useful for defining the data structures to be exchanged by applications within an integration scenario. Data transformation and validation requirements are derived from this analysis.

   - Document the analysis results, either in a text document with as much detail as possible or using a UML-based development tool. A use case analysis model captures the results of analysis in text form. Use case models identify the relationships between use cases, system boundaries, and entities interacting with the use cases. An example of a use case capturing a simple end-to-end integration scenario is shown in the section on "Documenting Integration Scenario."

3. Analyze the individual application architecture.

   - Identify the database structures (tables, objects, and so on) of each application required to complete the integration scenario.

   - Identify any available API, staging database tables, and other types of interfaces in the application. These interfaces could be used as points of integration for adapters. If no such interfaces are available, it is a good indication of the effort required to develop integration capabilities for the application.

- Identify third-party middleware technologies used in multitier applications. Generally, distributed applications are easier to integrate because they have more points of integration tied together by middleware platforms and tools.

- One of the most important design features that needs research is the applications support for synchronous and asynchronous transactions. Knowing which applications support either or both types of transactions helps in the design of a high-quality adapter. It is quite common for adapters to be burdened with additional work required to handle asynchronous interfaces in a synchronous transaction and vice versa.

- Document the available points of integration (PIN) and the type of PIN (database table, stored procedure, API, message, and so on). Also, document the business function exposed by the individual PIN. Document the sync-async mismatch between PINs because it will drive the individual adapter designs later in the process.

4. Identify programming constraints.

- Many times, integration project teams face the difficult task of integrating old business applications. Not only are the programming language and supporting tools an issue, but also knowledge about its architecture and design. Identifying the constraints, especially with respect to the non-availability of appropriate development tools, needs to be documented very early in the process. Project managers need to treat these as potential risks and try to develop alternate strategies.

- Differences in programming languages of the business applications should be taken into consideration when identifying constraints. Not all programming languages are easier to deal with when developing adapters. Java provides a JNI interface to call code developed in other languages. However, it is not easy, and not all languages are supported by JNI.

- The constraints identified by the adapter analysis teams are very useful for project managers in estimating the adapter development efforts as well as setting the right expectations.

This four-step process is very basic and is not supposed to be a full-fledged analysis process. Individual project teams and project managers need to verify whether their analysis process handles some of things stated above.

## Documenting the Integration Scenario

Integration scenarios can be simple point-to-point data exchange or complex distributed data synchronization. Other types of integration scenarios include accessing services over the Web or other proprietary platforms. Increasingly, process modeling and automation are seen as means to capture business processes and link them to applications using workflow and other tools.

Each type of integration scenario has unique requirements and can be implemented using different design patterns. But before you know which design patterns to use, it is important to document the integration scenario and identify all the participants as well as the different integration points. A common practice in software analysis today is defining the requirements in use cases. A *use case* is part of UML specifications, and is more often used to capture user requirements. However, use cases can also be used to capture integration requirements. Requirements of a simple integration scenario are shown in the example use case in Figure 7.4.

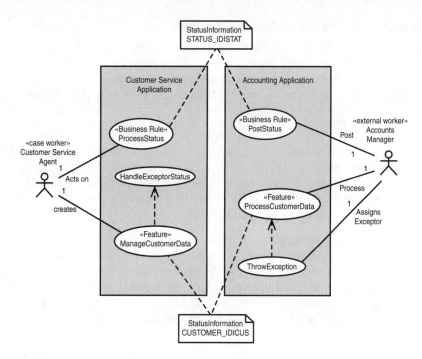

*FIGURE 7.4*   Example integration use case.

It may look odd at first that the diagram shows two system boundaries. Most business analysts using UML are perhaps used to a single system boundary that defines the business application for which the user requirements are captured. This diagram shows the difference between normal requirements analysis and integration analysis. More complex integration scenarios will have more system boundaries (systems) involved in the use case model.

Another difference is the identification of data structures that need to be exchanged between systems. In Figure 7.4, the data structures are shown as text notes outside the system boundaries. It is important to understand these requirements early on because they may require different project teams to spend significant time later on in supporting the integration projects.

From a project management perspective, a use case model is very useful for understanding the complexity of the integration scenario, the different systems involved, and the points of integration between the systems at a high level without any technical details. Project managers can then begin to estimate the effort and coordinate with other project managers the work required from members of other teams in successfully implementing the integration solution.

## Determining Hub and Spoke Scenarios

Sometimes, integration scenarios can be defined as a *hub and spoke* type of integration scenario. This is usually the case when one application is the master or controlling application, and all other applications are reacting to the state changes of the controlling application. Controlling application could be legacy applications, third-party packages, and even J2EE applications.

In a hub and spoke integration scenario, the controlling application's action determines the effect on all other applications in the scenario. If the controlling application (hub) changes any of its data, other applications (spokes) need to be notified of the change so that they can synchronize their database states as required. Changes to data in other applications besides the controlling application are not part of the integration scenario; they are considered to be local changes.

The benefits of identifying hub and spoke scenarios are evident when selecting integration technologies implementing the solution. However, from a project management perspective, it is quite likely that the project managers responsible for the controlling application (hub) need to take the leadership role and put in extra efforts to coordinate the integration efforts from other teams. Without a defined flow of project management activities, it is difficult to understand and manage the integration project.

## Determining Peer-to-peer Scenarios

A different type of integration scenario occurs when all participants have equal responsibilities. In a peer-to-peer integration scenario, the participants synchronize data between their databases by processing data updates from all applications. An update to one application is broadcast to all other applications in the scenario. There is no concept of a master application controlling the chain of events.

Peer-to-peer integration scenarios are more likely to emerge in the context of process automation rather then data integration. Most data-integration scenarios have one application as the data owner, and only this application triggers data updates. The hub and spoke scenario discussed earlier is more suitable for data integration. Examples of peer-to-peer scenarios include workflow and process automation-related integration scenarios in which participating applications are expected to generate events reflecting internal state changes, and to process incoming events by taking appropriate actions. In a workflow automation environment, all applications generate events or they process events and then trigger the associated actions. The coordination and propagation of the events are not controlled by any one application, but depend on a higher-level abstraction of the finite state machine.

In some special cases, one or more of the peers in a peer-to-peer integration scenario is a composite application. A *composite application* is an aggregation of other applications built to support specific integration requirements. The individual applications that are part of the composite application may have a hub-and-spoke or peer-to-peer relationship with other applications; but for analysis, the composite application can be considered as supporting the peer-to-peer scenario. Composite applications may not be common today, but over time they will be found in most enterprises.

It is always better to separate the peer-to-peer integration scenarios from hub and spoke scenarios. Most adapters only handle data integration. Event processing is not usually considered an adapter function. Sometimes, it is handled by a workflow automation tool, which maintains the state changes on the application's behalf. By identifying the peer-to-peer scenarios project, managers can choose to either enhance the workflow tool if one exists or include the functionality in adapters. Without proper support in the adapter frameworks, however, it is very difficult to have both data integration and event processing implemented as one adapter.

## Analyzing Application Architectures

Adapters are part of business applications, so one of the challenges of building adapters for existing applications is having the knowledge of application internals or the architecture. Very often, the application architecture and design are not explicitly documented or modeled. As a result, adapter developers need to spend a significant amount of time understanding the application internals. Integration teams often spend most of their time modeling the database structure and business rules—something that should have been done earlier by the application development teams that maintain the application. Project managers need to consider the impact of this when estimating the integration efforts. Depending on the size of the application, available documentation, and access to resources knowledgeable about the application, the architecture analysis effort can be reasonable or frustrating.

Project managers should not skip this activity because the result is a longer design and development cycle. In other words, the architecture analysis work cannot be avoided. It can be done as part of the integration analysis process or deferred to the development teams. Putting it off to the development teams usually results in a less-than-desirable integration solution.

## Analyzing Application Data Models

Data impedance or differences in data models between applications is the classic application integration problem. These issues are complicated by business rules attached to data models. For example, it is quite likely that the structure of an account number column in the accounting database is actually a composite of three business data elements: Customer ID, Geographical Area code, and Account type. These types of data fields and data models pose significant integration challenges during the development and implementation phase. It is not surprising to see integration projects fail due to lengthy implementation cycles as a result of hidden data impedance. Project managers need to understand the significance of these seemingly small technical issues. It is not just about transforming data from one format to another; it involves applying and verifying business rules, as well.

Experienced project managers tend to estimate additional time for data model analysis because generally it is one of those areas that comes back later as a major underestimated factor. The lack of any documentation on the business rules attached with data models means coordination and help from business analysts. Either way, this is a very important task of adapter development, especially when focused on data integration.

## Analyzing Application APIs

Sometimes we get lucky, and one such instance in the life of an adapter developer is when applications have a well-defined API. Adapter developers eventually develop a sense of respect for applications with well-documented APIs. However, not all APIs are useful for adapter development. Many times, low-level APIs that work with technical objects instead of higher-level business objects tend to be more work than they're worth. This is not to say that lower-level APIs are not useful, but in the context of adapter development, accessing technical objects such as data rows in an RDBMS table, or data objects in a ODBMS is faster and easier with the native interfaces such as SQL and OQL. Application-level APIs that encapsulate business logic are more useful for adapter development.

In the absence of a higher-level API, a decision needs to be made very early on in the project on the relative use of lower-level APIs in adapter development. If the lower-level APIs are expected to save time and encapsulate the adapter developers from many technical details, there is still value in using the APIs. However, if the difference between native interfaces and the lower-level APIs is not much and the value added by the APIs is more cosmetic, a better strategy would be to build a higher-level API as part of the adapter development project.

In the long term, adapter development time and maintenance time can be reduced by higher-level, business-oriented application APIs. Project managers need to consider and weigh the long-term benefits versus short-term time constraints.

## Analyzing Buy Versus Build Options

Having a good understanding of the end-to-end integration scenario, individual application architectures, data impedance between applications, availability of clearly defined APIs, and so on should enable project managers to contribute to the buy versus build decision-making process. Many integration solutions are available in the market. Some specialize in data transformation, and others provide integration brokers and application servers capable of simplifying integration.

This book is not about the various decision-making processes involved in selecting integration solutions, but the information generated during the analysis phase outlined in the chapter should enable project managers to contribute to that process. It is always a good strategy to engage application integration vendors and consultants and get the benefit of their expertise in managing and deploying integration solutions. The number of adapter vendors is increasing, and the availability of open standards such as JCA makes adapter development a better-understood technology. It will be easier to buy a JCA-compatible resource adapter and maintain it in-house than build a completely proprietary adapter technology. However, Chapter 10, "Overview of JCA," identifies some areas in which JCA is still missing critical specifications. It is very likely that adapter vendors will fill this gap in JCA specifications with their own proprietary solutions.

Building adapters in-house makes sense, especially when proprietary technology and applications are considered. No one understands the proprietary technologies better than the team that originally developed it. Some adapter vendors will probably provide tools that make JCA resource adapter development easier.

## Estimating Adapter Development

Software estimation is always a challenge, and adapter development projects have more variables to consider. The primary variables that affect adapter development include the following:

- The number of application interfaces (points of interface) to be included in the adapter. A good design principle is to implement not more than three to five interfaces in one adapter. If there are more then five interfaces, it is better to group them by business or technical functions, and implement one adapter for each group. You implement fewer interfaces in one adapter to keep the memory footprint as small as possible. Adapters are expected to scale a lot more than the applications. Hence, the smaller the adapter, the larger the number of instances the JVM can manage. It may not be possible in all cases to break down the adapter functionality into groups for better implementation. The optimum number of interfaces per adapter depends on the specific integration scenario and the technical complexities.

- The number of data models and databases, differences between them, and resulting data transformation requirements.

- The differences between the adapter development environment and the application development environment. For example, a JCA adapter developer may need to interface with a C or C++ API to access data objects stored in an object database. These paradigm differences require more time to understand, design, and develop the adapter.

- Internationalization requirements resulting in DBCS support in adapters and the resulting conversions always create unwanted surprises during development and deployment.

Other factors affect the overall estimation effort, but these depend on the individual team structures, IT environments, and the company culture. The objective of this chapter is to identify areas of concern, not define project management solutions.

## Adapter Design

The details of adapter architecture and design are explored in Chapter 4, "Adapter Reference Model." From a methodology perspective, the adapter architecture and design is no doubt impacted by the constraints identified in the analysis phase. The primary object of adapters is to encapsulate the application and expose integration functions and features. Hence, the adapter design should be driven by the right balance of long-term objectives enabling easier secure integration and short-term objectives of specific integration with specific applications and integration scenarios.

The complexities of interfacing with the application should not affect the long-term value of the adapter. Sometimes, this is hard to achieve with applications that have very closed architectures. Adapters for such applications can be very complex, and the benefits of integrating the application should be considered and weighed with the cost of developing complex adapters. If the application is strategic or mission-critical, then developing an adapter is always beneficial despite the possible complexities.

Adapter developers need to be some of the most creative programmers because they face challenging integration scenarios. Given the choice between constraining adapter functionality due to the underlying application architecture and developing complex integration adapters, the decision will be based on the significance of the application in the integration scenario. If the application is identified to be the master application that drives data synchronization actions, adapter developers may need to modify the application so it's more open to adapters.

Some of the design choices that adapter developers have to make involve the selection of point-to-point integration versus broker-enabled integration. Integration brokers are great tools for centralizing and managing complex integration scenarios involving intelligent routing of data and messages. However, you pay a price for the flexibility of using integration brokers. Sometimes when the integration scenario is simple, few applications are involved in the scenario (between three and five), and the volume of data is small, it might be better to develop a point-to-point adapter-based integration solution. This is more cost-effective and also easier to manage. However, the adapter design must be easy to migrate to a broker-enabled integration scenario without additional modifications in future.

Other design choices include persistence mechanisms that can include serialized objects, RDBMS, property files, and so on. Once again, the final decision should be guided by the foreseen integration scenarios. Obviously, large corporations need to plan for flexible integration platforms and adapter designs from the very beginning. Another design choice is the document model standard driving the data exchange mechanisms between adapters. Given the maturity and broad-based support for XML and XML-related technologies, it is logical to select XML as the document model. However, developers new to XML face a steep learning curve with many new technologies, and must assess the impact of learning on project estimates.

## Selecting an Implementation Environment

The implementation environment for an adapter depends on various things, including the integration context (data integration, Web service, process automation) and existing infrastructure. The implementation environment for adapters usually comprises the operating system, servers, and database.

### Operating System

It is quite possible for the adapter to run on the same platform as the business application. Many times, adapters need to support remote execution. This is especially required when the two applications collaborating in the integration scenario are located in remote locations or on different hardware and operating platforms. The operating system(s) on which the adapters are expected to run also define the choice of supporting software-like databases and other servers. The selection of appropriate types and versions of operating systems is critical to the final adapter implementation environment.

For example, an adapter can integrate with a CICS application on the IBM OS/390 platform to use CICS transaction gateways on Windows NT environment to access the CICS application data. In this case, the adapter implementation is simpler because it involves only Windows NT instead of both Windows NT and OS/390. However, if the integration scenario needs the adapter to run closer to the CICS application, then the adapter needs to support remote execution on the OS/390 platform, so it is much more complex.

### Servers

Depending on the type of adapter and the integration scenario, one or more servers may be required as adapter hosting environments or gateways. Application servers, database servers, Web servers, WAP servers, and transaction servers all become part of adapter implementation environments depending on the individual application architectures and the integration scenario.

### Database

Adapters need to store their configuration information in a fail-safe environment. Depending on the number of adapters and the frequency of changes to the configuration, a simple RDBMS-based configuration database or a high availability, data persistence solution may be required. Storing adapter configuration environments in a separate environment is a good design principle because it isolates adapter-generated control information (error messages, log files, and configuration data) from other application and system data.

## Constraints Identified During Analysis

As developers begin to analyze the application architecture and design, it is quite common to identify serious constraints. Often, legacy applications (and sometimes even newer applications) are not designed with integration capabilities. Database stored procedures are not always thread safe or re-entrant. Many stored procedures do not identify the actual user invoking them. Database security and access are often defined by user requirements, and do not include application integration requirements. Allowing applications to access the database as a different type of users (invisible user) may require changes to the security policies used by the database administration teams.

Architecture constraints are the most difficult to solve during adapter development. If no APIs are available to the adapter developer, the design choices are significantly reduced unless the application is changed. Even then, refactoring application architecture and design is always prone to errors and introduction of new bugs. It is typical and wise to expect new bugs or resurfacing of old application bugs in the context of integration projects. It is important to remember that adapters cannot add new functionality to the application; they can only increase its integration capabilities. However, you can change or enhance the application functionality at the same time the adapter is being developed.

## Adapter Hosting Environment

Adapters can be hosted in a multitude of environments, ranging from simple operating systems and application servers to sophisticated integration brokers. The difference between hosting environment and implementation environments are the supported services specific to adapters. For example, a J2EE-compliant application server can be an implementation environment; however, the JCA-compliant services define an adapter hosting environment. Adapters can be built with or without JCA support with the adapter architecture varying based on the adapter hosting environment.

Adapters can be hosted by different hosting environments. Some are sophisticated, like JCA-compliant application servers; and others are not so sophisticated, like the UNIX operating system. The level of sophistication expected is very specific to the requirements of managing adapters and providing adapters with system-level services. It is not always possible or even required to host adapters in an application server environment. Adapters can be hosted as UNIX processes, as standalone applications, as embedded components, or even as services and components of a distributed environment such as DCOM or CORBA.

Selecting the appropriate hosting environment depends on the integration scenario, requirements, and constraints identified. If the scenario is expected to achieve data synchronization between different databases, it is possible to host the adapters on the database servers, perhaps even including database triggers and procedures. The actual hosting environment can be selected based on the following criteria.

### Level of Manageability

Adapters requiring a higher level of management services (dynamic configuration capabilities, graphical representations, dynamic load balancing, fail over capabilities, and so on) will require a sophisticated environment such as J2EE and JCA-compliant application servers or a CORBA-based distributed object environment. On the other hand, some adapters may not be complex or may be more static in their configurations. These could be hosted in a simpler environment, such as a Web server or a UNIX/NT-based workstation.

### Performance Requirements

The volume of data, number of service messages, or number of workflow events to be processed can determine the hosting environment. Higher performance requirements will evidently require faster machines as well as high throughput environments. Higher-end application servers or those environments supporting clustering technologies will need to be considered.

### Operational Requirements

Transaction and security requirements impact the adapter hosting choices on the operational side. Single sign-on requirements, distributed transactions, two-phase commit, and other transactional requirements must be provided by the hosting environment when needed. For example, when you're using MQSeries as an adapter hosting environment, you may need to develop some additional transaction and security services to meet the adapter requirements. MQSeries is one of the best messaging and queuing platforms, but does not perform the functions of a transaction monitor.

It is clear that adapter hosting environments need to be analyzed and selected based on a number of different factors. Some adapters can be hosted in a simpler environment, whereas others cannot function without a sophisticated adapter hosting environment. It is always a good design principle to develop scalable adapters capable of working in a multitude of hosting environments.

## Building the Target Reference Model

In the previous sections, we have covered some of the important aspects of adapter analysis and design. Without a common reference model, the architecture of adapters probably will be different for each adapter. Consistency in design requires a common set of standards, and a reference model captures those critical parameters and design principles. Chapter 4 defines a target reference model for adapters. A similar model or a specialized version of this reference model should be accessible to adapter developers.

Reference models ensure a common design philosophy and a set of design patterns useful for developing adapters. The reference model is a good starting point when developing adapters. It provides you with a structural model of the adapter that can be extended and specialized for the specific adapter requirements without sacrificing a common infrastructure.

# Adapter Coding

Adapters can be developed in any programming language. However, some languages provide better support for adapters then others. For example, Java has an excellent component model in the form of Java Beans and Enterprise Java Beans. Java also has specific support for hosting adapters in J2EE-compliant servers. Java JNDI can be used to access code developed in other programming languages such as C and C++. Also, the multiplatform support of Java makes a strong case as the language of choice for adapter development.

Having said that, there will be cases in which other languages are better suited for specific environments. In the case of embedded operating systems and databases, C or C++ may be the only language available or may be better for performance-related issues. When faced with a proprietary platform that supports only specific programming languages, your choice could be limited. Hence, the logical architecture of an adapter is devoid of any programming language or platform. Regardless of the programming language used to develop the adapter, the basic principles of the development methodology described in this chapter are applicable to all adapter development projects.

## Using Appropriate Tools

The complex task of defining integration requirements, developing adapters, and deploying the integration solution requires good tools. Very little specialized development tool support exists for adapters. The basic tools needed for design, coding, and testing adapters are not very different from the standard development tools. However, specific features help to speed the developer and QA tasks in particular, as required for adapter development. Developing adapters generally involves external components such as parsers and mapping engines. For example, XML document editors are required to create, view, and edit document definitions. Ideally, development tools should support easy extensions such as adding editors, generating test data, and so on.

### Support for Top-Down and Bottom-Up Coding

Many very good development tools are available today. Most of the popular IDE tools are comprehensive and include modeling capabilities, code generation, version control, deployment management, and so on. Some of the more popular tools, especially for Java programming include Together Control Center, Rational Rose, Borland JBuilder, and IBM VisualAge. Apart from the features listed here, one very important feature especially for adapter development is the capability to support top-down and bottom up development.

Top-down development starts with a UML-based model, including business process definitions, requirements in the form of use cases, and so on. This type of development is more appropriate in the case in which adapters are built for a well-known set of integration requirements, and in the situation in which the applications involved have APIs and other documented points of interface. However, if the adapter is to be designed with little knowledge of the applications or no known points of integration, a more iterative method of coding and testing is required. This is where the development tools need to support easy transformation of code to higher-level models of abstraction. It is important to keep the code and the model in synchronization.

When selecting development tools for adapters and integration projects in general, you need to take into consideration the different coding methods and full lifecycle support. It is advisable to go for a high-end development tool when developing adapters because many applications could be involved. Being able to model the complex integration scenarios enables you to see the big picture and build the right adapter functionality. One such tool is Together Control Center from TogetherSoft Inc., which was used for developing the example JCA connector in this book. All the models (use case, class diagram, and so on) in this book were also generated by Together Control Center. (An overview of the Together Control Center tool with instructions of where to get further information is contained in the Appendix B, "References.")

## Adapter QA

Quality assurance is a tedious task but extremely important. The best architecture and design is not very useful if the software does not comply with requirements, and if it has too many bugs. Fixing software bugs is a continuous process that involves constant checking and fixing. Adapter QA is a more complicated task that considers the involvement of not one but many applications in a scenario. Two levels of QA are basic to adapter development: adapter unit tests and integration scenario tests.

*Adapter unit tests* are focused on testing the adapter features and capabilities with reference to the adapter requirements. They involve testing the connectivity between the adapter and the business application, the fail over, and other recovery mechanisms programmed into the adapter. Adapter unit tests are important to ensure the basic level of integration between the business application and adapter on a one-on-one basis.

However, adapter unit tests are not enough to certify the adapter fit for participating in integration scenarios. That is the job of integration scenario tests, sometimes known as *end-to-end testing*. These tests are more complex, and involve a series of adapters collaborating in a simulated integrating scenario using test data. Sometimes, these tests are run for days to ensure the adapters do their job over a long period of time without crashing or corrupting any data.

Ironically, these tests expose bugs in operating systems—bugs in business applications, middleware, and so on. It is only in the integration scenario tests that the entire infrastructure associated with the scenario (including hardware, operating systems, databases, applications, adapters, and other middleware) are tested as a single unit of operation.

The usual system tests or integrated system tests conducted as part of software development are slightly different from integration scenario testing. The objective of the system test is to identify bugs in a particular business application. The objective of integration scenario testing is to ensure that all points of integration work as expected. The scope of testing is therefore much bigger and involves many potential points of failure.

## Setup of the QA Environment

It is no surprise that setting up the QA environment for integration scenario testing, as well as a separate adapter unit test, is not a small task. Most QA teams prefer to maintain their test environments for a long time after they are set up. It takes a lot of effort to build a valid QA environment, complete with meaningful test data, decent hardware configurations, and defining appropriate scenarios. Automating the repetitive testing cycles is very important to maintain consistency between testing different versions of the adapters, and so on. Without a consistent QA environment, it is hard to isolate bugs, or even prove that past bugs don't exist in new versions of the software.

## Selecting Valid Test Data

Access to good quality test data is always a challenge. Sometimes, QA teams consider copies of production data (data from applications in production environments) as good test data. This principle is problematic, however, because in many instances production data only represents the valid conditions. Test exceptions, business rules, security policies, and so on require an incredibly comprehensive set of test data. Most of the time, the quality of test data increases with the number of testing cycles.

QA teams need to expand their testing procedures and include test data for end-to-end integration scenarios. This requires test data from potentially multiple applications in different databases. This task of defining the appropriate set of test data should begin as soon as the integration requirements are known. Test plans and test databases should be defined and populated as soon as possible to avoid lengthy QA cycles in the later half of the development schedules.

## Identifying Regression Test Cases

How many times should you test the adapter? If a minor change has been made to an adapter, or if an adapter has some bugs fixed, what kind of testing is required before it is deployed? These are some of the questions that QA engineers, project managers, and IT staff face regularly in any integration project. Regression tests define a set of test cases that represent critical aspects of the integration scenario. Not all adapter test cases are required for regression tests. Generally, each adapter has a specific set of features or functions relevant to a particular integration scenario. All features of all adapters probably are not deployed or even required to fulfill a specific integration scenario.

Hence, it is important to identify a series of test cases that represent the critical functionality in play for a particular integration scenario, and reference them as regression test cases. Regression test cases are useful for testing minor upgrades to adapters or bug fixes or maintenance releases of adapters. They provide the adapter QA team with enough testing procedures to test adapters quickly before deploying them in a production environment. However, if the adapters have undergone significant changes, it may be better to test using the full set of test cases.

### Developing a Test Harness

A very useful part of adapter QA is the availability of a test harness. A *test harness* is a self-contained testing tool that is part of the adapter. It helps in conducting quick and easy adapter unit tests without major QA infrastructure. It also helps developers test their adapters because other adapters or even applications may not be ready for a comprehensive adapter QA. Developers and project managers can decide to include a test harness as part of the development schedule. However, the effectiveness of such a harness is likely to go down if it is not kept in sync with the adapter and the business application.

## Deploying Adapters

Adapter deployment can be a tedious task, depending on the complexity of the integration scenarios and the integration platform. Specific challenges are involved in deploying internationalized adapters and deploying adapters on multiple platforms. Adapters are normally developed on a platform more suitable to development activities. Most adapter development is done in a Windows NT environment. If Java is the programming language, deploying the adapters on different platforms requires extensive testing. Not all platforms may support the same JDK or support all the features of J2EE specifications. This section identifies the critical tasks before and during adapter deployment.

One of the features frequently requested by adapter developers is the support for deploying adapters in different stages. A very real challenge of any integration solution deployment project is the simultaneous deployment of many interrelated components. Consider an integration scenario that involves 10 different applications hosted on different platforms in two different countries. Deploying adapters for all 10 applications at the same time is not an easy task. Quite often, a sequential deployment strategy is used to install the adapters. However, it is not a good idea to have individual adapters working in a production environment until all other adapters necessary are also installed and potentially tested.

It is also important that the integration platform on which adapters are installed is capable of recognizing and managing the adapters in different states. Adapters can exist in different states—including installed, tested, configured, deployed, and so on. Alternately, adapters that are already in the deployed state may need to be stopped for upgrades. Many times, deployment management tools are not sufficiently sophisticated. Hence, project managers need to fully understand the implication of installing adapters in stages, and define a schedule to complete the deployment successfully.

## Multiplatform Deployment Guidelines

One of the benefits of programming in Java is the multiplatform support it generates without specific porting of the code base. With adapters (especially JCA resource adapters), the definition of multiplatform support includes J2EE-compliant application servers. Although the J2EE specifications are comprehensive, application vendors have some flexibility in how the implement the specifications. Some vendors also add additional functionality and support for their other products. For example, BEA WebLogic's application server also includes the Tuxedo transaction engine as an option. IBM's WebSphere application server includes MQSeries and gateways to IBM mainframe platform and environments such as CICS.

In the case of JCA support in application servers, vendors have the necessary flexibility to implement connection pooling and other JCA services using proprietary designs. Hence, although the connection-pooling service interfaces are guaranteed across application servers, the actual implementation will be different. Some will have more additional features than others. These differences result in different deployment management and configurations.

Needless to say, the application server will have bugs just like any other software. Thus, it is critical to test JCA-compliant adapters on all application servers it is expected to support. Although it is the same JCA adapter, it may work in the J2EE reference implementation, but may not work with other application servers. J2EE compliance, as defined by SUN, does not require application server vendors to support all specifications of J2EE. This is another reason for adapter developers to check if the J2EE-compliant application server also supports JCA specifications.

The more committed adapter vendors try to get the products tested and certified on different operating systems and hardware configurations. JCA adapter vendors should do the same, and get the resource adapters certified on different application servers whenever possible. To summarize, the testing and deployment guidelines for JCA resource adapters are as follows:

- Test the JCA resource adapter with the reference implementation for J2EE 1.3.

- Test the JCA resource adapter with all other application servers used in the production environment.

- Test the resource adapter with the different operating systems supported by the J2EE application servers in the production environment.

- Deploy the resource adapter on one type of application server at a time. This helps to eliminate application server-specific problems more quickly. Application servers may have different configurations, which could result in varying results.

- Group the resource adapter deployment by operating system. If you are expected to deploy three resource adapters on a Windows NT environment and two resource adapters on Linux, it is better to complete all the Windows NT or Linux deployment first. Chances are, if one resource adapter encounters a problem with the operating system or a problem with the application server running in the operating system, other adapters will face the same issues.

## Deploying Internationalized Adapters

Not all adapters are internationalized or ready to support different languages and locales. But there are two parts to ensure that adapters are ready for international deployment. The first part is *internationalization*, which involves additional work and discipline from adapter developers. Developers need to ensure the use of appropriate mechanisms such as resource bundles to store literal strings, and so on. The second part is *localization*, which involves the creation of resource bundles in different languages.

Apart from the visual support for languages other than English, there is the issue of supporting double byte data and different input methods for languages. Several products enhance the native Java capabilities for internationalization by providing data input mechanisms for many different languages. UNICODE is the widely accepted standard for Double Byte Character Support (DBCS), but other specific standards (especially for Japanese and Chinese language support) may be more prevalent in different parts of the world.

Regardless of the level of DBCS support and the different input methods supported by the adapters, it is important to understand that testing and deploying adapters in different languages involves different versions of operating systems and perhaps different versions of business applications as well. Hence, QA of international versions of adapters is not simply restricted to testing the adapter using standard test cases. It involves a completely different test environment, including international versions operating systems (such as Chinese Windows), hardware that is more popular in different parts of the world, different versions of applications, and test data in the language matching the locale.

Project managers who plan to deploy adapters in a global environment using internationalized adapters should take into account the additional efforts required to test and support the adapters on hardware and operating systems that are more popular and relevant to the local environments. Support for Java is not equal on all platforms. Hardware and operating system vendors may be supporting various different versions of JDK, and it is important to understand those differences before the adapter development project starts.

# Adapter Maintenance

Adapter maintenance needs to be planned just like any other software or application maintenance. Although adapters are logically part of a specific business application, they usually require additional maintenance due to the dependencies with other adapters, applications, and infrastructure. The types of changes affecting adapters include enhancements to business applications, operating system upgrades, hardware upgrades, database upgrades, and platform upgrades (such as JDK upgrades). It is important for project managers to keep track of all these parameters and plan adapter enhancements accordingly. As such, the three basic tasks of adapter maintenance include planning adapter upgrades, deploying adapter fixes, and managing related vendor relationships. The following sections take a closer look at these three tasks, and provide some guidelines on adapter maintenance.

## Planning Adapter Upgrades

Because adapters are extensions of business applications, it is vital that adapters are always synchronized with changes and upgrades to application functions and databases. Some of the obvious challenges are when changes to one application can result in changes to adapters of other applications. This can happen, for example, when the database structure or the database model of an application drops elements and attributes. Not only the adapter of the changed application, but also adapters of dependent applications may need to be upgraded.

As a guideline, adapter upgrades should be analyzed with each release of the relevant application. The analysis should also cover adapter upgrades needed due to changes in other applications participating in the integration scenario. The planning activity should become a regular practice for project managers. One of the first tasks in any software and IT planning meetings should be integration planning, and it should involve adapters. Integration and adapters is not a one-time activity; it requires regular planning, analysis, and constant monitoring.

## Deploying Adapter Fixes

Because adapters are primarily built to enable integration, applying fixes or patches should be done with more than normal planning. The impact of changes to adapters could be felt by other applications integrating with the adapter. For that matter, testing adapter patches with all other adapters involved in the affected integration scenario is very important. The regression test scenarios identified in the adapter QA plan are useful when deploying patches and fixes to adapters.

Project managers should plan for extra time and resources when conducting regression tests before deploying adapter fixes. This is especially required in a distributed environment in which adapters can be on servers connected by a WAN. Distributed IT teams should inform all other IT teams about adapter deployments and other administration tasks.

## Importance of Vendor Relationships

Various integration products are available in the market. Some are message broker-based; others are application server-oriented. There aren't many adapter vendors yet, but the number of adapter vendors specializing in specific integration platforms (application servers, messaging platforms, and so on) and types of integration (data, Web service, process automation) is sure to grow rapidly.

Successful integration projects are partly dependent on close partnerships or relationships with technology vendors. Platform vendors continue to add significant support for integration. Major hardware and software vendors—including Microsoft, SUN, IBM, and others—have a comprehensive set of platform technology and services capable of supporting complex integration requirements. These platforms can host integration solutions such as adapters and integration brokers. On the other hand, business application vendors haven't been as aggressive in their efforts to support integration. Not surprisingly, most business software vendors, including ERP and CRM vendors, are likely to focus on better integration within their application modules and less on integration with other applications. The business integration issues faced by business application vendors are more complex and numerous when compared with platform integration issues.

For integration projects to succeed in the long term, it is vital that hardware, software, and infrastructure vendors share their product roadmaps, capabilities, and strategies more openly than before. Customers and end-users need to plan their integration strategies by working closely with their vendors. Without the visibility of the vendors' plans, customers will be forced to react to integration requirements instead of proactively planning to resolve integration issues. Corporate IT managers and development managers should actively seek closer partnerships with vendors, and include long-term information sharing as a prerequisite to acquiring new software and hardware technology.

A typical corporate IT department is likely to deal with various type of vendors, including application package vendors, hardware vendors, integration vendors, service providers, and so on. Each vendor will have a specific approach and visibility to integration issues and solutions. It is important to define a corporate integration strategy that fits the corporate technology and vendors supplying and supporting the technology. Integration is not a problem that can be solved in isolation.

One of the benefits of partnering with an adapter vendor is the consistency in adapter technology across platforms and business applications. Without a consistent adapter management environment, it will be almost impossible to manage the complex integration scenario. Adapter vendors are also more likely to better understand the challenges of adding integration features to applications. The motivation for adapter vendors should be to provide adapters independent of integration infrastructure, thus providing their customers the freedom to select infrastructure matching the business and budget requirements.

## Summary

Software project management is a difficult task in general, and is more complex and critical in the case of integration projects. By definition, there is more collaboration and planning required between development teams and project managers. You need to select development tools carefully to manage the complex adapter development projects. Understanding the differences between normal software development and adapter development mean that the end results (adapters) meet the business requirements, as well as handle complex technical infrastructures involved in the integration scenario.

Building close relationships with vendors of third-party packages is essential to knowing their product roadmap. Knowledge of what features and changes to expect in the near future, as well as what features will be deprecated, enables project managers to plan integration projects and requirements. Without a planned integration roadmap, it is difficult to upgrade third-party application packages without impacting any customization or integration between applications.

This chapter doesn't provide all the answers, but it helps identify some of the unique project management and development issues related to integration projects. Existing development methodologies may need some adjustments when applied to integration projects. As integration and adapter development become entrenched into mainstream development, the experience gained by the teams involved will influence future methodologies, techniques, and design patterns.

**8**

# Pitfalls of Adapter Development

**IN THIS CHAPTER**

- Strategy and Planning Pitfalls
- Architecture Pitfalls
- Analysis and Design Pitfalls
- Development and Implementation Pitfalls

"Your legacy should be that you made it better than it was when you got it."

—Lee Iacocca

Most software development projects can be managed better the second time around. Despite the best of intentions, management experience, tools, and budgets, projects are invariably delayed. A common problem is the underestimation of work involved and the technical complexity. Unclear requirements add to the usual frustrations of development teams. In this chapter, I have highlighted some of the pitfalls or mistakes made by development and project managers, architects, and developers during adapter projects. Sometimes, knowing what to avoid saves more time and raises the chance of overall project success.

Faced with new concepts, technologies, and little time to deliver the end product, development teams often compromise long-term benefits with short-term constraints. The pitfalls identified in this chapter are by no means exhaustive, but the intention is to help you understand common mistakes and the results of ignoring them. Mistakes made earlier in the development cycle are harder to fix and prove more costly over time. I have categorized the pitfalls into four groups:

- Strategy and planning pitfalls
- Architecture pitfalls
- Analysis and design pitfalls
- Development and implementation pitfalls

Avoiding known pitfalls during the strategy and planning stage will prove beneficial in the long term. Compromising development and implementation pitfalls may be unavoidable sometimes, but can be fixed in the future at lesser cost. Ultimately, individual project teams will have to ascertain pitfalls unique to their environments and avoid them.

## Strategy and Planning Pitfalls

Decisions made during the early stage of adapter projects have a lasting impact on the overall E-Business integration objectives. Choosing a strategic direction in terms of selecting adapter vendors, integration infrastructure, and so on is complex and hard. Avoiding the following specific mistakes during this critical planning phase will ensure greater flexibility in delivering the required integration solution.

### Assuming All Adapters Are Available as Prebuilt Components

This is a very common perception among those who are newly exposed to the adapter technologies. Although quite a few companies have built a whole list of adapters for off-the-shelf packages and middleware, the list is not complete by any stretch of the imagination. Also, prebuilt adapters are generally not flexible in terms of their capability to work with different integration infrastructures (integration brokers, messaging engines, process-modeling tools, etc.) Usually, prebuilt adapters have specific infrastructure requirements, and are sold as part of the integration software and hardware solution.

What about proprietary and home-grown applications? Where can you get adapters for these applications? The only solution is to build these adapters, and that requires a strong adapter framework capable of adapting to different infrastructures and environments. Although adapter vendors are known to provide customers with an adapter API, the functions and underlying framework of the adapters is not accessible or exposed for customization.

Instead of spending time and money searching for all the adapters you need, a better strategy is to select prebuilt adapters for off-the-shelf applications and to select an adapter framework for building all other adapters in-house. The ideal situation is if the prebuilt adapters are built on the same adapter framework. Failure to balance the advantages of prebuilt adapters and requirements for proprietary adapters leads to different adapter solutions. When this happens, the end goal of achieving complete application integration becomes more complex.

### Adapter Development Is Planned as a One-Time Effort

Sustaining adapter development is the most challenging part of the planning process. Continued support for adapter enhancements is rarely planned from the onset of an integration project. Most of the time and effort is spent on the actual integration infrastructure and the implementation, but most of the value-add is in application adapters. Before J2EE standards, application server vendors had mostly proprietary software, resulting in much higher costs to the customer. Because J2EE was accepted by major application server vendors such as IBM and BEA, the competition is more intense. It is quite possible that application servers are becoming more of a commodity and less of a proprietary software platform. This changes the customer focus from evaluating the application server to evaluating value-added components such as adapters that are packaged with the application server.

Even if a majority of the adapters you need are available as prebuilt adapters, the customization of these adapters leads to upgrades as the underlying application and infrastructure changes. Hence, it is wise to consider adapter development as an ongoing project, evolving with the applications and the infrastructure. With careful planning and modifications to development methodologies, as identified in Chapter 7, "Adapter Development Methodology," the effort required to maintain the adapters can be better predicted and managed.

On the other hand, you don't need to build or buy all adapters to start an integration project. Using the big bang approach of integrating all applications at the same time does not usually work. A phased approach of integrating critical business processes and the applications enabling these processes before integrating other applications is a better choice. Start with the few adapters required, and plan to sustain these adapters over a long time before expanding the integration project. Many companies have experienced success by using this approach instead of the all-or-nothing strategy.

## Lack of Vendor Relationship Management

Vendor relationships are very important to any integration project. A major task of the project management office or team is to coordinate activities between the different players and managing the cross-functional processes. Some of the players will be the package vendors, platform vendors (hardware), and integration experts or consultants.

From an adapter-development perspective, it is important to build a good relationship with the package vendor. If an ERP package or a CRM package is part of the integration scenario, it is better to consult with the vendor technical experts before finalizing the adapter architecture and design. Not all internal technical details are documented nor are the future plans for the package publicly disclosed by the vendor.

One way to get exposure to the technical details is to work with the vendor and explain your integration project objectives. Most vendors will give their long-term perspective as well as point you in the right technical direction. The really big package vendors such as SAP, Oracle, PeopleSoft, Siebel, and so on have documented their integration tools, API, and so on. But such information is hard to get with other package vendors who may not have a formal integration strategy.

Building adapters in isolation without consulting the package vendor is technically possible. But it will be hard to know if the adapter is interfacing with the application in the best possible way, or even plan or anticipate adapter changes driven by package upgrades.

## Not Understanding the Vendor Product Roadmap

From a technical perspective, this is the most dangerous situation, which usually means that more money is spent in constantly changing the adapter in a reactive way rather then in a planned proactive way. It is very important to understand the package roadmap from the respective vendors over an 18-to-24-month period. Many vendors announce their intentions publicly, but knowing when their technical visions and strategies will be implemented is vital for ensuring that adapters are kept in sync with the package.

Part of your adapter development strategy should be to identify the critical packaged applications that require adapters, and build a stronger relationship with the vendor with the intention of getting access to their product roadmaps. No amount of planning will result in perfect synchronization between the adapters and the package. However, the time required for the adapter to catch up with the changes to the package is greatly reduced by knowing the product roadmap. This applies to internally developed applications as well, and not just to packaged applications. However, getting the product roadmap may be easier for internal applications then external packages.

# Architecture Pitfalls

The architecture of any software determines how easy it is to maintain it over the long term. Closed architectures make change management difficult and very costly. Open architectures require more time to build the first time, but make change management easier. Although good software architectures and principles are all useful in adapter development, certain concepts and design patterns require specific focus.

## Assuming that Adapters Are Extensions of Integration Infrastructure

There is a major problem in the way adapters are conceptualized in terms of their role in application integration. Because adapters, especially the prebuilt adapters, are usually packaged as part of the integration infrastructure and solutions, it is easy to think of them as extensions of the infrastructure. However, this can lead to different adapters for the same application. For example, suppose that an application is required to exchange data with an application using MQSeries messaging engine and another application using CORBA as its middleware. In this scenario, it is better to have one adapter capable of working in both environments (MQSeries and CORBA) instead of two adapters, one for MQSeries and one for CORBA. This will require the adapters to be extensions of the application, and not of the underlying integration infrastructure.

The benefit of one adapter being capable of working in different infrastructures is obvious when changes are made to the application. Generally, integration infrastructure vendors would want customers to avoid taking this approach of a single adapter because it requires a single cross-platform adapter framework that most integration vendors don't provide yet. Nonetheless, it is important to maintain the idea of having a single adapter per application capable of running in different contexts, environments, and infrastructures. The alternative is many adapters for one application, each working on a specific infrastructure, which is very difficult and costly to maintain in the long run.

The JCA specifications are a step in the right direction, in the sense that it will work for any application server as long as it is J2EE 1.3-compliant. However, if we extend the requirement to include non-J2EE platforms such as CORBA, COM, and so on, then the concept of a single adapter framework becomes even more critical. Some adapter vendors are moving in that direction and will provide such a framework in the near future.

## Underestimating the Technical Impedance

The requirement to integrate applications is based on the reality that applications have different technical environments, architectures, and infrastructures. For adapter architects, it is vital that they understand the differences between the major technical environments of the applications before designing adapters. As architects dig deeper into the application, they find differences in database models, transaction management, session management, and so on. Each one of these differences makes it harder to integrate the applications. The job of an adapter is to bridge these differences, which are known as *technical impedance*. Some of the common differences are the following:

- Synchronous versus asynchronous sessions

- Object versus relational databases

- Transactional versus non-transactional systems

Each of these aspects of technical impedance requires a lot of bridging code, and most of it ends up in the adapter. For example, if a customer service application that is based on a two-tier client server architecture needs to integrate with a MQSeries-based Order Management system, it is possible that the adapter for the customer service application will have to do extra work in reading all the MQSeries messages before presenting the data as one data object to the customer service application. This additional work can be significant, and needs to be identified during the architecture phase to avoid costly delays later in the development process.

Similarly supporting XA-complaint transactions for an application that is not XA-complaint to start with is the job of an adapter. In some cases, this may require the adapter to directly access the applications database and expose its data as XA-compliant transactions.

More than one solution can solve these impedance issues, and the choice of the solution will determine how much additional work the adapter is required to do. Underestimating this work seriously impacts the success of the integration project. A good architecture will tackle common technical impedance issues such as integrating object-oriented databases and XML documents by implementing a framework for converting data objects into flat data structures. This framework can then be used for similar problems in other adapters.

Simulating synchronous sessions over asynchronous middleware requires state management with the adapters. This can also be isolated in a session management framework capable of being reused in other adapters. The failure to recognize these impedances and not implement a framework-based solution will result in delays to adapter projects.

## Analysis and Design Pitfalls

Assuming that a sound adapter development strategy is in place and a strong architecture reference model is available, the next step involves avoiding critical mistakes during the requirements analysis and design phase. Although an architecture reference model provides guidelines for the eventual design of the adapter, a great deal of effort is required to hone the right set of requirements and the physical design of the adapter.

### Not Understanding Hidden Integration Requirements

Where do you start to define the adapter requirements? Based on the concept that the adapter is an extension of the application, you might be tempted to analyze the application and derive adapter requirements from what the application does in terms of business functionality. Although this can be done, a better approach is to analyze the end-to-end integration scenario. These scenarios define the requirements from a collaboration perspective and identify the points of integration for the applications. Ignoring these requirements derived from the end-to-end integration scenario will lead to missing and inadequate adapter functionality.

For example, the integration scenario may point to the same data objects required in different formats and structures by two different applications. Unless you know these unique requirements that the adapter is expected to implement, it is not possible to design the right functionality.

Sometimes, adapter development teams take the approach that a generic adapter will solve the issue of satisfying unique requirements during the implementation phase, but this rarely works. More often than not, the adapter needs to be enhanced or reworked to include additional features, no matter how generic the design is. The problem is not the adapter's capability of supporting generic requirements, but different applications' having specific and unique requirements. If the adapter is capable of providing customer data in the form of a generic message, it may not be enough because some applications will dictate a different structure for the message. The objective of the adapter is to solve the problem of supporting different data requirements and not pushing that problem to some other entity.

These requirements will not be visible unless the entire end-to-end integration scenario is analyzed. Adapter teams should be prepared to look at bigger integration problems before deciding on the adapter requirements. Failure to do so results in hidden requirements left out of the adapter functionality, leading to disappointments.

## Managing Technical Constraints

Adapters are not without technical constraints imposed by the underlying applications and infrastructure. Adapter design teams have to constantly evaluate these constraints and compromise on the eventual design.

Some technical constraints could be managed by better design. For example, it is quite possible to have adapters run in a remote environment. Although the ideal scenario may demand that the adapter be hosted in the same environment as the application, it is not always technically possible. In the case of JCA resource adapters, it is more than likely that the resource adapter is communicating with a remote legacy application on a mainframe. This adds complications to the adapter because it has to manage the communication between the legacy application and the J2EE application server. An alternative solution could be to divide the resource adapter between two components: one hosted on the application server and the other hosted on the mainframe. Logically, both components are part of one adapter and have a common architecture and framework, but physically they are hosted in separate environments. Such solutions are required to manage some of the technical constraints that adapter developers are likely to face.

## Forgetting Customization

Although adapters are designed and developed to solve specific application-integration problems, customization is required to handle different platforms, locales, and so on. Externalizing adapter configurations as much as possible does ensure that most of the customization of adapter behavior is possible without code changes.

I18N (Internationalization) and L10N (Localization) are two such features that adapters should support. This ensures quick customization of the adapters to suit local languages and data requirements such as DBCS (Double Byte Characters) support. Also, adapters may be required to work in different environments and with different infrastructures in the future. Not providing an API for supporting these future requirements is not a good design principle. Although no one knows the future requirements fully, it is possible to make the job easier by designing an API to the adapter. If all applications were built with API integration, it would be that much simpler.

# Development and Implementation Pitfalls

So far, you have a good strategy, well-designed architecture, and solid design, but most of the development work is still to come. Although the actual coding task is largely dependent on the experience and quality of the programmers, some of the non-technical mistakes done in this phase have a more lasting impact. Having good programming practices, coding standards, documentation, and so on are integral parts of any development project including adapters.

## Importance of Test Data

This may not be a surprise to many developers, but it is worth mentioning. Adapters require a complex set of test data involving more than one application participating in the integration scenarios.

Sometimes, test data is not taken very seriously because it is hard to build a good test database. However, every attempt should be made to get the best quality test data available. This data is also useful in testing prebuilt adapters that are more often than not tested under different environments and conditions. It is always better to test third-party components (adapters) with real application data because it is a more accurate test of the business requirements. A prebuilt adapter may work and perhaps be certified by the package vendor, but it does not mean the adapter will work with your data.

In an integrated environment, in which applications share data and collaborate to implement enterprise processes, it is very easy for one application with a bug to propagate the errors to other applications. What was a standalone bug is now potentially affecting many other applications. To avoid this chain reaction of bad data spreading across the network, adapters need to be tested more stringently than the applications themselves. Before exposing an application to the network, it is prudent to test its readiness.

### Lack of Supporting Tools

How many times have you heard complaints from system administrators about the challenges of investigating what is wrong when things don't work? It is very rare for applications to include monitoring and administration tools. We leave that tedious task to the system administrators, and wonder why it takes so long to identify bugs in the production environment. You can imagine the scale of this problem in an integrated environment with many moving parts.

Componentization is a very good concept and base for application architectures because it promotes more flexible solutions. However, with it come more points of failures or potential failures. The more the number of parts in a machine, the more the likelihood of one of the parts breaking down.

To ensure a smooth implementation of the integrated solution, adapters should be developed to generate and maintain statistics. A good monitoring tool is required to identify which software component failed and what recovery path is available. Although a sophisticated GUI-driven tool is not yet available and will require more standardization, adapters can generate meaningful messages and respond to external administration events and triggers. As a bare-minimum solution, adapters should keep a log of failed activities and suggest corrective actions wherever possible.

This part of the development activity should not be ignored because it comes back to haunt everyone involved in the integration projects.

## Summary

In this chapter, you have seen some of the common mistakes most of us have made or could make in adapter and integration projects. The sooner you stop making these mistakes, the faster adapter projects progress, and the cheaper it will be to fix any problems. The pitfalls identified are not all of the possible mistakes likely to occur during the integration project, but are a good starting point to avoid known stumbling blocks.

As adapter development matures and methodologies are adapted to match the unique adapter development requirements, the process of application integration will improve. Adapter design patterns will emerge, and it will be easier to avoid some of the mistakes identified in this chapter. Knowing what to avoid is an important success factor.

# 9

# Testing Adapters

"Give them quality. That's the best kind of advertising in the world."

—*Milton S. Hershey, Founder of Hershey's Chocolate*

This chapter identifies some of the most important factors of adapter quality assurance. The application of the principles in this chapter depends on the methodology used for developing individual adapters. But it should be quite easy to incorporate and customize these adapter-testing concepts to suit your specific adapter projects.

## The Importance of Testing

Testing software is never easy, neither is it a very exciting task—especially for developers. Developing test plans and test cases, and executing them with the appropriate test data is a tedious task that needs to be repeated a number of times. The more you test software, the more bugs and faults you uncover. Good software development processes and tools make the testing cycles shorter by spreading the testing tasks throughout the development process. Although most developers understand the importance of software testing, very few development teams apply sufficient quality assurance (QA) practices. Despite the best planning efforts, in many cases, software testing turns out to be a hurried activity at the end of the development cycle. QA teams come under great pressure to test the software as fast as they can because it looks like they are holding the software release process. After all, developers have done enough testing, right?

Users have shown higher tolerance levels in accepting software bugs than in any other product or technology. We typically don't accept faults in consumer products, but are willing to work with less-than-perfect software. The situation is different in the corporate IT environment, in which large numbers of servers and applications are required to work in harmony. A buggy piece of software can be very frustrating, and will most likely be replaced with other acceptable software. Because adapters perform the critical task of integration, it is vitally important that their quality be higher. In fact, adapters need to be of higher quality than the adapted applications. High-quality adapters should expose bugs and faults in the adapted application, and not contribute to the list of problems.

Adapter testing has more variables than traditional software test environments. The adapter test environment can get quite complicated because some of the target systems the adapter works with are remote, or large ERP packages that are difficult to configure with the best talent available. Hence, the prudent thing to do is plan adapter QA from the beginning of the development process.

## Stages of Adapter Testing

Adapter QA can be done in two stages: The first stage focuses on application compliance, and the second stage focuses on platform compliance. Application compliance is focused on ensuring that the links between the adapter and business application function as expected. Application compliance could be triggered by a new version of the business application or the adapter. If a business application changes, all adapters associated with it will have to undergo application compliance tests. Platform compliance is ensuring that the adapter works in the production environments. The adapter platform is typically composed of appropriate hardware, operating systems, and middleware, such as an application server. Depending on the type of environments, adapters may have to undergo multiple platform compliance tests. In large corporate environments, adapters may have to work on different platforms in different geographical regions.

The JCA specifications allow J2EE vendors to implement additional functionality around the core specifications. This will lead to differences in how the JCA container or the J2EE application server is configured or behaves at run-time. In such circumstances, it is better to test the adapters in a simple environment first. The J2EE reference implementation from SUN is a good environment for conducting baseline adapter tests. Upon successfully demonstrating compliance with JCA and J2EE, further tests can be performed on specific application servers.

## Types of Adapter Testing

There are several types of adapter testing that are required to ensure the adapters' overall quality and readiness before deployment in a production environment. These tests range from simple unit tests performed by adapter developers on an ongoing basis to formal QA procedures involving test engineers and business analysts.

The actual QA procedures and the composition of the QA team depends on the organization, but the testing function can be categorized into four primary types of testing:

- Black box testing

- White box testing

- End-to-end testing

- Stress testing

## Black Box Testing

*Black box testing* is useful for verifying the adapter functionality as stated in the requirement models and documents. Black box test cases are not designed to test the internals of an adapter, but to test the adapter services and business functionality. In other words, black box test cases focus on "what" the adapter does, as opposed to "how" it does it. Usually this is what QA teams focus on, primarily because it doesn't require a lot of detailed knowledge about the adapter design and code. Testers expect the adapter to work as expected in the individual test cases. If the results are different, then the test case is considered to be a failure.

In the case of JCA-compliant resource adapters, a test client should be developed to simulate real-life scenarios and test the adapter's functionality.

## White Box Testing

*White box testing* handles the internal workings of the adapter. Test cases in white box testing are designed to test specific paths of the adapter code. Knowledge of the adapter architecture and design is vital for building white box test cases. Hence, most adapter development teams find it hard to conduct white box testing. Complex adapters should, however, pass at least some white box testing. Critical paths of the code base should be identified, so that show stopper bugs can be avoided during the software release cycles. Nothing is more harmful to software release and deployment than show stopper bugs. These bugs prevent the adapter from being deployed in production environments, resulting in lost opportunities and revenues.

White box testing techniques are generally used for testing the exception-handling capabilities of an adapter. This is harder than black box testing, in which the test data is designed to succeed and not fail. In white box testing, the test data is designed to ensure that the adapter fails, and tests its exception-handling behavior. If an adapter is expected to log debug messages when processing a null object or when certain business rules are violated, then white box testing ensures that the adapter behavior is consistent with this expectation.

Many times, software in general does not undergo white box testing due to the notion that the failure rate is much lower than the success rate. Some software engineers believe that software works adequately for 80% of its operational time, and fails 20% of the time. However, the time spent to rectify the failures is far more in proportion. So, although the software may fail only 20% of the time it requires 80% of the system administrators' time to fix it when it fails.

With adapters, this can be a real nightmare without proper monitoring and administration tools. There are many moving parts in an integration scenario, and determining where exactly the scenario failed and which component is responsible can take a frustratingly long time, with serious impact on the business. It takes only one major failure for customers to lose confidence. White box testing helps to avoid these situations by testing for exceptions, and ensuring that the adapters fail gracefully and don't crash or propagate errors throughout the network.

## End-to-End Testing

*End-to-end testing* involves more than one adapter, and is useful for proving the capability of the adapter to function in a larger integration scenario or context. Although the adapter may have passed all the black box and white box tests, its role as part of an integration scenario may expose its limitations, or even some bugs. Integration scenarios also ensure the robustness of the adapter. Memory leaks are often identified in simulations of real-world integration scenarios. These memory leaks affect the performance, as well as contribute to the eventual crash of the adapter and sometimes of the platform (operating system, hardware). Hence, end-to-end testing is a very important step in the adapter QA process. Typically, these tests are run for a week without any breaks unless warranted by the adapters failure.

## Stress Testing

*Stress tests* are a combination of black box, white box, and end-to-end test cases. The objective of stress tests is to identify the break point of the adapters. *Break point* can be defined by degrading performance or other observable effects due to large volumes of data and transactions. These tests often prove to be useful for system administrators who are required to fine-tune the platforms for optimum performance and reliability.

The definition of stress test depends on the number of expected users, transactions, and data volumes involved. Simultaneous user sessions should be simulated as far as possible to create real-life situations. The end result of stress testing is invariably the failure of adapters, applications, and the platform. Knowing when this failure happens determines how much stress the system can handle in a production environment. Eventually, the actual production environment will always be different for each customer and end-user, but the stress testing provides the necessary benchmarks useful to IT team in capacity planning. Professional IT teams always ask for stress test results from vendors because it helps them size the necessary hardware, software, bandwidth, and so on.

---

**VENDOR CERTIFICATION**

One of the most sought-after benefits of component-based application development is effective reuse. For reuse to be practical and real, components should be available off-the-shelf. However, there also should be a level of trust and confidence in the component by its users. Third-party certification is a good mechanism for gaining that confidence in a component.

Adapters are specialized types of application components, and yet vendor certification is indeed not very common. One of the reasons is the extensive process and support (technical and management) required to build a credible certification program. The return on investments is not so much to the vendor as it is to the component developer.

Leading package vendors such as SAP have an extensive software certification program. These programs are generic in nature, and only test the interfaces between the SAP modules and the third-party software. Getting SAP certification only proves that the interfaces between the adapter and the SAP modules are found to be correct and as required. It does not mean that the adapter has been tested for JCA compliance or any other platform compliance. Nonetheless, vendor certification is important because it is one more parameter to compare adapters for the same packages and applications. At the very least, it shows the component or adapter builder's commitment to quality and planning.

Vendor certification may not be very useful for adapters built in-house. There is no harm in seeking vendor certification, but the same can be achieved by extensive testing in-house. What is important are the test plans used by the package vendor to certify third-party software. These test plans provide good indicators about what is more important to the package vendor in terms of testing.

---

# Testing Environments

One of fundamental principles of software QA is to have a separate test environment. More often than not, developers claim that they have tested their code and that it works as required. However, developers usually test their code in development environments. Many of us who have created and published Web pages will be familiar with the situation in which the Web page works fine on our development machines, but fail or break when tested from a different machine. This happens because references to images and other links may be pointing to local files instead of files on the Web server. Similar things happen with adapters, and having a separate testing environment saves time and effort further down the line of the product lifecycle.

Having a standalone test environment totally separate from other environments (development, production, and so on) is expensive. In the case of JCA adapters, you are looking at a separate installation of the application server and the required hardware and operating systems. If more than one operating system needs to be supported, the test environments get bigger and more expensive to set up and maintain. The benefits of having a testing environment become clear over the long term. A consistent environment for testing different versions of the adapter helps to isolate factors contributing to the bugs and faults. Without a consistent test bed, it is not possible to isolate problems easily.

## Reference Implementation Test Environment

SUN Microsystems has made available a reference implementation of a J2EE-compliant application server that supports the JCA contracts. This reference implementation is a good candidate for setting up a baseline test environment. Adapter developers can use this environment to test their code, knowing that the tested adapter is expected to work on all other application servers. This also helps developers understand the expected run-time behavior of both the adapters and the application server.

After the adapter has passed all test cases in a reference implementation-based test environment, it is ready for specific tests on application servers from other vendors. Portability of the resource adapter across J2EE-compliant application servers may be important to resource adapter providers. In this case, the reference implementation test environment is useful for ensuring minimum compliance. However, more testing is required on specific application servers to ensure full compliance. The differences between J2EE-compliant application servers depend on the different vendors and their architectures. However, adapter developers should expect consistent behavior between the reference implementation and the vendor application servers.

## Application Server Test Environment

Because this book is focused on JCA from an implementation perspective, the application server is considered as part of the test environment. Other middleware may be required, depending on the adapter architecture. Although the reference implementation is a good sandbox for establishing basic JCA conformance, a fully supported J2EE-compliant application server is absolutely necessary for a production environment. The same version and brand of application server used in production should also be installed and maintained as part of the testing environment. Many leading application server vendors have certification guidelines and programs aimed at speeding the process of testing adapters and other application server-based components.

## Operating Systems

The operating system plays an important part in any test environment. With Java, it is especially important because the support for JVM varies on different platforms. There are also instances in which particular JVMs work better in specific operating systems. The version of the operating system, the JVM support, and the system parameters set up by the administrators are important factors in understanding the testing environment.

After a baseline operating system and its environment are established, test engineers should not change the configuration unless there is solid justification. For adapters, the operating system part of the test environment gets complex when the application demands or requires specific versions and parameters that conflict with the adapter requirements. For example, the application may be built using Java 1.2 and the adapter is Java 1.3, which could be a problem for some operating systems and platforms.

Although Java is intended to work on all platforms, Java support is not consistent, and varies with time. Hence, a safer approach to testing is to establish the baseline of the operating systems in conjunction with the application servers, the version of Java, and also the hardware platform.

## Hardware

This is the most stable part of the testing environment. Companies do not change hardware as often. Operating systems require upgrades; application servers require upgrades; and so do the adapters and business applications. Hardware, on the other hand, does not undergo significant change. The addition of CPUs, hard drives, and so on does not require software to be retested.

If the production environment has more than one type of hardware architectures on which the adapters are required to run, it is better to have all the types of hardware architectures in the testing environment, too. The likelihood of an adapter failing on different hardware platforms is due to the JVM or the application server version being different for the hardware. The JVM for SUN SPARC and JVM for Intel platforms will be different, and although both JVMs may be Java 1.3, there could be problems on one platform and not on the other. Even if both platforms are running the SUN Solaris operating system, it is not safe to assume that if the adapter works on SUN SPARC platform it will work on the Intel platform as well. Testing the adapter on both platforms is always a better strategy than allowing bugs to crop up in the production environment.

## Test Harness

So far, you have seen the testing environment from a platform-compliance perspective. You also need an environment from an application-compliance perspective. Adapter developers commonly run into situations in which they have to develop the adapters without access to the applications or with limited access to the applications. Under such circumstances, adapter test harnesses are ideal environments for testing application interfaces.

A test harness takes the place of the actual application, and simulates the interfaces between the adapters and the actual application. One drawback of a test harness is the additional time required to develop it. With careful planning, adapter developers can build simple, command line-driven test harness components that can be part of the testing environments in general. For example, if the target application is Web-based and uses HTTP-based servlets to process incoming data, the adapter developer can develop similar servlets, but replace the back-end process of the incoming data with a simple storage mechanism. This test harness allows you to send data to the servlet as if it were the real application. In reality, nothing happens at the back end, but the adapter thinks everything is working properly. Such test harnesses are useful for fixing adapter problems early on in the development cycles.

# Gathering Test Data

Perhaps the most difficult task of any testing activity is the availability of a good sample of test data. Meaningful test data does not mean only volume, but also the quality of the test data. The data should cover every business pattern and scenario that the adapter is likely to encounter. In practice, access to such test data is rare. Adapter developers and QA engineers have to spend time analyzing the available test data and then build the test database over time. Testing tools are capable of generating data based on some parameters, but the generated data is not the same as real data.

Leading package vendors such as Oracle include a test database with its application software. Oracle Applications includes a test database that is ideal for adapter developers and QA engineers. But not all applications provide such databases, and it is left to the development teams or the QA teams to build it from scratch. Test data are perhaps the biggest show stoppers in adapter testing, and require cooperation from application developers who have better domain knowledge in creating the test data.

---

**NOTE**

Personally, I always like to see the test data before I see the test plans. The best test plans and test cases do not mean much if the test data is weak and unable to cover the business patterns as much as possible.

---

Another reason for focusing on test data is getting predictable results. It is important to establish a known and stable set of test data. The data arms testers with predictable expected results every time the tests are performed. If the test data changes during different testing cycles, it is hard to identify the source of bugs when identified. Isolating bugs is very important, just as reproducing bugs is important to find where things are going wrong. In many instances, bugs cannot be isolated or reproduced, making the job of bug fixing extremely difficult. A good set of test data is generally useful to solve such problems (or, at the very least, to confirm a reported problem).

## Planning Regression Tests

As you have seen so far, there are many different types of tests that adapter developers and QA engineers need to perform. Testing is not a one-time deal. Changes to the adapters or any of its platform components may require retesting. Regression tests are useful for getting a quick feel for the adapters' compliance after any changes. Generally, regression tests are based on black box test cases, except in the case where the adapter has undergone significant re-engineering or the addition of new features and functions.

Many times, regression tests are also based on end-to-end tests that ensure that the larger integration scenario is not broken by changes to any of the participating adapters and applications. Identifying test cases as one of the regression test suite is important and should be based on the following parameters:

- The most complex test case of the adapter test plan
- The most time-consuming test case of the adapter test plan
- The most resource-intensive test case of the adapter test plan
- Test cases for the most frequently used adapter features and functions

Any test cases that match any one of the previous parameters is a good candidate for regression tests. Automating regression tests is always a good strategy, but may not be feasible at all times. Every effort must be made to automate regression tests because they are repeated most often of all test cases.

## Summary

Adapter QA is not a small task that can be finished in a day or two at the end of the development cycle. It needs careful planning, a proper testing environment, a comprehensive test data suite, and a host of test cases. All this requires time and resources that are in addition to the development resources.

Platform compliance and application compliance are separate tasks, and must be part of adapter testing. Vendor certification may be useful for boosting the confidence levels and trust in third-party components. Whether the adapters are built in-house or bought from an adapter vendor, a comprehensive adapter QA plan is required to ensure its long-term stability and robustness in a production environment.

Some platform and application vendors have specified compliance criteria that help determine the end goal of the test plans. However, in the absence of such criteria from the vendors, project teams should consult with system administrators and IT managers to determine a baseline platform compliance. This can be as simple as compliance with specific versions of the operating system, JVM, databases, and so on; or can be more complicated and include performance requirements, security requirements, and sometimes even certain administration requirements such as log messages created in the right directories.

This chapter has highlighted the importance of adapter testing, and identified the basic types of tests that every adapter team should plan and undertake. At the end of the day, quality differentiates between two adapters for the same application.

# 10

# Overview of JCA

"Honest criticism is hard to take, particularly from a relative, a friend, an acquaintance or a stranger."

—Franklin P. Jones

The J2EE Connector Architecture Specification version 1.0 is a comprehensive document outlining the objective and concept of JCA, as well as examples of potential integration scenarios in which they may be applicable. This chapter provides an overview and a perspective on the JCA specifications. It is intended to be complementary to the JCA specifications and intended to help you better understand JCA.

The JCA specification is the first serious attempt to formalize and standardize the infrastructure and architecture for application integration adapters. The specification does more than define an architecture model; it defines the different stakeholders and their roles and responsibilities, and it also provides a framework for building an adapter reference model in the context of J2EE-compliant application servers and applications. The specification also includes guidelines for testing and deploying adapters.

Although this book covers aspects of adapter development beyond the current scope of the JCA specifications, it is important to read and understand the entire JCA specification because it is the basis on which J2EE resource adapters are developed. The objective of this chapter is to clarify some of the goals and objectives of JCA, and in the process, enable quicker and easier implementations of JCA-compliant resource adapter.

## Objectives of JCA Specifications

The objective of JCA is quite simply to enable J2EE applications to integrate with legacy applications and other emerging technologies known in JCA terms as Enterprise Information Systems (EIS). From a J2EE application's perspective, an EIS manages information resources either in the form of databases or real-time information.

J2EE is a component-based application platform, and as such, a business application will be decomposed into many different types of components. One type of component is a JCA-compliant resource adapter. Although there are no restrictions on how many resource adapters can be developed and deployed, typically there is one resource adapter for an EIS. This does not mean that there cannot be more than one instances of the adapter running at the same time. In fact, it is very likely that there will be multiple instances of resource adapters required to access EIS—depending on the volume of users, data, and instances of EIS.

A JCA-compliant resource adapter will obviously be hosted by a J2EE server. In most cases, this means that the resource adapter will be accessing the actual EIS remotely using some form of middleware. This can be Java Database Connectivity (JDBC), messaging and distributed computing, or proprietary middleware. The JCA adapter model is somewhat different than what is commonly found in the EAI technologies, where the adapters are generally considered to be hosted in the same environment as the EIS. So if the legacy application is a mainframe accounting system, then most EAI solutions will have an adapter that executes in a mainframe environment, with the integration broker communicating with the adapter in the legacy application environment. In the case of JCA, that model has changed; the mainframe resource adapter (JCA resource adapter) will be hosted in a J2EE application server environment. It is important to remember this distinction because the resulting architecture and design of the resource adapter will be different.

Readers of the JCA specification may notice that there is no mention of integration scenarios in which legacy applications may need to integrate with J2EE applications. It is entirely possible that a mission-critical application in a mainframe environment may want to invoke a specific EJB or other J2EE application components. Although you can innovate and develop a solution to achieve this, the JCA specifications are not designed to solve this type of integration scenarios. Figure 10.1 shows a schematic diagram of JCA and its role in J2EE application integration.

Figure 10.1 contains two distinct domains: the J2EE domain and the Enterprise Information System (EIS) domain. The J2EE domain contains a J2EE-compliant application server, and the EIS domain contains the EIS-specific platforms and servers. The J2EE domain consists of three environments: the JCA environment, managed application environment, and non-managed application environment. Of these, the managed application environment and JCA environment are hosted by a J2EE-compliant application server. The non-managed application environment is for standalone Java applications, which can also communicate with resource adapters.

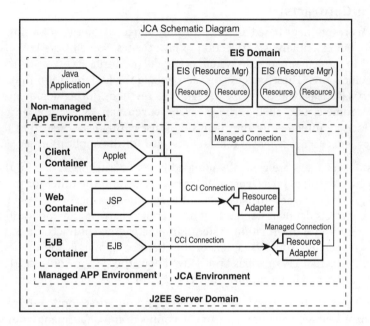

*FIGURE 10.1*    JCA schematic diagram.

Each environment hosts software components of different granularity. The JCA environment hosts JCA resource adapters, and the managed application environment hosts J2EE application components. There are different types of J2EE application components, each hosted by a specific container. Figure 10.1 shows three containers: a client component container, an EJB container, and a Web component container. The non-managed environment includes Java applications or standalone two tier Java applications.

The objective of JCA is to extend the application server's integration capabilities. This is significant from a design perspective, especially because it means that JCA resource adapters are not the same as business components (EJB). The resource adapters are not managed by a JCA container, but are extensions of the application server. Hence, the need for system contracts that enable application servers to access these extensions or resource adapters. However, it also means that the application server acts like a broker between the business components (EJB) and the resource adapters. Understanding the system contracts as well as the connection mechanisms between EJB and the resource adapters is very important for the design of the resource adapters as well as the EJB.

## System Contracts

True to its component-based architecture, a resource adapter is not a single Java program, but essentially is a collection of Java classes. Some of the Java classes are required to implement specific system contracts (Java interfaces), as defined by the JCA specifications. These system contracts enable the J2EE platform to discover the necessary Java classes and invoke the required methods during deployment and at runtime. Some classes, such as the `javax.resource.cci.ConnectionFactory` implementation, are intended for the client's (EJB) use. Other classes, such as `javax.resource.spi.ManagedConnection`, are intended for the application server.

The system contracts are generally grouped into two categories, one for the clients of the resource adapter (`javax.resource.cci` package) and the other for the application server (`javax.resource.spi` package). Although the specifications say that the system contracts define a standard set of interfaces between an applications server and EIS (Enterprise Information System), in practice the contracts are between application servers and resource adapters or the client components and the resource adapter. The actual EIS now has knowledge about the system contracts. For a JCA resource adapter to function properly, a compatible J2EE server is essential.

Some of the system contracts are mandatory, and others are optional. For example, all resource adapters must implement the connection management contracts, whereas the transaction contracts could be implemented only if the underlying EIS supports transactions.

Figure 10.2 shows the JCA contracts that are part of the resource adapter domain. A JCA contract is specified as an interface, which ensures a consistent method of invoking the resource adapter, but not necessarily the associated implementation or behavior. For example, a resource adapter for Oracle database may support Oracle SQL extensions, whereas another resource adapter for Oracle database may not. The JCA contract does not specify any EIS-related attributes, methods, or interfaces.

The same applies to system contracts between the resource adapter and the application server. Neither resource adapter developers nor users of resource adapters should assume that the implementations of system contracts by the application servers will be consistent. One application server may support connection pooling, and another application server may not. If there is a need to handle aspects of connection pooling (especially dynamic content-based connection pooling) with EIS, then it may be possible that the resource adapter will have to implement connection pooling.

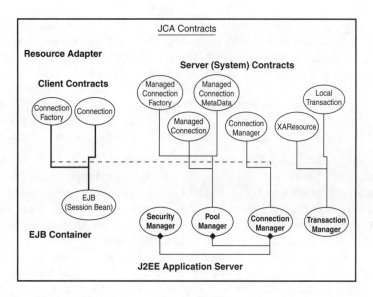

*FIGURE 10.2*   JCA contracts.

JCA resource adapter developers need to understand all the system contracts, including transaction management and security management, even if they may not be implemented in all resource adapters.

## Roles Specified in the JCA Specifications

There are multiple roles defined for stakeholder responsibilities in the JCA specifications:

- Resource adapter provider—An entity with expertise in a particular EIS that is therefore capable of providing a resource adapter for that EIS. This entity could be the EIS vendors in the case of packaged applications, corporate development teams in the case of in-house proprietary applications, and system integrators or consulting companies specializing in custom adapter development. Even some EAI vendors can be resource adapter providers, depending on their experience with the EIS and J2EE environments. Expertise in the EIS alone is not enough to become a resource adapter provider. Along with the domain knowledge of the EIS, resource adapter providers must be experts in J2EE and JCA.

- Application server vendor—Provides an implementation of the J2EE specifications. In the case of JCA, the application server vendor is responsible for supporting the JCA contracts that ensure proper management of resource adapters and implementation of support services such as connection pooling and so on.

- Container provider—Generally, the same entity as the application server vendor. Container providers develop EJB and Web component containers for JSP, servlets, and so on as part of the application server. In terms of JCA, the containers (EJB, JSP, servlets, and so on) are expected to use the system-level contracts (security, transaction, and so on) provided by the resource adapter and manage connectivity to the EIS on behalf of the application components. Container-managed transactions or container-managed security is possible due to the support for these features in the J2EE component containers.

- Application component provider—In the context of JCA, a supplier of components that accesses one or more EIS. This means it's typically a domain expert or an EIS expert who builds EJB and other components who use the CCI-based interfaces of resource adapters. For all practical purposes, an application component provider is the end user of JCA resource adapters. In the case of an end-to-end integration scenario, as described earlier in Chapter 7, "Adapter Development Methodology and Best Practices," an application component provider is responsible for understanding the scenario and supplies components that can be configured at deployment time to interface with different resource adapters as required to enable the scenario.

- Enterprise tool vendors—As described in the JCA specifications, supplies a comprehensive application development tool that involves much more than traditional analysis, design, and debugging capabilities. A J2EE application development tool needs to support component assembly or composition, explore available resource adapters capabilities, manage deployment (install and configuration) of modules, and so on. Although many IDEs are good, they still lack the capability to explore resource adapters. Perhaps in the near future, leading Java IDEs may support that, too, because it will make the job of an application assembler simpler.

- Deployer—Responsible for the installation and configuration of modules in the target operational environment, which is generally comprised of the application server and the various other EIS connected to it over the network.

- System administrator—Responsible for maintaining the operational environment, and will work with the deployer to ensure that applications are deployed correctly.

One person can assume different roles at different times. It is quite possible that in a relatively small operational environment, the system administrator, deployer, and in some cases even the application assembler are the same person. Also, it is possible that a team of developers assumes the role of resource adapter provider as well as application component provider. Identifying the roles as opposed to actual end-users results in better distribution of responsibilities and tasks. The intention is to become more efficient in developing and deploying distributed applications using J2EE and JCA.

## Understanding Connection Management

Connection management can be a very confusing subject, especially for programmers who are new to J2EE and JCA. But it is also one of the most important aspects of the JCA architecture. In the context of JCA, *connection management* means creating and managing the connections between J2EE applications and connected EIS. This task is distributed between the resource adapter and the application server. After all, the resource adapter is supposed to connect applications components (EJB) hosted by application servers with one or more instances of EIS. It is this distributed nature of managing connections that may be intimidating to some programmers.

The client contracts in Figure 10.2 define connections and connection management contracts between application components (EJB) and the resource adapter. These connection contracts are not the actual connections to EIS. Thus, an EJB is not really connecting with the EIS when it interacts with the resource adapter. The EJB gets a connection handle that represents an actual physical connection to EIS, which is maintained by another connection type called `ManagedConnection`.

### Managed and Non-managed Applications

Before getting into the details of connection management, it is important to remember the two application scenarios:

- Managed application—Application components depend on the application server to manage system services such as transactions, security, persistence, and so on. In this scenario, the application components contain only the business logic. At deployment time, the deployer looks at the deployment descriptor for the application component, and configures the required system services. With the addition of JCA specifications, one of the system services can be access to an EIS, as supported by the associated resource adapter.

- Non-managed application—The application components (which are also part of the application, and not managed by any server) include interfaces to system services. Therefore, a non-managed application is typically a two-tiered Java application with JDBC, transaction, and code for other system services embedded in it.

Resource adapters must support connectivity to EIS for both managed applications and non-managed applications. A resource adapter must support two types of connections:

- Connections between the client and the adapter

- Connections between the adapter and EIS

In a managed application scenario, the application server acts like a broker that manages these connections and ensures proper load balancing (connection pooling) between client usage, server performance, and EIS connection bandwidth. Client usage is dictated by the number of application components requesting connections to a resource adapter, server performance is dictated partly by the algorithms used for load balancing, and the EIS connection bandwidth depends on the type of EIS.

The connections between client and adapter are represented by the interfaces (contracts) defined in the `javax.resource.cci` package. These include `javax.resource.cci.ConnectionFactory`, `javax.resource.cci.Connection`. Every resource adapter must define a class that implements these or derived interfaces. The deployment descriptor has a tag, `<connection-impl-class>`, whose value is the fully qualified name of the class that implements the `Connection` interface. For example, if the class name is `ClientAccess.ExConnection.java`, then the deployment descriptor entry will be

```
<connection-impl-class>ClientAccess.ExConnection</connection-impl-class>
```

Instead of creating instances of the `Connection` class directly, clients of the resource adapter should use an implementation of the `ConnectionFactory` interface (contract). Any object factory is used to create instances of one or more classes, depending on a key supplied by the client. For example, the key could be an EIS name, or it could include an EIS name and some security parameters such as user name and password. The key value is used by `ConnectionFactory` to determine what type of connection is appropriate for the client.

The association between a client application component and a resource adapter's connection factory is handled by the application component's deployment descriptor. The deployment descriptor for the application component states the resource reference name defined in the JNDI name space and the resource type, which is the fully qualified name of the Java interface implemented by the connection factory.

From an application component's perspective, getting a connection to the EIS is quite simple; but a heck of a lot of things are happening under the covers to create an instance of the connection. The application component creates a default initial JNDI-naming context and does a lookup of the connection factory instance, as defined in its deployment descriptor. The connection factory has methods such as `getConnection` that return a connection to the EIS. The application component then uses the connection to perform EIS-related tasks and services before closing the connection.

In the case of a non-managed application, the sequence of getting a connection to the EIS via a resource adapter is very much the same. However, the resource adapter must support both managed and non-managed clients. There are some differences in how these two types of clients (applications) are handled by the resource adapter. Most of the work of supporting these clients is done by the managed connection factory, as described in subsequent sections of this chapter.

Managing the connections, and especially the distributed flow of connection-related tasks, is the responsibility of a `ConnectionManager`. An application server provides a `ConnectionManager` that deals with the details of coordinating connection pooling with the creation of new connections, and so on. A resource adapter is required to provide an implementation of a `ConnectionManager` to support the case of a non-managed application accessing the resource adapter. Remember, in a non-managed application scenario, the application server does not take responsibility for coordinating the flow of connection-related tasks. This includes connection pooling, and so on. Hence, if a resource adapter is expected to support many standalone two-tiered Java applications, it may have to do a lot of work in terms of implementing connection pooling, transactions, security, and so on.

But in the case of a managed application, the connection factory of a resource adapter delegates the job of creating connections to the `ConnectionManager` instance created by the application server. When the application server creates an instance of the connection factory, as requested by the application component, the application server hands an instance of a `ConnectionManager` to the connection factory. The connection factory is expected to preserve the connection manager and use it when the application component asks it to create a connection instance.

Figure 10.3 shows a simplified depiction of two connection-managed flows. One is the lookup of a connection factory, and the other is creating an application-level connection to an external EIS via a resource adapter.

**Flow 1: Look Up a Connection Factory**
Figure 10.3 shows a session bean creating a context (1.1) and invoking the JNDI lookup function on the context (1.2). This results in the JNDI delegating the request to a server process (1.3), which creates an instance of a `ConnectionManager` (1.4) if required, as well as creating an instance of the `ManagedConnectionFactory` (1.5) and invoking the `getConnectionFactory` method on the managed connection factory (which creates an instance of `ConnectionFactory`). The connection factory instance is then bound to the JNDI namespace. In a managed environment, the deployment tool does most of the job of creating and configuring the connection factory and binding it to the JNDI name space. In a non-managed environment, the application needs to do the work.

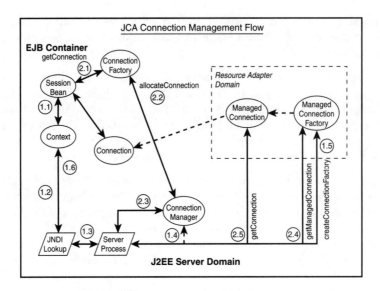

*FIGURE 10.3*    Connection management flows.

### Flow 2: Get an Application Level Connection

Figure 10.3 also shows a session bean getting a connection by invoking the
getConnection method on the connection factory instance. The connection factory
delegates the request for connection to the ConnectionManager instance associated
with the factory. The allocateConnection method of the connection manager
receives a ManagedConnectionFactory instance as a parameter. This managed connection factory provides two kinds of services to the application server: It either creates
a new managed connection (physical connection to the EIS) or matches an existing
set of managed connections with the properties set as part of the
ConnectionRequestInfo instance, which is another parameter to the
allocateConnection method.

If there is a matching connection, then the server process invokes the getConnection
method on the managed connection instance. This method creates a new
Connection instance that is associated with the managed connection. If there are no
matching managed connections, then the server process invokes
createManagedConnection method on the managed connection factory, resulting in
a new managed connection. The server process then invokes the getConnection
method on the managed connection, resulting in a new Connection instance being
created and associated with the managed connection. The Connection instance is
returned to the connection manager, which returns it to the connection factory,
which returns it to the application component.

The benefits of this rather roundabout way of getting connections to EIS are the layers of abstraction that result in a consistent connection management interface for application components. Regardless of the underlying EIS and its connection mechanisms, the application component always uses an instance of the Connection class to interact with the EIS. It also ensures that the application server can manage connection pooling without affecting the physical connections with EIS. Although all this sounds complex and at times confusing, a couple of implementations of resource adapters will make it clear how the different classes collaborate to manage EIS connections.

# Understanding Transaction Management

The transaction management contracts specified in the JCA specifications are system-level interfaces between the application server and the EIS. A resource adapter is expected to support the transaction contracts used by the application server to manage transactions across resource managers (EIS). An EIS can support two types of transactions:

- Java Transaction API (JTA) or X/Open's transaction demarcation protocol (XA) transactions—Transactions controlled and coordinated by an external transaction manager such as BEA Tuxedo

- Resource Manager (RM) local transactions—Transactions managed entirely by the EIS

A transaction manager, which is part of the application server, manages/coordinates transactions across multiple EIS. It propagates the transaction context across all EIS participating in a transaction. The transaction manager is invisible to the application component; the JCA transaction contracts define interfaces between the application server (transaction manager) and the EIS. There are two contracts: javax. transaction.xa.XAResource and javax.resource.spi.LocalTransaction. It is obvious from these interfaces that an XA transaction is managed by the transaction manager, and a local transaction is managed directly by the application server.

## Local Transactions

There are two types of local transactions. In one type, the transaction demarcation is managed by the component container (*container-managed transaction*); in the other type, the demarcation is coded by the application component (*component-managed transaction*). In the case of a component-managed transaction, the application component can use the UserTransaction interface defined in the JTA (Java Transaction API) package, or use an API specific to the EIS (for example, JDBC). In terms of J2EE applications, the EJB container is required to support both container-managed and component-managed local transactions. Web component containers, on the other hand, support only component-managed transactions.

The interface for local transactions is included in the `javax.resource.spi` package. A resource adapter implements the interface `javax.resource.spi.LocalTransaction` to provide support for local transactions performed on the EIS. The application server uses the `LocalTransaction` interface to manage the transaction. The `LocalTransaction` interface is shown here:

```
public interface javax.resource.spi.LocalTransaction {
    public void being() throws ResourceException;
    public void commit() throws ResourceException;
    public void rollback() throws ResourceException;
}
```

## Role of `ManagedConnection` Objects

Transactions happen over a physical connection to the EIS, which is represented by the `ManagedConnection` instances. These instances are also factories for connection handles used by client components. `ManagedConnection` interfaces also support transaction management contracts by creating `LocalTransaction` and `XAResource` instances. The interface defines two methods, `getLocalTransaction()` and `getXAResource()`, which return instances of the respective transaction management objects.

There is a one-to-one correspondence between an XA resource and the managed connection to the underlying EIS. The `ManagedConnection` instance, which represents the physical connection, is responsible for returning the same instance of `XAResource` across calls to the `getXAResource` method. Hence, the `ManagedConnection` instance also acts as a factory of `LocalTransaction` and `XAResource` instances.

Supporting `XAResource`-based transaction (XA transactions) is not mandatory, and resource adapters need not implement it if the underlying EIS does not support XA-compliant transactions. The decision on transaction support for the resource adapter is dictated by the capabilities of the EIS. If the EIS is an ASCII file, for example, then the resource adapter will most likely not support any transaction that is also allowed as an option in the deployment descriptor of the adapter.

In most cases, the resource adapter will be required to support container-managed local transactions and XA transactions. Unless the resource adapter is expected to support standalone Java applications or other forms of non-managed applications, it is not necessary to implement transaction demarcation code in the resource adapter classes. The transaction contracts specified in the JCA specifications make the often-onerous task of managing distributed transactions simpler and more manageable.

They also formalize the resource adapter's responsibility in supporting XA-compliant and local transactions.

# Understanding Common Client Interface

The term *common client interface* implies that it is intended for any type of client that needs access to the resource adapter. The section on CCI in the JCA specifications could be clearer and less ambiguous in explaining the actual role of CCI. Some of the unclear and confusing objectives of CCI are as follows.

Implementing a CCI-compatible interface is not mandatory. This will invariably lead to different designs and implementation of access mechanisms to resource adapters. This is not entirely bad because the usage patterns or used cases of resource adapters are too big in number to be constrained by a small set of interfaces or APIs. However, a better solution would have been to design a flexible extendable client API, which was also a mandatory requirement for resource adapters. Building a CCI-compliant API for resource adapters brings a structured and more manageable method of granting access to resource adapters. Without the API, users will build their own interfaces, which will result in maintenance nightmares over time.

Common Client Interface (CCI) is the API for clients of resource adapters, and defines services (interactions) supported by the resource adapter. The features and functionality of the resource adapter is presented to the client in the form of CCI-compliant API. The JCA specifications state that the CCI APIs do not replace other Java APIs, such as the JDBC API. However, the JCA specifications do not stop developers from encapsulating JDBC API in CCI classes. This gives adapter developers the flexibility to encapsulate database access to the EIS as part of the client API.

Although the CCI does not define any EIS-specific characteristics, it is possible to develop EIS-specific APIs. For example, a resource adapter for SAP can define a CCI-compatible API that offers SAP-specific services (interactions) such as invoking BAPI objects. The example adapter in this book has a CCI interface with services (interactions) capable of parsing ASCII data files and converting the contents to Java objects. It is not mandatory that all resource adapters implement or extend the CCI interface. Neither is it mandatory that if a resource adapter has an API, it must be CCI-compliant. However, because any client API will have to deal with connection management (as specified in the JCA specifications), extending CCI is the better approach for defining EIS-specific client APIs.

## Categories of CCI

CCI is composed of four parts or categories of interfaces: connection-related interfaces, interaction (service)-related interfaces, data-related interfaces, and metadata-related interfaces. Each category has a set of interfaces that must be implemented to enable the respective category of API. The connection-related interfaces represent an application (J2EE application) level connection to the EIS. The interfaces in this category include

```
javax.resource.cci.ConnectionFactory
javax.resource.cci.Connection
javax.resource.cci.LocalTransaction
```

The ConnectionFactory interface enables resource adapters to define EIS-specific connection factories that can contain simple or complex logic for determining the appropriate type of connection to the underlying EIS. If there are multiple instances of an EIS in a distributed environment, for example, and the client demands connection to a specific instance of the EIS, the CCI connection factory can choose the appropriate connection type associated with the EIS. This will require the resource adapter to extend ConnectionFactory and Connection interfaces to support the previous connection requirements.

A ConnectionFactory implementation is an extension of java.io.Serializable and javax.resource.Referenceable classes. This means that a ConnectionFactory instance can be looked up in the JNDI namespace. The client component (an EJB) uses an instance of javax.naming.context to look up the specific ConnectionFactory. The ConnectionFactory instance has a method, getConnection(), which returns the Connection object (instance) that represents a connection to the EIS.

The getConnection method has two signatures: one without parameters, getConnection(); and one with a parameter which is an instance of java.util.Map class, getConnection(java.util.Map properties). The getConnection() method is used when the EIS sign-on (logon) is managed by the J2EE containers. The client invoking the getConnection() method does not specify any sign-on-related information such as user name, password, or other credentials. This is useful when many clients share a common user-id, password combination to access the EIS, or when there is a single sign-on process managed by the application server. Many databases have a user license, and sometimes it is more cost-effective to share a physical connection to the database. In other instances when a client is required to provide a unique user-id and password for security and privileged access, the getConnection(java.util.Map properties) method should be used. If an EIS requires custom connection management services and behavior, additional EIS-specific getConnection methods can be defined.

## Overview of Interaction

An *interaction* represents a function or service (or a sequence of functions and services) provided by an EIS and accessible by the application component via the resource adapter. For example, if an order-tracking system has a service or function Add Purchase Order that can be accessed by the resource adapter, then the Add Purchase Order could be one of the interactions supported by the adapter. Adapters can support one or more interactions, and each interaction is a separate class that implements the javax.resource.cci.Interaction interface. There are two interfaces related to Interaction in the CCI:

```
javax.resource.cci.Interaction
javax.resource.cci.InteractionSpec
```

An interaction supports two styles of executing a function:

```
public void execute(InteractionSpec iSpec, Record input, Record output) throws
ResourceException;
public Record execute(InteractionSpec iSpec, Record input) throws
ResourceException;
```

The InteractionSpec class execute methods define parameters or quality of service attributes for specific instances of Interaction classes. The InteractionSpec interface can be extended or implemented as is. The standard InteractionSpec interface defines a set of standard properties, including the name of the EIS function that should be accessed, an integer describing the integration scenario type (SYNC_SEND, SYNC_SEND_RECEIVE, SYNC_RECEIVE), and an integer representing the execution timeout (in milliseconds).

The SYNC_SEND scenario (interaction) type is useful if the resource adapter enables a function such as data upload, or when sending a service request and not waiting for the response.

The SYNC_SEND_SYNC_RECEIVE scenario (interaction) type is useful when the interaction is about sending a request and waiting for immediate response. The execution timeout value determines how long the Interaction should wait for the response from EIS before throwing an exception or taking corrective actions.

The SYNC_RECEIVE scenario (interaction) type is useful when retrieving message from a queue, extracting information from a staging table, and so on.

Figure 10.4 shows examples of the three interactions (patterns) just described. The first interaction (1) shows a SYNC_SEND_SYNC_RECEIVE type of interaction, in which the session bean sends a request to the resource adapter and then waits for the response from EIS. The second interaction (2) shows a session bean that sends a request to the resource adapter, but does not wait for the response from the EIS. The resource adapter sends the request to a message queue monitored by the EIS. The EIS sends its response to the reply queue that is monitored by a message-driven bean. In this instance, the interaction is a SYNC_SEND interaction. The last type of interaction occurs when an application component invokes a method on the resource adapter to read messages from a reply queue. It is quite possible that there are several messages on the queue, and the application component wants to receive all messages before processing them. This is a SYNC_RECEIVE type of interaction.

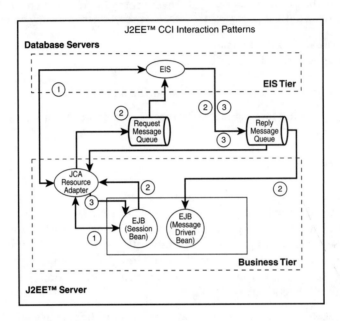

**FIGURE 10.4**    CCI interaction patterns.

Apart from the standard properties, the InteractionSpec interface can be extended to define EIS interaction-specific properties. For example, the interactions defined in the example adapter included in this book require the ASCII filename and the name of the metadata file. These can be added as properties of the interaction spec, enabling client components to set different filenames to parse every time the resource adapter is used:

```
public interface myEISInteractionSpec1 extends javax.resource.cci.InteractionSpec {

    public static final String asciiFileName;
    public static final String asciiMetadataFileName;
    public String getasciiFileName();
    public void setasciiFileName(String filename);
    public String getasciiMetadataFileName();
    public void setasciiMetadataFileName(String filename);


}
```

An adapter need not support all the standard properties defined for an `InteractionSpec`. For example, not all adapters will return a result set as the return value of an interaction. Result sets are very database-oriented, and do not make sense if the resource adapter is reading messages off a queue, or reading records in an ASCII file and converting them to Java objects. Irrespective of the properties supported by the `InteractionSpec`, the specifications do state that the interface must be implemented as a JavaBean.

Another way to store `InteractionSpec` instances is by registering them as administered objects in the JNDI namespace. This gives the instance a logical name that is easier to read and more meaningful to the application component and the EIS. The deployment tool can be used to manage the registration process. Just like the application component looks up the connection factory in the JNDI space, the application component can look up an `InteractionSpec` by using a logical name before handling it to the *execute* method in the `Interaction` interface. `InteractionSpec` instances provide runtime flexibility of invoking an EIS service (interaction) with different parameters, as required by the application component.

## Understanding Metadata Interfaces and Records

There are several reasons why metadata information is important and useful. Self-describing messages have been designed and deployed for many years, and the XML standard is a classic example of the benefits of including metadata information along with the actual data. Metadata information describes the associated data independent of the implementation. Because the `Connection` interface is not bound to any specific EIS, connection-related metadata information is useful for determining the attributes of the underlying physical connection and EIS environment.

The interface `javax.resource.cci.ConnectionMetaData` provides information about an EIS instance connected through a `Connection` instance. A client (application) component interested in knowing the metadata information calls the `Connection.getMetaData` method to get an instance of `ConnectionMetaData`. Some of the information that can be retrieved from the metadata interface include the EIS (product) name, EIS version number, and even the user name used to connect to the EIS. As you have seen in earlier sections in this chapter, the user name used to connect to the EIS can be different from the user name used to get a `Connection` instance.

There is another class of metadata information, known as `ResourceAdapterMetaData`, which describes information related to the resource adapter—and not the underlying EIS. It is quite possible that the resource adapter will support different versions of the JCA specification in the future, although the EIS version may be the same. Even information about the resource adapter's capabilities, in terms of supporting local transactions and so on, can be retrieved from the `ResourceAdapterMetaData` instance. Resource adapters that have more EIS-specific or adapter-specific metadata information to offer their clients can extend the `ConnectionMetaData` and `ResourceAdapterMetaData` interfaces.

A `Record` is a Java representation of a data structure used as input or output to an EIS function. Because the data structures of the EIS can vary and will most likely not be Java, a generic `Record` implementation that uses a metadata repository at run-time is a basic requirement for resource adapters. This type of abstraction or indirection shields the adapter from changes in the data structure of the EIS, too. There is a catch to this solution of a generic `Record`, and that is the requirement to map EIS data structures (or data models) to the `Record` data structure. Without mapping, the attributes of the data structures will not be converted to and from Java data types properly.

It is possible to not use the `Record` data structure in an adapter. Instead, either a derived interface (a more specialized form of `Record` interface) or an entirely different custom interface may be used to interface and transform EIS data into Java data, and vice versa. With the widespread use of XML, it might make more sense to use XML as the data structure between the resource adapter and the external applications. However, the external application (EIS) must be able to exchange XML documents.

Other aspects of using the generic `Record` implementation, such as the use of the `ResultSet` interface to return data extracted from a RDBMS using a JDBC interface, may not be useful when the EIS is not database-centric. It is not a surprise that `ResultSet` cannot be of much use for adapters that interface with messages or other forms of data representations besides RDBMS. There may be instances when a `ResultSet` can still be used to convert a flat data structure to a `ResultSet`-compatible data set, but the overhead may not be justified. The one instance in which the overhead may be justified is when all or most application components (Entity beans) that interface with the resource adapter are capable of processing a `ResultSet`.

The CCI architecture is free of any implementation details and specifics of the underlying EIS. This gives the JCA architecture the flexibility required to maintain the design patterns of a J2EE application. But it also makes presumably simple tasks, such as getting a connection and invoking a function, more tedious. However, the long-term benefits of a common interface far outweigh the extra efforts required to implement the required CCI interfaces.

## Overview of JCA Security

The security architecture defined in the JCA specifications extends the end-to-end security model for J2EE application by including integration with EIS-based resource adapters. Users accessing EIS are authenticated and authorized before being allowed to interface with the EIS. One problem with multiple EISs is that the security infra-structures can be different, as will the security capabilities. Hence, keeping the secu-rity neutral is one of the most important goals of JCA security. In most cases, access to EISs will be over networks (local or remote), which means that support for secured communications is a basic requirement.

Some of the terms used to describe the JCA security architecture are defined here:

- A *principal* is an entity that can be authenticated by the enterprise authentica-tion platform. So it can be an individual with a valid ID that can be authenti-cated. Each principal has a principal name, and it is authenticated by using authentication data. The actual contents of both the name and data depend on the authentication platform. So, if the authentication is a magnetic card, then a magnetic card reader is required as part of the enterprise security platform.

- *Security attributes* are associated with the security environment or platform. There can be more than one security environment or platform, in which case there will be more than one set of security attributes for the principal.

- A *credential* is a set of security information that the principal acquires upon authentication. A credential can be a valid credential or an invalid credential. If the principal is carrying an expired identification card, the authentication mechanism will fail, resulting in invalid credentials. Principals with invalid credentials must not be allowed to access enterprise systems.

- An *end-user* is the source of application requests; and it can be a human being or another application, component, or service. An end-user is represented as a security principal in a `Subject` instance. A subject is an instance of `javax.security.auth.Subject` class. This class holds a subject's identity (one or more) and its security-related attributes (user names, passwords, digital certificates, and so on).

- An *initiating principal* represents the end-user that interacts directly with the application. So, if an application component is not initiating an authentication process, it is not an initiating principal. User authentication can be done either with a Web client or an application client (component).

- A *caller principal* is associated with an application component instance when a method is invoked. This is used to identify the caller of a specific method within the current security context. In a managed environment, when an application component method is invoked, the principal associated with the component instance is called a caller principal.

- A *resource principal* is a security principal under whose security context a connection to the EIS is established. A resource principal can be different from a caller principal. This means that there can be one set of security attributes and credentials for the resource principal when an application component requests a connection to be established. If the resource adapter has a `user-Id` = `"myUserID"` and `password` = `"xyz"`, then every connection made under this security context has the same user-id and password, allowing for the sharing of security credentials.

- A *security domain* defines the security mechanisms and policies that are enforced. There can be different security domains in an enterprise (for example, inside the firewall, outside the firewall, in the DMZ (demilitarized) zones, and so on). It is possible for the application server and the EIS to be in different security domains, and hence have different security policies and mechanisms.

The purpose of these terms is to define security in the larger context of J2EE applications, with the intention of extending its capabilities to different EIS environments.

An application component provider has two choices for supporting EIS sign-on: allow the component deployer to set up the resource principal and EIS sign-on information, or allow components to sign on to EIS using explicit and potentially different security information for the resource principal. The application component provider uses the deployment descriptor element <res-auth> to indicate the choice of the preceding two choices. If <res-auth> is set to `Application`, the component performs the EIS sign-on; if it's set to `Container`, then the application server does the EIS sign-on.

Sometimes, a physical connection to the EIS is shared by more than one end-user (principal), in which case the reauthentication of security attributes may be required. Not all EIS or physical connections or security platforms can support reauthentication on open connections.

## Security Contract

The classes and interfaces of the security contract actually extend the connection management contract to include security-specific details. The objective of the security contract is to support EIS sign-on by the application server. This is achieved by passing connection requests (`ConnectionFactory.getConnecion();`) from resource adapter clients to the application server's *ConnectionManager*.instance. This allows the application server to add security services before continuing with connection management. After the EIS sign-on is completed, the security credentials are propagated back to the resource adapter.

The security contract includes the following classes and interfaces:

- `javax.security.auth.Subject`
- `javax.security.Principal`

- `javax.resource.spi.security.GenericCredential`

- `javax.resource.spi.security.PasswordCredential`

An instance of `Subject` is a composite object containing the identity (represented by one or more instances of `Principal`), as well as credentials. If there are multiple identities as part of the `Subject` instance, the `getPrincipals` method retrieves all the principals associated with the `Subject`. Other methods, such as `getPublicCredentials` and `getPrivateCredentials`, retrieve the public and private credentials, respectively.

The interface `GenericCredential` provides a mechanism to retrieve credential-related data, independent of the security platform. So a PKI (Public Key Interface) or digital certificate data can be encapsulated inside the `GenericCredential` implementation. If the credentials are composed of a user name and password, only then the `PasswordCredential` interface will be better suited to hold the credential data.

The connection management flow involves delegating the request for a connection to the `ConnectionManager` associated with the `ConnectionFactory` instance. The `allocateConnection` method can be invoked by the connection factory without any security-related data or with the security information provided by the application component. The first method is used by the connection factory when the application server is managing the sign-on to EIS. In this case, the configuration parameters (security policies) define the user name and password, or any other security data required for the sign-on process. The second method is used when the security is managed by the application component.

Under both circumstances, the actual physical connection and sign-on are done by the managed connection. The difference is where the security-related information comes from—the application server or the component. In either case, the resource adapter makes the connection and sign-on.

### Role of `ManagedConnectionFactory`
The `createManagedConnection` method of the `ManagedConnectionFactory` instance of a resource adapter is the security hook between the resource adapter (and therefore the EIS) and the application server. One of the parameters to the `createManagedConnection` method is of type `javax.security.auth.Subject`. The application server can perform one or more security-related tasks before invoking the `createManagedConnection` method with the appropriate credentials. The application component is unaware of the application server's security related tasks, which can include a single sign-on service.

If the EIS sign-on is to be managed by the application component without any involvement of the application server, the resource adapter's createManagedConnection does not receive a null javax.security.auth.Subject object. The user information contained in the ConnectionRequestInfo object passed by the application component in the getConnection method is used by the resource adapter's createManagedConnection to perform the appropriate EIS sign-on.

The decision to delegate the authentication task to the resource adapter or configure the application server to manage it depends on the type of authentication mechanism supported by the EIS. Irrespective of who manages the sign-on process, the J2EE security contracts hide the authentication tasks from the application client. In this way, the security contracts also hide the security mechanisms and platform from the application component and ensure the end-to-end security between application components and the EIS.

## Support for Packaging and Deployment

A resource adapter is essentially a set of classes; some implement JCA contracts or interfaces, and others implement the services and functions interacting with the EIS. There can also be external libraries and drivers, such as JDBC drivers, or network drivers, or middleware drivers necessary for the resource adapter to interact with the EIS. All these classes, together with a deployment descriptor, are packaged as a resource adapter module. This module is an extension of the application server, and the deployment descriptor defines a contract between the resource adapter provider (developers) and the resource adapter deployer.

A J2EE application is composed of one or more J2EE modules, such as an EJB module, Web client modules, and a resource adapter module, if required. A resource adapter can be deployed directly into an application server or as a standalone component. Another mechanism for deploying a resource adapter is by deploying it as part of an application. Chapter 12, "Deploying Adapters," goes into the details of the deployment descriptor and deployment scenarios; this chapter focuses on the deployment code requirements and some of the details of the deployment descriptor.

### Deployment Descriptors and Deployment Tools

A resource adapter provider declares deployment hints by defining the properties in a deployment descriptor. If multiple managed connection factories are supported by the resource adapter, there will be a deployment descriptor for each managed connection factory class. A deployment descriptor becomes the contract between the adapter provider and the adapter deployer.

An application server provides a deployment tool that supports the deployment of multiple resource adapters. Deployment tools can be sourced from third-party vendors as well as IDE vendors, for example. The basic requirement for a deployment tool is the capability to read the deployment descriptor from a resource adapter module and configure multiple property sets (one per configured `ManagedConnectionFactory` instance). It should also help the deployer in adding or removing resource adapters from the operational environment. The set of standard properties for `ManagedConnectionFactory` include

- `ServerName` (Name of the server hosting the EIS instance.)

- `PortNumber` (Port number used to establish the connection.)

- `UserName` (Name of the user establishing a connection to the EIS.)

- `Password` (Password for the user establishing a connection. This can be different from the client credentials using the resource adapter.)

- `ConnectionURL` (URL for the target EIS instance.)

The managed connection factory is not required to support all the standard properties; but for the properties it does support, the implementation class must implement setter and getter methods for each property. In addition to the standard properties, the managed connection factory can support other EIS-specific properties required to create connections.

Another function of the deployment tool is to generate deployment code that ties the resource adapter to the application server. Part of the code registers the connection factory instance in the JNDI name space. If there are any administered objects, then those are also registered in the JNDI name space. The more sophisticated deployment tools generate the necessary code to configure the resource adapter and other external modules the adapter depends on. The J2EE reference implementation includes a deployment tool that can be used as a default deployment tool.

## Summary

This chapter is an overview of the JCA specifications and is intended to help you understand the specifications more easily. You should refer to the JCA specifications, as well as EJB and J2EE specifications, for further details.

The JCA specifications define a set of APIs for extending the application server's capability of integrating external EISs (legacy applications and other non-J2EE enterprise applications). A resource adapter must support two types of application environments: a managed application environment and a non-managed application environment.

In a managed application environment, the application server and the containers do most of the system-level work, such as managing physical connections with the EIS, transactions, security, and so on. This allows configuration to be handled at deployment time, ensuring more flexibility. In the non-managed application environment, the application does not depend on the server to do the system-level tasks. A resource adapter must implement connection management functions such as connection pooling, signing on with the EIS, managing transaction demarcation, and so on to support a non-managed application environment.

The JCA specifications are defined in terms of contracts or interfaces that should be implemented by a resource adapter. These contracts are either system- or server-related interfaces (connection management, security, transaction management) or client- (application component) related interfaces (CCI). EIS-specific interfaces are outside the scope of the JCA specifications. The concept of JCA contracts allows a resource adapter to provide a consistent interface to its clients and to the application server while maintaining application-specific interfaces to the EIS encapsulated in the resource adapter.

Resource adapters support two types of connections: one set of connections and connection factories for the client (application components), and the other set of managed connections and managed connection factories for the application server. The application server is responsible for providing a connection manager, as well as services such as connection pooling, security, and transaction management. This is to ensure that in a container-managed environment, the application server can interact with the appropriate contracts of interfaces of the resource adapter.

The connection flow between an application component, the application server, the resource adapter, and the EIS is quite complicated and distributed across a number of classes. Understanding the exact sequence in a managed and non-managed application environment may take time and the actual implementation of a resource adapter.

The current specifications are still restricted in what they can achieve in terms of interactions with EIS. All interactions are synchronous, although there are ways to work around this limitation and support asynchronous interactions under some specific conditions. Using a combination of a resource adapter and a message-driven bean, you can support simple asynchronous design patterns.

The next version of JCA specifications will attempt to solve some of the problems or restrictions of the JCA 1.0 specifications. It is anybody's guess whether XML will play a bigger role in JCA, as well as whether the CCI interfaces will be stronger in terms of supporting XML and other metadata along with the interaction specifications. The concept of message-driven beans is quite powerful, but JCA needs more inherit support for asynchronous services with EIS. But even in its current form, JCA represents a big step forward in application integration, and promises to leave its mark on the J2EE world.

# 11

# Developing J2EE Resource Adapters

"The truth of the matter is that you always know the right thing to do. The hard part is doing it."

—General H. Norman Schwarzkopf

This chapter is focused on applying the adapter development process, adapter reference model, and other best practices discussed throughout the book. As an example of a simple resource adapter, this book includes the full source code for an ASCII file adapter in Chapter 17, "Source Code for ASCII File J2EE Adapter." This resource adapter can read the contents of an ASCII file, depending on the associated metadata supplied to it as on of the parameters. The intention is to use the various concepts and principles of the previous 10 chapters, and implement them in practice using the ASCII file resource adapter as the example.

The process of developing a resource adapter begins with the end-to-end requirements analysis, and this chapter captures the process and the resulting artifacts. The code for the ASCII resource adapter is available for download at www.samspublishing.com, or it can be installed from the CD-ROM at the back of this book.

The integration scenario described here is a very common situation found in many organizations. An ASCII file or a text file has a stream of ASCII characters representing application data. One of the obvious problems is the lack of structural information for this data. Usually, there are no metadata describing what the ASCII characters represent. Reading such a file and interpreting the data is typically done by inserting all the logic and functions required for parsing the file, extracting the data, validating the data, and so on, in the receiving application. If the format of the data in the ASCII file is simple and without any implied logic or ordering/sequencing, then the database can probably import the ASCII file without much help. But usually, even the slightest complication in the data structure results in failed data uploads. You will develop a generic resource adapter capable of reading ASCII files with different data formats maintained by the application using the resource adapter. You can use similar techniques, and build more powerful and feature-rich ASCII file resource adapters.

# Documenting ASCII File Adapter Integration Scenarios

If there is one habit that adapter programmers must develop, it is the habit of analyzing end-to-end integration requirements before focusing on specific adapter requirements. Therefore, you start the process of analyzing the ASCII file adapter requirements by documenting the end-to-end integration scenario involving all the applications and their components participating in the scenario, and capturing the adapter requirements by defining a problem domain model.

## Integration Scenario Description

A J2EE application that maintains customer information and allows customers to update their profiles needs to synchronize changes to the customer information maintained by other enterprise and departmental applications. One such departmental system is a legacy customer information application used by sales and customer service agents. This legacy application maintains the current customer status, including the number of outstanding customer complaints and queries as well as the account status in terms of outstanding balance. Figure 11.1 shows a schematic diagram of the different domains and components and their relationships.

The legacy application exports changes to the customer information in the form of an ASCII text file on a daily basis. These changes include adding new customers (by sales and customer service agents); updating customer information; suspending customers, especially when the outstanding balance is higher than the allocated limits; and deleting customer records in the legacy application. The ASCII file does not contain any structural information (metadata). The J2EE application administrator has defined a metadata file after discussing the details of the ASCII text file with the developers of the legacy application.

The J2EE application has an administration task that creates an EJB (Customer Data Synchronization EJB). This EJB reads the name of the ASCII text file as well as the associated metadata file, and invokes the ASCII resource adapter using the adapter's CCI-based services. The resource adapter opens the ASCII text file, and parses the data contained in the file depending on the rules defined in the metadata file. If the parsing is successful, the end result is that the customer data is stored in a `Vector` object (list), which is available to the calling EJB. It is the responsibility of the EJB to process each customer record in the `Vector` object and take appropriate action. In this example, the EJB reads each record from the `Vector`, and displays it.

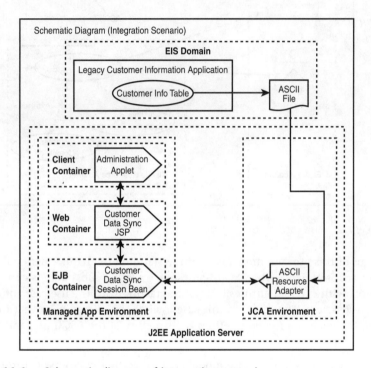

*FIGURE 11.1*    Schematic diagram of integration scenario.

## Use Case Model

The use case model is a more detailed decomposition of the integration scenario just described. The resource adapter's features are captured in use cases, and described as a sequence of steps. Apart from individual use cases, the model also defines the system boundaries that help to identify the required access mechanisms to access remote resources. Figure 11.2 shows the use case model for the ASCII file resource adapter. Because this is an example, some of the more complicated aspects of use case models, such as inheritance of actors and so on, are not included.

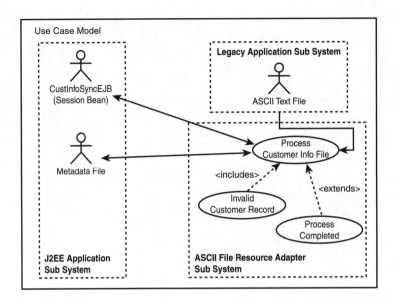

*FIGURE 11.2*    Use case model.

The focus of this use case model is on understanding the requirements of the resource adapter. Hence, the ASCII file resource adapter subsystem is considered the black box, with external entities (actors) interacting with the use cases of resource adapter subsystem. The actors in this case include the session bean that invokes the adapter, the metadata file that defines the structure of the ASCII file, and the ASCII text file itself.

The primary flow of the use case model is captured by the Process Customer Info File use case. Alternate use cases include Invalid Customer Record and Process Completed. Notice that the Invalid Customer Record use case has an `<includes>` relationship with the primary use case. This indicates that the Process Customer Info File use case knows about the Invalid Customer Record use case, and makes specific reference to it when exceptions are detected.

On the other hand, the Process Completed use case has an `<extends>` relationship with the Process Customer Info File use case. This means the Process Customer Info File use cases does not make any reference to the Process Completed use case, which is triggered by the event that indicates that the process of ASCII file is complete. The Process Completed use case captures statistics such as number of records processed, number of bad records, and so on, and logs them to an ASCII log file. The benefit of the `<extends>` relationship is that it's a loose coupling between two use cases, and the extended use case may not exist at run-time without impacting the primary use case. On the other hand, any use case with the <includes> relationship must exist at all times for the primary use case to function.

All three use cases are documented here, with each use case description containing its objective, assumptions (if any), preconditions that need to be true before the use case is initiated, the process that defines the sequence and steps of the use case, any post conditions that ensure that the use case is in the proper state before ending, and a list of exceptions thrown in case of errors.

### Use Case: Process Customer Info File (Primary Use Case)
We'll begin by examining the Process Customer Info File use case.

**Objective**    The primary objective of this use case is to open and parse the contents of an ASCII text file whose structure is defined in a separate metadata file.

**Assumptions**    The use case relies on these assumptions:

- Each ASCII text file has an associated metadata file that defines the internal structure of the text file. The metadata file defines the layout of record and fields in the ASCII text file.

- All data in the ASCII text file are delimited by a delimiting character defined in the metadata file.

**Pre-conditions**    The use case assumes that these pre-conditions are true:

- The ASCII text file to be parsed exists, and is accessible and readable.

- The metadata file that defines the structure of the ASCII file is also accessible and readable.

**Process**    The use case follows this process:

1. If the metadata filename is not specified, then retrieve the default metadata filename from the adapter configuration parameters.

2. Open the metadata file, and parse the metadata records. There should be one control record and one or more file_layout records. The control record specifies the delimiting character to be used in parsing the ASCII data file. The file_layout records define the structure of the customer records contained in the ASCII data file.

3. Upon the successful parsing of the metadata file, open the ASCII data file, and parse all customer records. Each customer record must be validated with the file_layout record extracted from the metadata file.

4. If the customer record does not match the file_layout log, throw an exception, and copy the bad customer record to a log file named BADCREC.DAT.

**Post-conditions**    Update the total number of customer records successfully parsed and the total number of bad records.

**Exceptions**    The use case raises exceptions under these conditions:

- If the metadata file is missing or not accessible
- If the ASCII text file is missing or not accessible

### Use Case: Invalid Customer Record (Alternate Use Case)

Next, let's examine the Invalid Customer Record use case.

**Objective**    The primary objective of this use case is to log the invalid customer record in a log file named BADREC.DAT.

**Assumptions**    This use case is invoked as soon as a bad customer record is detected by the ASCII file parser.

**Pre-conditions**    This use case assumes that the customer record is either incomplete or invalid.

**Process**    The use case follows this process:

1. If the file BADREC.DAT is not open, then open the file in append mode.

2. Log the bad customer data, and timestamp it.

3. Also, for each bad record logged to the file, increment the counter; this will be useful for administrators.

**Post-conditions**    The file BADREC.DAT remains open until all the records are parsed.

**Exceptions**    If the BADREC.DAT file can't be opened, raise an exception.

### Use Case: Process Completed (Alternate Use Case)

Finally, let's look at the Process Completed use case.

**Objective**    The primary objective of this use case is to log the total number of good records in a log file: PSTATS.DAT. The intention is to keep a historical record of how many customer records were successfully processed by the resource adapter.

**Assumptions**    This use case assumes that the parsing process has been successfully completed. This alternate use case does not get triggered if the processing was stopped due to any exceptions.

**Pre-conditions**    This use case assumes that the primary use case Process Customer Info File has completed its sequence of actions successfully.

**Process**    The use case follows this process:

1. Open the ASCII text file PSTATS.DAT.

2. Log the total number of records successfully parsed in the text file. The start time and end time of the parsing cycle should also be logged in the ASCII text file.

3. Close the ASCII text file PSTATS.DAT.

**Post-conditions**    This use case has no post-conditions.

**Exceptions**    If the file PSTATS.DAT cannot be opened, raise an exception.

# Designing the Logical Reference Model

The logical architecture model for the ASCII file resource adapter will be based on the reference model presented in Chapter 4, "Adapter Reference Model." Only a subset of the modules identified in the logical reference module will be needed for the ASCII file adapter. Figure 11.3 shows the logical architecture for the adapter in terms of the relevant modules. The APIs in the logical model are expressed by a set of Java interfaces that define the primary methods (services) provided by each module in the model. These API are implemented as part of the resource adapter, and will provide the non-JCA contracts for the adapter.

## Access Layer Modules

The role of access layer modules, as explained in Chapter 4, is to define APIs and interfaces or channels for accessing the adapter functionality. The modules and the classes they contain implement application-specific contracts. In the case of the example adapter, these contracts are about parsing an ASCII file containing customer records and transforming the records into Java objects. The Java interfaces (APIs) defined for each module of the access layer are the following:

- clientAPI

- adminAPI

- configAPI

The source files for these APIs are given in Listings 11.1 through 11.3. These interfaces will be implemented by associated classes that will be used to invoke the adapter services. The host connectivity module in the foundation layer implements the JCA interfaces (ConnectionFactory, Connection, and so on), which will invoke the methods described in these interfaces.

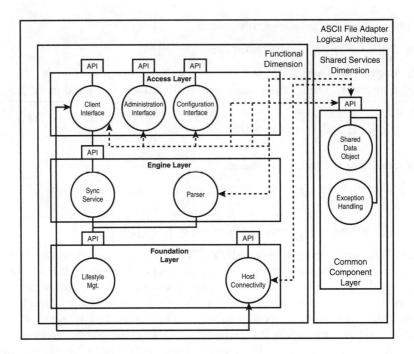

**FIGURE 11.3**   Logical architecture model.

**LISTING 11.1**   clientAPI.java

```
/**
 * Title:        ASCII File Adapter<p>
 * Description:  This package contains all non-JCA classes of the
 * ASCII file adapter.<p>
 * Copyright:    Copyright (c) Atul Apte<p>
 * Company:      iConexio Technologies Inc.<p>
 * @author Atul Apte
 * @version 1.0
 */
package com.iconexio.asciiFileAdapter;

import java.util.Vector;

/*
 * This is the API for all client services offered by the ASCII File
 * resource adapter. Since the contents of the ASCII file can change
 * their structure the adapter services accept metadata
```

**LISTING 11.1**   Continued

```java
 * information in a different file.
 * All customer objects created as a result of the
 * process are stored in a Vector instance.
 */

public interface ClientAPI
{

  // This API uses the default metaData filename set by the configuration
  // interface. If there is no default metaData filename then this API
  // returns an exception. The metaData file contains the filename of the
  // customer data ASCII file
  // Pre-condition: The calling method must check for the files existence
  // The implementation of this method assumes the file is accessible and
  // readable
  public void extractRecords() throws Exception;
  // This API requires the invoking method to define a specific metadata
  // and customer data filename
  // Pre-condition: The calling method must check for the files existence and
  //                and if it's readable
  public void extractRecords(String dataFileName, String metadataFileName)
                                        throws Exception;
  // This API returns the Vector holding the parsed customer record objects.
  // objects.
  // Pre-condition: Either one of the processASCIIFile methods has been
  //                successfully executed.
  public Vector getCustomerRecordList();
  // This API checks the validity of the customer record
  public boolean isCustomerRecordValid(CustomerRec aRec);
}
```

**LISTING 11.2**   adminAPI.java

```java
/**
 * Title:       ASCII File Adapter<p>
 * Description: This package contains all non-JCA classes of the
 * ASCII file adapter.<p>
 * Copyright:   Copyright (c) Atul Apte<p>
 * Company:     iConexio Technologies Inc.<p>
 * @author Atul Apte
```

**LISTING 11.2**    Continued

```
 * @version 1.0
 */
package com.iconexio.asciiFileAdapter;


/*
 * This is the API for all administration services offered by the
 * ASCII File resource adapter. This interface can be implemented by an EJB
 * or even integrated with a system management tool. However in the
 * example adapter this interface will be implemented by a simple Java class
 */

public interface AdminAPI
{
  // This API returns the total number of records parsed by
  // the resource adapter
  // since it was instantiated. The implementation can be serial
  // ized to store
  // the statistics if required.
  // Pre-condition: None
  public int getNoOfRecordsProcessed() throws Exception;
  // This API returns the total number of bad records parsed by
  //  the resource
  // adapter since it was instantiated. The implementation can
  // be serialized
  // to store the statistics if required.
  // Pre-condition: None
  public int getNoOfBadRecords();
}
```

**LISTING 11.3**    configAPI.java

```
/**
 * Title:        ASCII File Adapter<p>
 * Description:  This package contains all non-JCA classes of the
 * ASCII file adapter.<p>
 * Copyright:    Copyright (c) Atul Apte<p>
 * Company:      iConexio Technologies Inc.<p>
 * @author Atul Apte
 * @version 1.0
```

**LISTING 11.3**  Continued

```java
*/
package com.iconexio.asciiFileAdapter;

/*
 * This is the API for all configuration services offered by the
 * ASCII File resource adapter. This interface can be implemented by an EJB
 *  or any other Java class besides the resource adapter.
 * However in the example adapter
 * this interface will be implemented by a simple Java class which
 * is used by
 * other classes to get and set the default metaData filename.
 */

public interface ConfigAPI
{
    // This API sets the default metaData filename.
    // Pre-condition: None
    public void setDefaultMetadataFileName(String metadataFileName);
    // This API returns the default metaData filename
    public String getDefaultMetadataFileName();
}
```

## Engine Layer Modules

The role of engine layer modules is to define and implement the core functionality of the adapter. This is done as a set of services supported by other modules such as parsers and mapping engines. For the example adapter, there are only two modules: the synchronous service module and the parser module.

The customerDataServiceAPI in Listing 11.4 defines methods that enable the client to load customer records from the ASCII text file as Java objects. This is a synchronous type of service, with the caller waiting for the service to complete (parse the ASCII text file).

**LISTING 11.4**  customerDataServiceAPI.java

```java
/**
 * Title:       ASCII File Adapter<p>
 * Description: This package contains all non-JCA classes of the
 * ASCII file adapter.<p>
 * Copyright:   Copyright (c) Atul Apte<p>
```

*LISTING 11.4*   Continued

```
* Company:        iConexio Technologies Inc.<p>
* @author Atul Apte
* @version 1.0
*/
package com.iconexio.asciiFileAdapter;

// The customerDataServiceAPI interface defines the methods representing
// the services offered by sync-servic module of the engine layer.
// These services enable the client to load customer records from an
// ASCII file whose structure is defined by a metaData file.

import java.util.Vector;
import java.io.IOException;

public interface CustomerDataServiceAPI
{
  // This method parses and load the customer data from the data filename
  // stated in the metaData file. The structure of the customer data file is
  // also defined in metaData file.
  public void loadCustomerRecords(String metaDataFileName) throws Exception,
                  ParserException, IOException;

  // This method does the same function as above except the data filename is
  // explicit.
  public void loadCustomerRecords(String metaDataFileName, String dataFileName)
                        throws Exception, ParserException, IOException;

  // This method allows client to verify if the customer record is valid
  public boolean isCustomerRecordValid(CustomerRec aRec);

  // This method returns the Vector instance holding all the
  // customer records
  public Vector getCustomerRecordTable();

  // This method returns a specific customer record with matching ID
  public CustomerRec getCustomerRecord(String ID);
```

## Foundation Layer Modules

The most important module in the foundation layer is the host connectivity module, which contains classes that implement the JCA contracts. Although the access layer modules define the client services and interfaces from an end user perspective, the host connectivity module classes tie the client services to the client environment. In the case of the example adapter in this chapter, the host connectivity classes invoke the appropriate client services (interfaces) as part of the JCA connection implementation classes.

This separation of adapter services from the host connectivity results in a loosely coupled interaction between application connectivity contracts implemented by the access layer and engine layer modules and the J2EE connectivity contracts implemented by the foundation layer modules.

The following two classes implement the CCI interfaces:

- `ASCIIFileConnection` (implements `Connection` interface). Listing 11.5 shows the source code for this class. Note that the class returns the actual filename managed by the adapter so that the client application knows which connection is associated with which file.

- `AFConnectionFactory` (implements `ConnectionFactory` interface). Listing 11.6 shows the source code for this class. This class is responsible for delegating the call to get a new connection to the application server's connection manager.

The following three classes implement the SPI interfaces:

- `ASCIIFileManagedConnection` (implements `ManagedConnection` interface). Listing 11.7 shows the source code for this class. The managed connection class ensures that one instance of `ASCIIFileManagedConnection` is associated with only one file at a time.

- `AFManagedConnectionFactory` (implements `ManagedConnectionFactory` interface). Listing 11.8 shows the source code for this class. The managed connection factory is responsible for creating instances of managed connections as well as connection factories.

- `AFManagedConnectionMetaData` (implements `ManagedConnectionMetaData` interface). Listing 11.9 shows the source code for this class. This class provides more descriptive information of the resource adapter and especially what resources it is managing.

**LISTING 11.5**   `ASCIIFileConnection.java`

```
/**
 * Title:       ASCII File Resource Adapter<p>
 * Description:  This project is about building a JCA 1.0 compatible
 * resource adapter as part of the book on developing
```

*LISTING 11.5*    Continued

```
 * JCA adapters.<p>
 * Copyright:    Copyright (c) Atul Apte<p>
 * Company:      iConexio Technologies Inc.<p>
 * @author Atul Apte
 * @version 1.0
 */
package com.iConexio.jca.asciiFileRA;

import javax.resource.cci.*;
import javax.resource.NotSupportedException;
import java.util.Map;
import javax.resource.ResourceException;
import javax.resource.spi.ConnectionEvent;
import javax.resource.spi.IllegalStateException;
import javax.resource.spi.*;

/** This class represents the connection handle between the ASCII file
 * adapter and the application component or client.
 * The ASCII file adapter can be part of a local transaction however the entire
 * ASCII file will be parsed as a single step with a begin and an end as
 * transaction demarcations
 */
public class ASCIIFileConnection implements javax.resource.cci.Connection {

  /** Each connection handle has a reference to the managed connection
   * that interfaces or represents the actual ASCII file.
   */
  public ASCIIFileConnection(ASCIIFileManagedConnection mc)
  {
    this.mc = mc;
  }
  ASCIIFileManagedConnection getManagedConnection()
  {
    return(mc);
  }

  public String getASCIIFileName() throws javax.resource.ResourceException
  {
    if (mc == null)
    {
```

## LISTING 11.5    Continued

```
        throw new ResourceException("Connection is already closed");
  }
  return(mc.getASCIIFileName());
}

public javax.resource.cci.LocalTransaction getLocalTransaction() throws
                          javax.resource.ResourceException
{
  // Since the ASCII file itself does not have a any support for transactions
  // the adapter only supports local transactions for this adapter.
  return(new AFLocalTransactionImpl(mc));
}
public void setAutoCommit(boolean autoCommit) throws ResourceException
{
  throw new ResourceException(" Auto Commit is not supported");
}

public boolean getAutoCommit() throws ResourceException
{
  return false;
}

/** This adapter does not use the ResultSetInfo class to return data
 * ResultSetInfo is more useful when accessing a database rather than
 * a flat file. The Interaction class of this adapter returns a vector of
 * customer records instead
 */
public javax.resource.cci.ResultSetInfo getResultSetInfo() throws
                          javax.resource.ResourceException {
  NotSupportedException e = new
      NotSupportedException("Result Set Info Not Supported");
  throw e;
}

public void close() throws ResourceException {
    if (mc == null) return;  // already closed
    mc.removeAFConnection(this); // Remove this connection from the set of
                                 // connections in the managed connection
                                 // instance
    mc = null;
```

*LISTING 11.5*    Continued

```
      connectionDestroyed = true;
  }

  public javax.resource.cci.ConnectionMetaData getMetaData() throws
                              javax.resource.ResourceException {
    ASCIIFileMetaData md = new ASCIIFileMetaData();
    return(md);
  }

  /** The createInteraction method returns an instance of ASCIIFileInteraction
   * This object contains services or methods that provide the capability of
   * parsing customer data files in ASCII format.
   */
  public javax.resource.cci.Interaction createInteraction() throws
                              javax.resource.ResourceException
  {
    ASCIIFileInteraction aint = new ASCIIFileInteraction(this);
    return(aint);
  }

  // This method is called by the application server when needed.
  // The application server wants the connection to be associated with a
  // new or different managed connection instance.
  void associateConnection(ASCIIFileManagedConnection newMc)
      throws ResourceException
  {
      if (mc == null)
      {
          // Then the connection was closed and therefore no need to
          // associate it with the new or different managed connection
          throw new IllegalStateException("Connection is either closed or "+
                                          "invalid");
      }
      else
      {
          // dissociate handle with current managed connection
          mc.removeAFConnection(this);
          // associate handle with new managed connection
          newMc.addAFConnection(this);
```

**LISTING 11.5**   Continued

```
        mc = newMc;
    }
}

private void checkIfDestroyed() throws ResourceException {
    if (connectionDestroyed) {
        throw new IllegalStateException("Managed connection is closed");
    }
}

public void invalidate()
{
  mc = null;
}

// private member variables
private ASCIIFileManagedConnection mc; // Represents the physical connection
                                // to the ASCII data file
private boolean connectionDestroyed; // Flag to indicate that the connection
                                // is destroyed.
}
```

**LISTING 11.6**   AFConnectionFactory.java

```
/**
 * Title:        ASCII File Resource Adapter<p>
 * Description:  This project is about building a JCA 1.0 compatible
 * resource adapter as part of the book on developing
 * JCA adapters.<p>
 * Copyright:    Copyright (c) Atul Apte<p>
 * Company:      iConexio Technologies Inc.<p>
 * @author Atul Apte
 * @version 1.0
 */
package com.iConexio.jca.asciiFileRA;

import java.io.*;
import java.io.Serializable;
import javax.resource.Referenceable;
import javax.resource.*;
import javax.resource.spi.*;
```

*LISTING 11.6*    Continued

```java
import javax.naming.Reference;
import javax.resource.cci.*;

public class AFConnectionFactory implements
                javax.resource.cci.ConnectionFactory,
                java.io.Serializable, javax.resource.Referenceable
{

    public AFConnectionFactory(ManagedConnectionFactory mcf,
                        ConnectionManager cm)
    {
        this.mcf = mcf;
        if (cm == null)
        {
            this.cm = new AFConnectionManager(); // This is the default
                                                 // Connection Manager
        }
        else
        {
            this.cm = cm;
        }
    }

    public AFConnectionFactory(ManagedConnectionFactory mcf)
    {
        this.mcf = mcf;
    }

    public javax.resource.cci.Connection getConnection()
      throws ResourceException
    {
      javax.resource.cci.Connection con = null;
      // Delegate the getConnection function to connection manager
      // and its allocate connection method
      con =
        (javax.resource.cci.Connection) cm.allocateConnection(mcf, null);
      return con;
    }

    public javax.resource.cci.Connection
            getConnection(ConnectionSpec properties) throws ResourceException
    {
```

*LISTING 11.6*   Continued

```java
        javax.resource.cci.Connection con = null;
        // Create a connection request info object from connection properties
        // This connection request info object is sent to the managed connection
        AFConnectionRequestInfo info =
                new AFConnectionRequestInfo(
                        ((AFConnectionSpec)properties).getUser(),
                        ((AFConnectionSpec)properties).getPassword(),
                        ((AFConnectionSpec)properties).getASCIIFileName(),
                        ((AFConnectionSpec)properties).getMetadataFileName());
        con = (javax.resource.cci.Connection)
                cm.allocateConnection(mcf,info);
        return con;
    }

    public ASCIIFileMetaData getMetaData() throws ResourceException
    {
        return new ASCIIFileAdapterMetaData();
    }

    public RecordFactory getRecordFactory() throws ResourceException
    {
        throw new ResourceException("Record Factory not supported");
    }

    public void setReference(Reference reference)
    {
        this.reference = reference;
    }

    public Reference getReference()
    {
        return reference;
    }

    // Private variables
    private ManagedConnectionFactory mcf;
    private ConnectionManager cm;
    private Reference reference;
}
```

*LISTING 11.7*    ASCIIFileManagedConnection.java

```java
/**
 * Title:        ASCII File Resource Adapter<p>
 * Description:  This project is about using existing Java
 * application level classes and encapsulating them
 * in a JCA 1.0 compliant resource adapter<p>
 * Copyright:    Copyright (c) Atul Apte<p>
 * Company:      iConexio Technologies Inc.<p>
 * @author Atul Apte
 * @version 1.0
 */
package com.iConexio.jca.asciiFileRA;

import javax.resource.*;
import javax.resource.spi.*;
import javax.resource.spi.security.PasswordCredential;
import javax.resource.spi.IllegalStateException;
import javax.resource.spi.SecurityException;
import javax.resource.NotSupportedException;
import java.io.*;
import java.util.*;
import javax.security.auth.Subject;

public class ASCIIFileManagedConnection implements ManagedConnection

{

    ASCIIFileManagedConnection(ManagedConnectionFactory mcf,
                        PasswordCredential passCred)
    {
        this.mcf = mcf;
        theCredentials = passCred;
        this.asciiFileName = null;
        this.metadataFileName = null;
        connectionSet = new HashSet();
    }

    public void setManagedConnectionFactory(ManagedConnectionFactory mcf)
    {
        this.mcf = mcf;
    }
```

**LISTING 11.7**   Continued

```
public ManagedConnectionFactory getManagedConnectionFactory()
{
    return this.mcf;
}


// This method is called by the application server on behalf of the
// application component. The application component passes information
// to the application server via connectionRequestInfo instance.
public Object getConnection(Subject subject,
                            ConnectionRequestInfo cRequestInfo)
    throws ResourceException
{
  // Retrieve the password credentials passed in the ConnectionRegInfo
    PasswordCredential pc =
        Util.getPasswordCredential(mcf, subject, cRequestInfo);
    if (!Util.isPasswordCredentialEqual(pc, theCredentials)) {
        throw new SecurityException("Principal does not match." +
                                    "Reauthentication not supported");
    }

    AFConnectionRequestInfo afcri = (AFConnectionRequestInfo)cRequestInfo;
    if (this.asciiFileName == null)
    {
      this.asciiFileName = new String(afcri.getASCIIFileName());
      this.metadataFileName = new String(afcri.getMetadataFileName());
    }
    if (afcri.getASCIIFileName().equalsIgnoreCase(this.asciiFileName)
            == false)
    {
        // This managed connection is not managing the file requested by the
        // application component in the connection request info
        throw new ResourceException("ASCII file name and managed connection"
                                    + " do not match");
    }
    // Ensure that this managed connection is still valid.
    checkIfDestroyed();
    ASCIIFileConnection aCon = new ASCIIFileConnection(this);
    addCciConnection(aCon); // Add the new connection to the set
    return aCon;
}
```

*LISTING 11.7*    Continued

```
public void destroy() throws ResourceException
{
  if (destroyed) return;
  destroyed = true;
  Iterator it = connectionSet.iterator();
  while (it.hasNext())
  {
    ASCIIFileConnection afCon = (ASCIIFileConnection) it.next();
    afCon.invalidate();
  }
  connectionSet.clear();
}

public void cleanup() throws ResourceException
{
  checkIfDestroyed();
  Iterator it = connectionSet.iterator();
  while (it.hasNext())
  {
    ASCIIFileConnection afCon = (ASCIIFileConnection) it.next();
    afCon.invalidate();
  }
  connectionSet.clear();
}

public void associateConnection(Object theCon)
    throws ResourceException
{
  checkIfDestroyed();
  if (theCon instanceof ASCIIFileConnection)
  {
      ASCIIFileConnection afCon = (ASCIIFIleConnection) theCon;
      afCon.associateConnection(this);
  }
  else
  {
    throw new IllegalStateException("Invalid connection object: " +
                            theCon);
  }
}
```

**LISTING 11.7**  Continued

```java
public ManagedConnectionMetaData getMetaData() throws ResourceException
{
    checkIfDestroyed();
    return new AFManagedConnectionMetaData(this);
}

public void setLogWriter(PrintWriter out) throws ResourceException
{
    this.logWriter = out;
}

public PrintWriter getLogWriter() throws ResourceException
{
    return logWriter;
}

boolean isDestroyed()
{
    return destroyed;
}

PasswordCredential getPasswordCredential()
{
    return passCred;
}

public void removeASCIIFileConnection(ASCIIFileConnection afCon)
{
    connectionSet.remove(afCon);
}

public void addASCIIFileConnection(CciConnection afCon)
{
    connectionSet.add(afCon);
}

private void checkIfDestroyed() throws ResourceException
{
    if (destroyed)
    {
```

**LISTING 11.7** Continued

```
            throw new IllegalStateException("Managed connection is closed");
      }
   }
public String getASCIIFileName()
{
  return(asciiFileName);
}

// The managed connection instance keeps track of the data filename it
// manages as well as the metaData filename associated with it.
// The example adapter assumes that these files are accessible on the local
// machine. If these files exist on a remote machine then a different set
// of functions may be necessary to access the files over the network.
private String asciiFileName;
private String metadataFileName;

// These variables hold the managed connection factory used to create this
// instance and the a container (set) to hold application level connections
// or handles to the adapter.
private ManagedConnectionFactory mcf;
private Set connectionSet;

// This adapter supports the basic password credentials. These credentials
// have no bearing on the ASCII data file and its permissions although it
// can be programmed to check the ASCII files ownership in a UNIX file system.
private PasswordCredential theCredentials;

private PrintWriter logWriter;
private boolean connectionDestroyed; // Flag indicating that the connection
                                     // is destroyed.
}
```

**LISTING 11.8** AFManagedConnectionFactory.java

```
/**
 * Title:        ASCII File Resource Adapter<p>
 * Description:  This project is about using existing Java
 * application level classes and encapsulating them
 * in a JCA 1.0 compliant resource adapter<p>
 * Copyright:    Copyright (c) Atul Apte<p>
```

**LISTING 11.8**   Continued

```
 * Company:        iConexio Technologies Inc.<p>
 * @author Atul Apte
 * @version 1.0
 */
package com.iConexio.jca.asciiFileRA;


import javax.resource.ResourceException;
import javax.resource.spi.*;
import javax.resource.*;
import javax.resource.spi.security.PasswordCredential;
import java.io.Serializable;
import javax.resource.spi.security.PasswordCredential;
import javax.resource.spi.SecurityException;
import java.io.*;
import javax.security.auth.Subject;
import java.util.*;
import javax.naming.Context;
import javax.naming.InitialContext;


/** The AFManagedConnectionFactory instance create instances of
 * AFConnectionFactory as well as ASCIIFileManagedConnection
 */
public class AFManagedConnectionFactory implements ManagedConnectionFactory,
                                                Serializable
{

  public AFManagedConnectionFactory()
  {
    factoryID = new String("ASCII File");
  }

  /** This method creates a connection factory instance. The parameter
   * connection manager is passed by the application server. The constructor
   * for the connection factory also accepts a managed connection factory
   * instance for future reference. The connection manager instance is there to
   * support connection pooling by the application server.
   */
  public Object createConnectionFactory(ConnectionManager cm) throws
                    ResourceException
  {
```

*LISTING 11.8*   Continued

```
    AFConnectionFactory afcf;
    afcf = new AFConnectionFactory(this, cm);
    return(afcf);
}


/** This method creates a connection factory instance without any
 * associated connection manager. The application server does not perform
 * any connection pooling when connections are retrieved from this type
 * of connection factory later.
 */
public Object createConnectionFactory() throws ResourceException
{
    AFConnectionFactory afcf;
    afcf = new AFConnectionFactory(this, null);
    return(afcf);
}


public ManagedConnection
    createManagedConnection(Subject subject,
                            ConnectionRequestInfo info)
    throws ResourceException
{

    String userName = null;
    PasswordCredential pc =
        Util.getPasswordCredential(this, subject, info);
    if (pc != null) {
        userName = pc.getUserName();
    }
    return new ASCIIFileManagedConnection(this,pc);
}


public ManagedConnection
        matchManagedConnections(Set connectionSet,
                                Subject subject,
                                ConnectionRequestInfo info)
    throws ResourceException
{

    PasswordCredential pc =
        Util.getPasswordCredential(this, subject, info);
```

**LISTING 11.8**  Continued

```java
        Iterator it = connectionSet.iterator();
        while (it.hasNext())
        {
            Object obj = it.next();
            if (obj instanceof ASCIIFileManagedConnection)
            {
                ASCIIFileManagedConnection mc =
                                (ASCIIFileManagedConnection) obj;
                ManagedConnectionFactory mcf =
                    mc.getManagedConnectionFactory();
                if (Util.isPasswordCredentialEqual
                    (mc.getPasswordCredential(), pc) &&
                    mcf.equals(this))
                {
                    AFConnectionRequestInfo afcri =
                                (AFConnectionRequestInfo)info;
                    String s = afcri.getASCIIFileName();
                    if (mc.getASCIIFileName().equalsIgnoreCase(s) == true)
                        return mc;
                }
            }
        }
        return null;
    }

    public boolean equals(Object obj) {
        if (obj == null) return false;
        if (obj instanceof AFManagedConnectionFactory) {
            String v1 = ((AFManagedConnectionFactory) obj).
                getFactoryID();
            String v2 = this.getFactoryID();
            return (v1 == null) ? (v2 == null) : (v1.equals(v2));
        } else {
            return false;
        }
    }

    public int hashCode() {
        if (getFactoryID() == null) {
            return (new String("")).hashCode();
        } else {
```

*LISTING 11.8*   Continued

```
            return getFactoryID().hashCode();
        }
    }

    private transient Context ctx;
    private String factoryID;
}
```

*LISTING 11.9*   AFManagedConnectionMetaData.java

```
/**
 * Title:        ASCII File Resource Adapter<p>
 * Description:  This project is about using existing Java
 * application level classes and encapsulating them
 * in a JCA 1.0 compliant resource adapter<p>
 * Copyright:    Copyright (c) Atul Apte<p>
 * Company:      iConexio Technologies Inc.<p>
 * @author Atul Apte
 * @version 1.0
 */
package com.iConexio.jca.asciiFileRA;

import javax.resource.ResourceException;
import javax.resource.spi.*;

/** This class will return information about the managed connections and the
 * resource managed by it.
 */
public class AFManagedConnectionMetaData implements ManagedConnectionMetaData
{

  public AFManagedConnectionMetaData(ASCIIFileManagedConnection afmc)
  {
    this.afmc = afmc;
  }
  /** This method returns the name of the EIS and can be the ASCII
   * filename of the customer data file
   */
  public String getEISProductName() throws ResourceException
  {
```

*LISTING 11.9*   Continued

```java
    if (mc.isDestroyed()) {
      throw new ResourceException
        ("ManagedConnection has been destroyed");
    }
    // If the managed connection instance stores the customer data filename
    // it can be returned here.
    return(afmc.getASCIIFileName());
  }

  public String getEISProductVersion() throws ResourceException
  {
    /** The version number of the ASCII file cannot be retrieved in most
     * cases
     */
    String versionNo = new String("Version number unknown");
    return(versionNo);
  }

  public int getMaxConnections() throws ResourceException
  {
    // The number of connections to the ASCII file will depend on
    // how many files can be opened by a user or in a session etc.
    // Hence for this example we just return the number 16
    return((int)16);
  }

  public String getUserName() throws ResourceException
  {
    if (mc.isDestroyed()) {
      throw new ResourceException
        ("ManagedConnection has been destroyed");
    }
    // Return the user name stored as part of the credentials
    return(afmc.getPasswordCredentail.getUserName());
  }

  private ASCIIFileManagedConnection afmc;
}
```

The example adapter does not implement any XA transaction interfaces because it does not support XA-compliant transactions. The ASCII file can be parsed outside the context of a transaction or be part of a local transaction. This might be useful when parsing the customer data file (ASCII file) and updating the customer database in a single transaction. The full source code for the ASCII file resource adapter including all the support classes can be downloaded from the Web site `www.samspublishing.com`. Chapter 17 presents all the functional (application level) classes used by the adapter.

## Common Component Layer Modules

The modules of this layer represent shared services and data objects. In other words, the classes contained in these modules will be used by more than one class across other layers. For the example resource adapter, there are two shared data objects: customer record and customer file metadata. There is only one shared service: exception handling, which uses the log manager framework (the source code is presented in Chapter 13, "Customizing Adapters").

### Shared Data Objects

The Java classes representing the shared data objects are also referred to as integration data objects because they represent the data that is used to integrate different target environments and applications.

The customer record (shown in Listing 11.10) is a read-only object because it is derived from the ASCII file that is parsed by the resource adapter. Data encapsulated by the customer record object cannot be changed by the adapter because it will mean that the customer record object would be out of sync with its source, the ASCII file. Hence, the setter methods in the customer record are declared private, and are used only by the constructor. If, on the other hand, the integration scenario were bidirectional, with the resource adapter changing the customer records before sending the changed data back in the form of a new ASCII file, then the customer records would have the setter methods as public methods.

*LISTING 11.10*    CustomerRec.java

```
/**
 * Title:       ASCII File Adapter<p>
 * Description: This package contains all non-JCA classes of the
 * ASCII file adapter.<p>
 * Copyright:   Copyright (c) Atul Apte<p>
 * Company:     iConexio Technologies Inc.<p>
 * @author Atul Apte
 * @version 1.0
```

*LISTING 11.10*  Continued

```java
*/
package com.iconexio.asciiFileAdapter;

// Objects of CustomerRec class hold the parsed customer data information
// Each customer record has a unique ID. There can be more than one record
// with the same ID as there can be multiple actions performed on a record
// including add, update, delete

public class CustomerRec
{
  public CustomerRec()
  {
    ID = null;
    name = null;
    actionID = 0x00;
    address = null;
    status = null;
    outstandingBal = (float)0.00;
  }

  // Since this customer record is supposed to be read-only all the setters are
  // declared as private methods accessible from the constuctor

  public CustomerRec(String ID, String name, String actionID, String address,
                     String status, String balance) {
    setID(ID);
    setName(name);
    setRecAction(actionID.charAt(0));
    setAddress(address);
    setStatus(status);
    Float x = new Float(1.00);
    x.parseFloat(balance);
    setOutstandingBal(x.parseFloat(balance));
  }
  public String getID() {
    return(ID);
  }
  private void setID(String theID) {
    ID = new String(theID);
  }
  public String getName() {
```

*LISTING 11.10*   Continued

```java
      return(name);
  }
  private void setName(String theName) {
    name = new String(theName);
  }
  public char getRecAction() {
    return(actionID);
  }
  private void setRecAction(char theAction) {
    actionID = theAction;
  }
  public String getAddress() {
    return(address);
  }
  private void setAddress(String theAddress) {
    address = new String(theAddress);
  }
  public float getOutstandingBal() {
    return(outstandingBal);
  }
  private void setOutstandingBal(float theBal) {
    outstandingBal = theBal;
  }
  private void setStatus(String theStatus) {
    status = new String(theStatus);
  }
  public String getStatus() {
    return(status);
  }
  public boolean isCustomerAccountActive() {
    if (status.equalsIgnoreCase("Active") == true)
       return(true);
    return(false);
  }

  private String ID;
  private String name;
  private char actionID; // A = Add, U = Update, D = Delete
  private String address;
  private float outstandingBal; // Default = 0.00
  private String status; // Active, Dormant, Bad Account
}
```

There are two types of metadata records that describe the layout of the ASCII file, as well as the control information necessary to parse the ASCII files. The control information is stored in `MetaDataControl` objects (see Listing 11.11); the file layout (structure) objects are stored in `MetaDataLayout` (see Listing 11.12) objects. The `MetaDataRec` (see Listing 11.13) object holds an instance of the control object, as well as one or more instances of layout objects.

*LISTING 11.11*   `MetaDataControl.java`

```java
/**
 * Title:        ASCII File Adapter<p>
 * Description:  This package contains all non-JCA classes of the
 * ASCII file adapter.<p>
 * Copyright:    Copyright (c) Atul Apte<p>
 * Company:      iConexio Technologies Inc.<p>
 * @author Atul Apte
 * @version 1.0
 */
package com.iconexio.asciiFileAdapter;

// This class contains the basic control data required to parse any ASCII
// file namely the field delimiter. This class can be extended for more complex
// control data.

public class MetadataControl extends Object
{
  public MetadataControl()
  {
  }
  public MetadataControl(int afID, String fName, String fValue)
  {
    fID = afID;
    fname = new String(fName);
    fvalue = new String(fValue);
  }
  public int getID()
  {
    return(fID);
  }
  public String getName()
  {
    return(fname);
  }
```

**LISTING 11.11**   Continued

```
public String getValue()
{
  return(fvalue);
}
private int fID;
private String fname;
private String fvalue;
}
```

**LISTING 11.12**   MetaDataLayout.java

```java
/**
 * Title:        ASCII File Adapter<p>
 * Description:  This package contains all non-JCA classes of the
 * ASCII file adapter.<p>
 * Copyright:    Copyright (c) Atul Apte<p>
 * Company:      iConexio Technologies Inc.<p>
 * @author Atul Apte
 * @version 1.0
 */
package com.iconexio.asciiFileAdapter;

// This class defines the structure of a field including its name, type, and
// the actual value. An example of MetaDataLayout instance is:
// fID = 1
// fName = ACCOUNT_STATUS
// fType = String
// fDomain = ACTIVE,DORMANT (values that define the domain of this field.)
// The domain parameter is optional and can be used by the parser to validate
// any values assigned to the field.

public class MetadataLayout
{

  public MetadataLayout()
  {
  }
  public MetadataLayout(int afID, String fName, String fType, String fDomain) {
    fID = afID;
    fname = new String(fName);
```

### LISTING 11.12     Continued

```java
      ftype = new String(fType);
      fdomain = new String(fDomain);
    }
    public int getID() {
      return(fID);
    }
    public String getName() {
      return(fname);
    }
    public String getDomainValue() {
      return(fdomain);
    }
    public String getType() {
      return(ftype);
    }
    private int fID;
    private String fname;
    private String ftype;
    private String fdomain;
}
```

### LISTING 11.13     MetaDataRec.java

```java
/**
 * Title:        ASCII File Adapter<p>
 * Description:  This package contains all non-JCA classes of the
 * ASCII file adapter.<p>
 * Copyright:    Copyright (c) Atul Apte<p>
 * Company:      iConexio Technologies Inc.<p>
 * @author Atul Apte
 * @version 1.0
 */
package com.iconexio.asciiFileAdapter;

import java.util.Hashtable;

public class MetadataRec
{

  public MetadataRec()
  {
```

*LISTING 11.13*   Continued

```
  controlRec = new Hashtable();
  layoutRec = new Hashtable();
}
public MetadataControl getControlRecord(String tag)
{
  return((MetadataControl)controlRec.get(tag));
}
public void addControlRecord (MetadataControl cRec)
{
  controlRec.put(cRec.getName(), cRec);
}
public void addLayoutRecord (MetadataLayout lRec)
{
  layoutRec.put(lRec.getName(),lRec);
}
public MetadataLayout getLayoutRecord(String tag)
{
  return((MetadataLayout)layoutRec.get(tag));
}
private Hashtable controlRec;
private Hashtable layoutRec;
```

### Exception Handling

The exception handling module of the common component layer defines a log file manager framework. Details of this framework (including the code) are included in Chapter 13. This log manager framework enables the adapter to open multiple log files (ASCII text files) and store error messages, bad data, and processing statistics.

## Testing the Resource Adapter

The test cases for the ASCII file resource adapters are grouped into white box test cases and black box test cases. Black box test cases are designed to test the functionality of the adapter and its proper behavior, as expected by the adapter users. The white box test cases are designed to test the internal design of the adapter including testing for exceptions and how they are handled by the adapter. White box test cases will require test data that has wrong data or bad data so that the appropriate exceptions are raised by the adapter.

### Black Box Test Cases

Test Case 1 processes a valid ASCII text file with an associated metadata file:

- Objective: Ensure that the resource adapter works per the requirements described in the primary use case Process Customer Info File.

- Expected results: All customer records contained in the ASCII file and defined by the metadata file are parsed successfully.

Test Case 2 processes a valid ASCII text file with the default metadata file:

- Objective: To test the adapter's capability to process a valid ASCII text file using the default metadata filename.

- Expected results: All customer records contained in the ASCII file and defined by the default metadata file are parsed successfully.

### White Box Test Cases

Test Case 1 processes a valid ASCII text file with an invalid metadata file:

- Objective: To test the resource adapter's capability to detect a mismatch between the ASCII text file (data) and the contents of the metadata file.

- Expected results: The parser is expected to detect the mismatch between actual data structure and the metadata definitions. The parser should throw an exception that is caught by the `customerRecService` class and logged using the exception handling service.

Test Case 2 processes an incomplete ASCII text file with a valid metadata file:

- Objective: To test the resource adapter's capability to detect an incomplete ASCII text file.

- Expected results: The parser is expected to detect the first incomplete record and throw an exception that is caught by the `customerRecService` class and logged using the exception handling service. The parser then continues to process other records if any in the ASCII text file.

## Packaging and Release

Normally, when adapters or any other software is packaged for distribution, it does not include test data or test case documentation. There are exceptions to this rule, but the majority of the software you buy does not have a test harness that will allow you to test the software if you change the configuration or customize the software.

With adapters, it is better to ship the product with any available test data, test plans, or test harness (test tools) that may be useful to the adapter users.

One reason vendors don't like to ship their products with testing tools is the fear of discovering bugs, especially at the customer site. However, in reality, customers do find bugs after installing the software. In the case of adapters, the adapter providers can be different vendors; so it is important to have access to testing tools to ensure that the adapters are working properly.

Resource adapters are packaged in resource archive files, also known as RAR files. A RAR is actually a Java jar file that contains all the classes of the resource adapter, including those classes that implement the JCA system contracts; any external classes; and packages that may be used by the adapter, configuration files, deployment descriptor, and other adapter-specific files.

The order in which these files appear in the RAR file may be significant, depending on the interdependencies between the classes. The example adapter is packaged as `ExRA.rar` file.

## Summary

This chapter is an example of how to implement some of the concepts, techniques, and best practices present in the book in the real world. The resource adapter developed in this chapter is capable of reading data from an ASCII file and converting it into Java objects. The client of this resource adapter is a session bean that displays the Java objects on screen.

The full source code (including the implementations of all interfaces defined in this chapter) for the example adapter, and the configuration of the J2EE environment in which it has been successfully tested is available in Chapter 17. The code is also available for download on the Web site `www.samspublishing.com` and on the attached CD-ROM.

The important thing to remember is the importance of following a methodology. Even for a seemingly simple adapter such as the ASCII file adapter, quite a few things need to be done, including understanding the end-to-end integration scenario, defining test plans and test data, and actually developing the adapter. The benefit of using an architecture reference model is easier and quicker adapter design because the model provides a starting point for adapter designers.

# 12

# Deploying Adapters

"Once was enough."

—Christophe Auguin, French teacher and sailor, after sailing around the world solo in 106 days in 1997

$S$oftware deployment is the final make-or-break situation in which the software is either successfully installed, configured, and operational in a product environment; or rejected for one of several reasons, including failing to operate properly, too many unknown dependencies, and so on. This is the phase in the software development life-cycle that determines the value of months of hard work and what impact the software has on the enterprise and its business. Deployment in a distributed environment is never easy, especially when you're upgrading the hosting environment components such as the operating systems, middleware, hardware, and so on. In the case of adapters, many of the deployment management options depend on the underlying platform features. If an integration broker is managing the adapters, then ease of deploying and configuration of the adapter depend on the broker's tools and features for system administration.

Automatic software distribution, applying adapter patches, and so on are essential features, but not many platforms support them. The J2EE specifications define deployment descriptors with the intention of making adapter and other component (J2EE modules) deployment easier. Regardless of the type of support that adapters get from the plat-forms, some basic functionality is helpful for making the task of deploying and managing the adapter easier. This chapter identifies these features, and provides high-level guidelines for implementing good deployment practices.

# Deployment Objectives

Let's begin with the fundamental objects of deploying an adapter. Apart from its role in application integration, the adapter must facilitate easy support for different deployment scenarios. Although the use case models of adapters capture some of the end user requirements, they do not capture the deployment scenarios, which are based on the underlying systems, network architecture, distributed platforms, and the overall dependencies between applications.

The primary objective of any deployment can be categorized into three broad deployment types:

- New deployment
- Software upgrade
- Software patch

Each type has different dynamics associated with it; for example, new deployments are easier to manage because there is no need to consider existing environments, users, and so on. However, upgrades and patches to already deployed adapters require more planning. After all, the last thing system administrators need to hear is that upgrading software and hardware has resulted in disruption of services. It is better to be prepared with a deployment plan to ensure a smooth deployment.

Every deployment consists of three basic activities or tasks: installation, configuration, and operational testing. Each task needs pertinent information, and some of it needs to come from the software developers—in this case, adapter developers. With JCA resource adapters, the deployment descriptor is responsible for carrying that information from the developers to system administrators who use deployment tools to read the descriptor and set any values to match the specific run-time environment.

## Adapter Dependencies

In each type of deployment, one of the most nagging problems is not knowing the dependencies between the adapter and its environment. Often, not knowing these dependencies results in failed or delayed adapter deployment. Although many vendors have J2EE-compliant servers, it does not mean that the run-time environment is the same across these servers. Because vendors can implement their own design patterns, it is quite likely that the adapter deployment descriptors vary with application servers. One application server may use multiple class loaders to load different types of modules (EJB, Resource Adapters, JSP, and so on), whereas other application servers may not. But there are more dependencies than just the application server that the system administrator needs to worry about.

An adapter depends on the application server for the run-time environment, and also depends on the target application it connects to and the infrastructure of the target application, including any middleware and databases that the application uses. Adding to this complication, the legacy system may have multiple instances or copies deployed in a geographically distributed environment. The resource adapter for this legacy system has to be configured to connect with a potentially different legacy system environment. If one instance is running on a SUN Solaris operating system and another instance is running on an IBM AIX operating system, then the resource adapter may need different configuration parameters.

In general, adapter dependencies can include multiple operating systems, multiple databases, and multiple versions of applications. The simplest case is one in which there is only one instance of each, and therefore the resource adapter deployment is simple as well. Some of the deployment requirements can be identified during the use case model phase; in particular, system attributes can be captured and documented. However, there are other, more granular dependencies such as shared libraries, dynamically linked libraries and components, device drivers, and so on. Some of these component dependencies are sensitive to the order in which they are loaded during run-time. System-level dependencies such as these must be identified and verified during QA, and documented in the system admin guide or release notes. Without this information, system administrators are left with little choice but to use trial-and-error methods. When deploying new adapters, doing so might not be as dangerous and potentially disruptive as when you are upgrading adapters or applying bug fix patches.

## Adapter Version Control

The level of version control needed for an adapter depends on the scope of the target application(s) being supported by the adapter as well as the scope of the hosting environment (J2EE application server versions, JDK versions, and so on). Version control can be defined in the context of a specific implementation environment or a set of implementation environments. If the adapter is being developed for a particular end user, then the dependencies are known and can be specified. For example, if a resource adapter was developed for an instance of an Oracle Application installation, then the specific version of Oracle Application and its underlying operating system are known. The adapter has to work with those specific versions of the different components of its environment. However, if a resource adapter provider (a third-party ISV that provides resource adapters) is developing a similar Oracle Applications adapter, then the context in which version control and dependencies are defined is more complex. The resource adapters from adapter providers need to be more generic in their support of the target applications and its environments. This affects the version control required in the adapter because it has to interface with different versions of Oracle Applications, in different operating environments, and with different configurations.

Also, if the target system is large and has many features, it is likely that there will be more than one adapter developed, each handling a group of related features. For the sake of performance and manageability, it may not be wise to write one adapter for all the features and modules of Oracle Applications, for example. Some adapters require version control at a method level, whereas others may not. In the case of adapters that support more than one version of the target application, some of the adapter services may need to know the version of the target application before interfacing with it. It is quite possible that the database table structures are different between different versions of an application. If the adapter is accessing that table for any reason, then the method responsible for it may need to know which version of the database tables it is interfacing with.

Sometimes, messages that carry information between applications also have version numbers. These message version numbers may indicate different message structures or even different semantics. If the resource adapter is receiving, processing, or generating these messages, a more granular method-level version control may be required in the adapter. From a deployment perspective, version control is absolutely necessary to maintain backward compatibility.

The resource adapter deployment descriptor does not support method-level version control. It only defines the version of the adapter and the version of the EIS the adapter interacts with. The XML DTD that defines the descriptor has to be extended to include additional information. This information should be stored in a different XML file, and should refer to the standard deployment descriptor. The DTD describing the descriptor can be found at `http://java.sun.com/j2ee/dtds/connector_1_0.dtd`. Note that the standard properties (information) defined in this DTD cannot be changed.

## Deployment Scenarios

There are many different deployment scenarios that can exist in a production environment. These scenarios can be specific to the environment, but some basic deployment scenarios can be identified. You can think of these scenarios as deployment patterns that are useful for understanding the deployment requirements and the definition of the deployment descriptor. Figure 12.1 captures the basic deployment scenarios for resource adapters. These scenarios can be extended to include specific run-time environments and other attributes of the distributed computing environment.

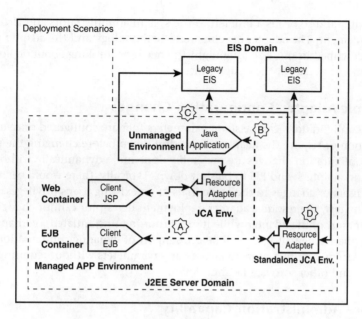

**FIGURE 12.1**    Basic adapter deployment scenarios.

In Figure 12.1, there are four deployment scenarios:

- A component of a managed application invokes two resource adapters

- An unmanaged Java application invokes a standalone resource adapter

- A resource adapter interfaces with one and only one EIS

- A resource adapter interfaces with two instances of the same EIS

Other permutations of these scenarios are also possible, such as an unmanaged Java application invoking more than one adapter. Identifying the deployment scenarios for each resource adapter enables the system administrator to configure the environments appropriately.

## Defining Deployment Requirements

Something that is often not part of most software requirements is the specific deployment requirement. Most development methodologies focus on end user requirements, but do little to capture the run-time environment and its requirements. Part of the reason is that these requirements are not known until the developers start designing the system. Capacity planning (hardware, memory, network bandwidth, and so on) is a task left to the system administrators and IT to define and implement. The adapter development methodology and the adapter reference model described in this book highlight the need for thinking about deployment requirements as part of the design process.

## Dynamic Adapter Configuration Changes

Not all configurations can be static parameters that are configured once during installation or require the adapters to be shut down before changing the parameters. Some configuration changes are preferably done more dynamically without requiring the client, adapters, and EIS to be shut down. Typically, there would be an addition of new users or changes to the credentials of an existing user's privileges. Unfortunately, the resource adapter deployment descriptor cannot change the configuration of the adapter while it's still running (instantiated). Perhaps one of the future enhancements to JCA will be the support of dynamic configurations that will enable system administrators to change any parameters without requiring that the adapters and other software be shut down.

## Remote Administration Capability

In a distributed environment, the capability to monitor and administer the adapter from a remote location is a critical requirement. The deployment tools used by system administrators to configure resource adapters must ideally support this capability. The use of Web-based deployment tools provides system administrators the flexibility to manage the adapters from remote sites.

# JCA Adapter Deployment Descriptor

Per the JCA specification, a *deployment descriptor* defines the contract between a resource adapter provider (developer) and a deployer (or system administrator). The descriptor is an XML document that conforms to the `connector_1_0.dtd` file. The root element in this DTD is `<connector>`, and it has many elements—including `display-name`, `description`, `icon`, `vendor-name`, `spec-version`, `eis-type`, `version`, `license`, and `resourceadapter`. Of these, the `description`, `icon`, and `license` elements are optional; and if they do exist in the descriptor, then only one instance is allowed. Hence, there can be only one `description` for the resource adapter, or none. All the other elements are required.

The `resourceadapter` element is further broken down into child elements—including `managedconnectionfactory-class`, `connectionfactory-interface`, `connectionfactory-impl-class`, `connection-interface`, `connection-impl-class`, `transaction-support`, `config-property`, `auth-mechanism`, `reauthentication-support`, and `security-permission`. Of all these elements, the `config-property`,

auth-mechanism, and security-permission elements can have more than one
instance or element. This means there can be multiple config-properties for a
resource adapter. Also, there can be more than one authentication mechanism—from
the simplest user-ID password combinations to more sophisticated digital certificates.

One thing to note is that the authentication mechanism does not relate to the EIS
authentication mechanism. Hence, the adapter may support digital certificate-based
authentication, even if the EIS has a much simpler authentication mechanism (or no
authentication mechanism at all). Another important factor of the resourceadapter
element is the connectionfactory-interface and connectionfactory-impl-class.
They signify that the standard connection factory interface (and, similarly, the
connection interface) can be extended before implementing the respective interfaces.
However, the managedconnectionfactory interface cannot be extended. The skeleton
structure of a resource adapter deployment descriptor is shown here:

```
<!DOCTYPE connector PUBLIC
➡     "-//Sun Microsystems, Inc.//DTD Connector 1.0/EN"
➡     http://java.sun.com/j2ee/dtds/connector_1_0.dtd>
<connector>
    <display-name> Legacy System Adapter </display-name>
    <vendor-name> Developed Inhouse </vendor-name>
    <spec-version>1.0</spec-version>
    <eis-type> AccountingSys in CICS Environment </eis-type>
    <version> 2.1.1 </version>
    <resourceadapter>
        <connectionfactory-interface>javax.resource.cci.ConnectionFactory
➡           </connectionfactory-interface>
        <connectionfactory-impl-class>myCFImplClass
➡           </connectionfactory-impl-class>
        <connection-interface>javax.resource.cci.Connection
➡           </connection-interface>
        <connection-impl-class>myConnection</connection-impl-class>
        <managedconnectionfactory-class>myMCClass
➡           </managedconnectionfactoryclass>
        ...
    </resourceadapter>
</connector>
```

The deployment descriptor is packaged as part of the resource adapter archive file.
The archive file is in JAR (Java Archive) format with a .RAR extension. The descriptor
itself must have the specific name META-INF/ra.xml. Thus, if the .rar file has a
descriptor with a different name, it is not recognized, which also means that there

cannot be more than one deployment descriptors in a .rar file. If an adapter supports different deployment environments, it has to be packaged as different .rar files, or the deployment descriptor has to be extended, if possible. The .rar file must also contain all external third-party libraries and components that the resource adapter classes depend on and requires at run-time. If the order in which the jar files are loaded is significant, then it should reflect that in the .rar file too.

If an adapter supports more than one instance of the EIS (target application), there has to be a corresponding deployment descriptor for each instance of the supported EIS. A deployment descriptor is used to configure an instance of the managed connection factory that enables connections to the EIS.

## Deployment Plan Template

The *deployment plan template* provides a guideline for defining a comprehensive plan that needs to be produced jointly by the development team and the system administration team. Deployment descriptors are part of a much broader deployment plan that includes the following information:

- **Objective**: The objective of the deployment can be one of the three identified earlier in this chapter: deploying new adapters, upgrading to existing adapters, or applying bug fix patches to existing adapters.

- **Components**: The components of the package that needs to be deployed must be listed in the correct order of significance. Some of the components of the package may not be installed in the target environment, and these should be highlighted. Other components may be required only during the installation process, and are deleted after the installation process is complete. These types of components should be listed so that they can be automatically deleted or manually removed after successful deployment.

- **Configuration of each component**: For each component, the configuration parameters and their default values, if any, must be clearly stated. If the component can be used without further configuration, then the component must be identified as a self-configuring or out-of-the-box component, enabling system administrators to see whether the environments are set up correctly. Developers sometimes like to keep the component configuration constant, and change the environment instead.

- **Deployment test cases**: The system administrator needs to know whether the installation and deployment are successful or not. Simply installing all the components, modules, files, and so on does not mean the adapters will work as expected. It is better to include a small set of test cases to check and certify the deployment.

- **Deployment rollback guidelines**: Despite the best efforts and best plans, there are instances when the deployment fails, and any problems identified need to be fixed. Having deployment rollback guidelines helps system administrators make those decisions more quickly and be better informed in general.

## Summary

Adapter deployment can be simple or complex, depending on the target environment. It is better to be prepared for deployment challenges, and having a deployment plan helps system administrators achieve successful deployments. Many times, the information required during deployment comes from software developers; and in the case of resource adapters, deployment descriptors fill that role of capturing deployment and configuration information.

Knowing the various dependencies between the adapter and its environment, as well as the potential deployment scenarios that may need to be supported by the resource adapter, ensures a successful transition of the resource adapter from a development stage to production stage. Some of the best-designed and developed software do not see the light of day because of inadequate deployment information. Developers need to remember that a resource adapter may be simple to develop, but the deployment environment may not be that simple.

# 13

# Customizing Adapters

"You can learn a lot from the client. Some 70% doesn't matter, but that 30% will kill you."

—Paul J. Paulson

One of the universal facts of e-Business projects is the need for customizing applications and components of e-Business infrastructure. Adapter customization is a necessity that can be rarely avoided. The deployment of an adapter in an e-Business environment results in changes to the adapter configuration or even changes to the adapter code. The extent of customization depends on how much customization the adapted business application has undergone, or if there are proprietary deployment and administration policy requirements that require additional functionality in the adapters. There are many forces resulting in customization requirements on adapters, but the real question is whether the adapter is conducive to customization. Unless the adapter was developed to support customization, it will be very hard, time-intensive, and costly to make the required changes in the adapter. This chapter focuses on some of the aspects of adapter customization, and how to be prepared for the inevitable question: "Can I change this feature of the adapter?"

Perhaps this chapter is more relevant in the cases in which prebuilt adapters are selected for deployment or if adapters have been acquired from more than one source (adapter providers). In that case, it is very likely that the architecture of the adapters will be different. Under such circumstances, the administration of the adapters will be difficult if there is no consistent interface to manage it. But customization is not limited to prebuilt adapters only; it applies even to custom-built adapters. The need to customize is not a one-time requirement, but an ongoing process driven by business requirements.

Consideration for adapter customization should be one of the major aspects of adapter development from the very beginning. This chapter identifies some specific areas of an adapter that tend to need customization more often. The intention is to help adapter architects and developers give some thought to future requirements in terms of extending the behavior of the adapter, or even using them in different deployment environments. The chapter also includes an example of how to build extendable and easily customizable adapter designs by using some of the more well-known design patterns. The code presented in this chapter is part of the example resource adapter described in Chapter 17, "Source Code for ASCII File J2EE Adapter," and shows a simple design for extendable log (audit trail) management.

## Adapter Customization Domains

It is very hard to predict when and what sort of customization may be needed of any adapter. There are almost infinite business patterns, each slightly different from the each other but requiring varying degrees of customization. There are, however, some very common areas or domains of an adapter that appear frequently during adapter customization projects. The four major adapter customization domains include the following:

- Administration interfaces

- Environment settings

- Host interface

- Persistence management

Figure 13.1 shows the major domains and the feature categories most often customized in each domain. The list of domains and the feature categories are by no means complete, but cover the most frequent adapter customizations.

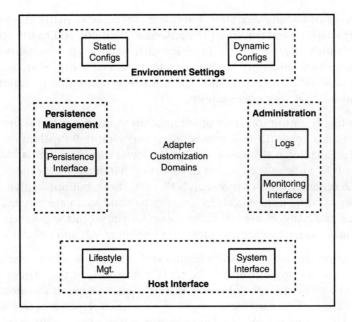

**FIGURE 13.1**    Adapter customization domains.

## Administration Interfaces

Any well-designed adapter keeps track of its actions and states in a log or an audit trail in varying levels of details. These logs are very useful for determining the exact cause of system and application errors, maintaining a proof of e-Business transactions, as well as capturing statistics that are useful in system monitoring in general. There are several methods of creating logs, maintaining them, and analyzing them. More sophisticated adapter designs integrate with system management and network management environments and tools such as IBM Tivoli and others. It is not uncommon to have more the one type of log maintained on different servers in a distributed environment. With JDK 1.4, Java has a logging API that will be useful for developing a custom log manager.

Administration policies and infrastructure are mostly customized to suit the organization's needs and available resources. Deploying adapters in a heterogeneous IT environment does require that the adapters interface with and support the administration policies and guidelines of the organization. Often, adapters are customized to enhance their audit trail capabilities, or new interfaces to system-management environments are added to the adapter. There is a tendency to think of audit trails and logs in the context of system events and exception handling. But with the adapter's participation in e-Business transactions, audit trails of transactions at a higher level are also required, especially in the case of supporting any dispute resolutions.

The typical end-to-end integration use case is composed of many moving parts, including adapters, and tracking the transaction from one end to the other is almost impossible without an audit trail in which each adapter logs its actions and data in one or more logs. Obviously, audit trails add considerable overhead, depending on their features and complexity. Once again, the level of detail to be captured in an audit trail varies among organizations.

Hence, a highly customizable set of administration interfaces increases the long-term value of an adapter. Without administration and audit trail capabilities, the significance of an adapter in e-Business tends to be lower than its potential. Many of us know the 80-20 rule in the context of exception handling. Applications or software in general function without problems 80% of the time, but during that 20% of the time when it fails, business costs in lost revenues and so on are very high. Problems will occur, and adapters need to make it easy for you to customize their administration features to match specific deployment environments and policies.

Another important administration feature that generally requires some customization is the monitoring capability. The actual monitoring of the adapter is usually managed by an external tool, but the adapter needs to support the monitoring capabilities of the tool. Generating appropriate events and responding to external triggers generated by the monitoring tool are essential features of an adapter. After all, monitoring tools cannot be effective without support from the monitored applications and components (adapters). Monitoring features sometimes also include performance statistics such as number of transactions processed within a given period or number of errors, bad data, and so on. Adapters need to generate these statistics or (at a minimum) generate the required data for some other tool to generate the statistics.

It is not possible for an adapter to have interfaces to all different logging and monitoring mechanisms and tools. Hence, a flexible architecture, including a log manager that can be easily customized to incorporate specific logging mechanisms, must be included in the basic adapter designs. Things would be a lot simpler if there were a standard interface to manage audit In the current environment, because there is no such standard available, the next best thing to do is be prepared for customization and design administration interfaces and frameworks to achieve easy customization.

## Environment Settings

Good programmers always externalize as much of the internal adapter behavior as possible. *Externalizing* adapter behavior means identifying parameters that define the different possible choices of specific adapter functions and features, and extracting the values of these parameters from an external source. Many times in the Java environment, the external source is a Java property file or Java resource bundle. But there is more to it than just reading parameters and their values from a property files. Some behaviors need more dynamic changes than others. Some parameters depend on specific business and system conditions.

For example, if the adapter is writing data to one database that happens to be unavailable, then the adapter writes to a secondary database. Another example of a business condition driving behavior is an adapter that interfaces with different message queues depending on the type of the customer account (investment account, savings account, and so on). These message queues may change in the future, and hard coding the association between account type and message queue is not appropriate or advisable—even if it works. In such situations, programmers externalize the parameters (message queue names, associated account types, and so on) in an external file (property file). More complicated business rules are stored in a business rules engine (database). An example of such complex business rules is an order management system that distributes orders based on order amount or number of items. Larger orders may get preference or may be routed to a different order fulfillment cycle. Customer service calls routed by severity, geographical areas, or customer account is also a valid example of business rules being stored in a database of some sort.

Adapters to these systems will have to interface with the business rules engines and the databases to extract the appropriate parameters and their values. Thus, a flexible interface to get and set environment variables alone is not enough. A more comprehensive interface to support static and dynamic environment settings is required. Not all adapters may need an advanced environment settings API, but if such an API is available as part of the adapter framework, it is better to use it. Even in the case of resource adapters, there will be times when external parameters may need to be retrieved from databases instead of property files.

## Host Interface

Integration components such as adapters are required to plug into various different types of infrastructures. Even in the case of resource adapters, although the system interfaces are well-defined (system contracts between resource adapters and the application server) and should not change from one J2EE application server to another, there is no restriction on additional system interfaces provided by application server vendors. It is quite possible to find application server vendors that include more than the standard JCA-defined system interfaces to differentiate their servers from competition. Load balancing, state management, and interfaces to messaging and transaction infrastructures are some of the additional system interfaces that you can find in application servers. Resource adapters may also need to interface with these system interfaces besides the JCA contracts.

A critical part of any integration component including adapters is the state management capability. Adapters can exist in different states throughout their lifecycle, from creation to final destruction. In-between these two states, an adapter may suspend its execution while performing housekeeping activities or while waiting for a critical system resource to be available. A lifecycle management interface makes the task of changing the adapter states much easier and more manageable and consistent. Changes to an adapter environment or regular system maintenance tasks should not require all adapters to stop or be completely shut down. Adapters should have the capability of temporarily suspending their normal processing, allowing for system management tasks to complete or allowing for dynamic configuration changes without affecting the executing of the adapters. State management is not usually considered critical, but its value is obvious when dealing with multithreaded or distributed software and components.

## Persistence Management

Persistence management,  in the form of supporting different databases and storage mechanisms, is a very familiar customization domain. For example, an SAP adapter may be using an Oracle database as its staging area for moving data between SAP and external systems, but the customer may be using a completely different database, such as an object database or a flat file, as a storage mechanism. The capability to change the persistence management features is very important if the SAP adapter has to function well with other databases. Without an API or a set of abstract interfaces, defining the persistence interface for the adapter will be very difficult if not impossible. Adapters that store data in a staging or intermediary database tables should not be tied to any specific database or even to any type of database. It should be possible to use any popular storage mechanism as a data staging area. It is easier said than done, but a persistence framework generally does the trick.

With resource adapters, the use of JDBC and JNDI helps to support different storage mechanisms, as long as they support either one of the interfaces. The need for a persistence framework does not stop at data staging areas. Adapters store their internal states and configuration in external storage media. Even a simple serialization of adapter objects is better off with a higher-level API that is capable of moving from a serialized object file to a more sophisticated RDBMS or other database.

Sometimes, the reverse is true, and adapters that originally stored everything in a database may need to be customized to store part or all of the data in memory or shared memory. This may be required when adapters are deployed in a high-volume environment in which the frequency of updates and data access is fast and furious, as with a stock market ticker. Even in such conditions, a persistence framework makes customization easier and more localized. Without the framework, it is very hard to isolate the functions or classes and interfaces that need to be changed.

## Example of Customizable Frameworks

The example resource adapter developed as part of this book uses a simple Log package that contains a log manager framework capable of creating instances of multiple types of log managers. Each log manager is capable of managing one or more individual logs.

By designing a simple interface to the log manager functions, it is possible to extend the features and support—not just simple ASCII files for logs, but also to interact with logs maintained by RDBMS or even remote RMI-capable logging mechanisms. The objective of the framework is simply to allow developers to add new features (log managers) without affecting existing features. The log manager package uses the well-known factory pattern to accept log manager types as a key, which the factory uses to create instances of appropriate log managers. Figure 13.2 shows the interfaces and classes of the log manager package included with the example adapter of this book.

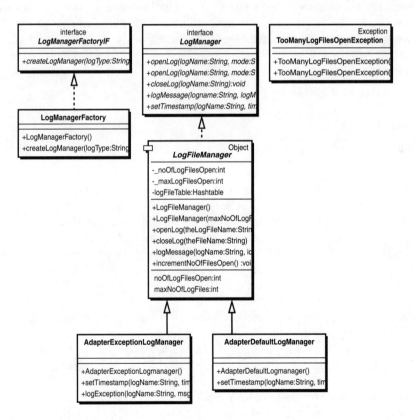

*FIGURE 13.2* Log package.

Listings 13.1 through 13.7 show the source code for all the classes in the Log package.

The design of the abstract class LogManager is very simple, and in the real world needs to be more rich in functionality as well as design. But even in its rather simple form, the current design is capable of supporting new log managers or even new methods of logging messages very easily. The biggest benefit is obviously the fact that developers know the precise location where changes are required and the effect the change will have on the Log package and its users.

A quick analysis of the LogManager class reveals that it is a simple abstraction of normal operations such as open and close logs, log messages, add a time stamp, and so on. These methods can be easily extended or overridden to support more complex features. For example, the openLog method in the LogManager class has two signatures: One is open and accessible to all users, and the other requires a valid user ID and password to open a particular log. Also notice that the use of factory pattern means that the decision to associate log types with specific instances of log managers is handled by the factory. This provides additional flexibility to change the associations or create new log manager types easily and quickly.

*LISTING 13.1*   The LogManager Class

```
/* Generated by Together */

package LogPackage;

/**
 * A log manager is a generic interface to different types of audit
 * trails that track different aspects of the resource adapter.
 * Some of the audit trail will be managed local to the resource
 * adapter (on the same J2EE application server) while other audit
 * trails will be remote to the adapter. For example if a resource
 * adapter is integrating a CICS COBOL application then it may well
 * be necessary to maintain a log in the CICS environment as well as
 * the application server environment.
 *
 * Designing a log manager independent of the actual location and
 * implementation is important part of adapter customization and
 * flexibility. In more advanced IT centers a NMS (Network Monitoring
 * System) based log manager may be needed.

 * An adapter may have to open more than one log at the same time.
 * One of the customization could be to I18N one or more of the log
```

## LISTING 13.1  Continued

```
* files. This will ensure that geographically distributed centers
* and users get messages in local languages.
*
* @author Atul Apte
* @version 1.0
*/
import java.io.*;

public interface LogManager {

    /* The LogManager implementation can open and manage more then one
     * log of different types including transaction logs, system logs,
     * exception logs, and performance logs
     */
    public void openLog(String logName, String mode) throws Exception;

    /* Some logs may need a secured access especially if the log file is
     * maintaining details of a business transaction and not just system
     * information
     */
    public void
      openLog(String logName, String mode, String userID, String password)
            throws Exception;

    public void closeLog(String logName) throws IOException;
    public void logMessage(String logName, String logMessage)
            throws Exception;

    public void setTimestamp(String logName) throws Exception;

}
```

## LISTING 13.2  LogFileManager.java

```
/* Generated by Together */
/* The LogFileManager provides a class for managing file based logs
 * This class must be extended to manage specific types of log files
 *
 * @author Atul Apte
```

***LISTING 13.2***   Continued

```
 * @version 1.0
 */

package LogPackage;

import java.io.*;
import java.util.*;
import java.lang.*;

abstract public class LogFileManager extends Object implements LogManager {
    public LogFileManager() {
        // The default constructor allows for only one log file
        // to be open at any given time
        _noOfLogFilesOpen = 0;
        _maxLogFilesOpen = 1;
        logFileTable = new Hashtable();
    }
    public LogFileManager(int maxNoOfLogFiles) {
        // If you need more than one log file open at the same
        // time use this constructor. The actual maximum files open
        // in any environment is defined by the system kernel.
        _maxLogFilesOpen = maxNoOfLogFiles;
        _noOfLogFilesOpen = 0;
        logFileTable = new Hashtable();
    }

    // mode can be a string with the value WRITE or APPEND
    public void openLog(String theLogFileName, String mode) throws
        TooManyLogFilesOpenException, Exception {
        // Check to see if there is any room to open more files
        if (getNoOfLogFilesOpen() >=  getMaxNoOfLogFiles()) {
            TooManyLogFilesOpenException e = new
                TooManyLogFilesOpenException("Cannot open " +
                    theLogFileName + "Too many log files open");
          throw e;
        }

            // Open a log file and store the handle in a hash table

            File logFile = new File(theLogFileName);
            FileOutputStream logFileStream;
```

**LISTING 13.2**  Continued

```java
            if (logFile.isFile() == false) {
// File doesnot exist
                if (mode.equalsIgnoreCase("WRITE") == true) {
        try {
            // Open file in write mode
            logFileStream = new
                    FileOutputStream(theLogFileName, false);
        } catch (Exception e) {
            throw e;
        }
        // Store the FileOutputStream object in the hashtable
            logFileTable.put(theLogFileName, logFileStream);
    }
            else if (mode.equalsIgnoreCase("APPEND") == true) {
        try {
            // Open file in write mode
            logFileStream = new
                FileOutputStream(theLogFileName, true);
        } catch (Exception e) {
            throw e;
        }
        // Store the FileOutputStream object in the hashtable
            logFileTable.put(theLogFileName, logFileStream);
        }
        incrementNoOfFilesOpen();
        }
        else {
                if (mode.equalsIgnoreCase("APPEND") == true) {
        try {
            // Open file in write mode
            logFileStream = new
                FileOutputStream(theLogFileName, true);
        } catch (Exception e) {
            throw e;
        }
        // Store the FileOutputStream object in the hashtable
            logFileTable.put(theLogFileName, logFileStream);
                incrementNoOfFilesOpen();
        }
        else {
            // Throw an exception
```

***LISTING 13.2***    Continued

```
                TooManyLogFilesOpenException e = new
                    TooManyLogFilesOpenException("File " +
                        theLogFileName +
                        " exists. Cannot open in WRITE mode");
                throw e;
            }
          }
    }

    public void openLog(String theLogFileName, String mode,
            String userID, String password)
            throws TooManyLogFilesOpenException, Exception {
        openLog(theLogFileName,mode);
    }

    public void closeLog(String theFileName) throws IOException {
        Object logFileStream = (Object)logFileTable.remove(theFileName);
        if (logFileStream != null) {
            Class logClass = logFileStream.getClass();
            String className = logClass.getName();
            if (className.equalsIgnoreCase("FileOutputStream") == true) {
                FileOutputStream theStream = (FileOutputStream)logFileStream;
                try {
                theStream.close();
                } catch (IOException e) {
                  throw e;
                }
            }
        }
    }

    public void logMessage(String logName, String logMsg) throws Exception {
        // Retrieve the correct file stream object matching the log name
        Object theFileStream;
        theFileStream = logFileTable.get(logName);
        if (theFileStream == (Object)null) {
            NullPointerException e = new
                NullPointerException("Cannot find matching file stream for "
                    + logName);
```

## LISTING 13.2  Continued

```java
            throw e;
        }
        FileOutputStream logFileStream;
        logFileStream = (FileOutputStream)theFileStream;
        byte[] msgInBytes = logMsg.getBytes();
        logFileStream.write(msgInBytes);
        logFileStream.write((int)nl);
    }

    public int getNoOfLogFilesOpen() {
        return(_noOfLogFilesOpen);
    }

    public int getMaxNoOfLogFiles() {
        return(_maxLogFilesOpen);
    }

    public void incrementNoOfFilesOpen() {
        _noOfLogFilesOpen++;
    }

    public void decrementNoOfFilesOpen() {
        _noOfLogFilesOpen--;
    }

    private int _noOfLogFilesOpen;
    private int _maxLogFilesOpen;
    private Hashtable logFileTable;
    private final char nl = '\n';
}
```

## LISTING 13.3  AdapterDefaultLogManager.java

```java
/* Generated by Together */
/* The AdapterDefaultLogManager extends LogFileManager class
 * The example resource adapter in this book uses this
 * as the default log manager.
 *
```

**LISTING 13.3** Continued

```
 * @author Atul Apte
 * @version 1.0
 */

package LogPackage;

import java.util.*;
import java.text.*;

public class AdapterDefaultLogManager extends LogFileManager {
    public AdapterDefaultLogManager() {
        super(1); // Only one default log manager
    }
    public void setTimestamp(String logName) throws Exception {
        Date now = new Date();
        DateFormat fmt = DateFormat.getDateTimeInstance();
        String timeStamp = fmt.format(now);
        try {
            logMessage(logName, timeStamp);
        } catch (Exception e) {
            throw e;
        }
    }
}
```

**LISTING 13.4** AdapterExceptionLogManager.java

```
/* Generated by Together */
/* The AdapterExceptionLogManager extends LogFileManager class
 * The example resource adapter in this book uses this
 * as the exception log manager.
 * Notice the logException method has been extended to support
 * severity of the exception
 *
 * @author Atul Apte
 * @version 1.0
 */

package LogPackage;
```

*LISTING 13.4*    Continued

```java
import java.lang.*;
import java.util.*;
import java.text.*;

public class AdapterExceptionLogManager extends LogFileManager {
    public AdapterExceptionLogManager() {
        // set max number of files that can be opened to 3
        super(3);
    }
    public void setTimestamp(String logName) throws Exception {
        Date now = new Date();
        DateFormat fmt = DateFormat.getDateTimeInstance();
        String timeStamp = fmt.format(now);
        try {
          logMessage(logName, timeStamp);
        } catch (Exception e) {
            throw e;
        }
    }
    public void logException(String logName, String msg,
            String severity) throws Exception {
        try {
          logMessage(logName,severity);
        } catch (Exception e) {
            throw e;
        }
        try {
          logMessage(logName,msg);
        } catch (Exception e) {
            throw e;
        }
    }
}
```

*LISTING 13.5*    LogManagerFactoryIF.java

```java
/* Generated by Together */
/* This factory interface creates a log manager depending
 * on the key defined by the parameter logType
 * The benefits of having a factory create instances of
```

*LISTING 13.5*    Continued

```
 * log managers is that the decision to associate a specific
 * key or log type to appropriate class is localized in
 * this class and easier to change in future without
 * affecting the other classes.
 *
 * @author Atul Apte
 * @version 1.0
 */

package LogPackage;

public interface LogManagerFactoryIF {
    public LogManager createLogManager(String logType);
}
```

*LISTING 13.6*    LogManagerFactory.java

```
/* Generated by Together */
/* This is the implementation of the log manager factory
 * interface
 * If the logType is == Adapter Exception Log then
 * an instance of the exception log manager is created.
 * Otherwise the default log manager is created
 * If the exceptions need to be directed to the system
 * admin by an email, the AdapterExceptionLogManager can
 * be extended to send an email using SMTP or other mail
 * protocols
 *
 * @author Atul Apte
 * @version 1.0
 */

package LogPackage;

public class LogManagerFactory implements LogManagerFactoryIF {
    public LogManagerFactory() {
    }
    public LogManager createLogManager(String logType) {
        LogManager aNewManager;
        if (logType.equalsIgnoreCase("Adapter Exception Log") == true)
```

**LISTING 13.6**   Continued

```
        aNewManager = new AdapterExceptionLogManager();
    else
        aNewManager = new AdapterDefaultLogManager();
    return(aNewManager);
    }
}
```

**LISTING 13.7**   `TooManyLogFilesOpenException.java`

```java
/* Generated by Together */
/* This is the exception thrown when too many log files are
 * open at the same time.
 *
 * @author Atul Apte
 * @version 1.0
 */

package LogPackage;

public class TooManyLogFilesOpenException extends Exception {
    public TooManyLogFilesOpenException() {
        super("Too many log files opened at the same time");
    }
    public TooManyLogFilesOpenException(String s) {
        super(s);
    }
}
```

Agreeing to use a single framework to manage different types of logs proves to be extremely useful, both in the short and long term. Perhaps in future versions of JCA, log management will also be standardized across different logging mechanisms.

## Summary

Adapter customization is inevitable, and the degree of customization depends on the environment and context. In an ideal situation, there will be APIs for every aspect of the adapter that may need changing. In reality, however, it is not possible or necessary to build APIs for every little function of the adapter. There are some features and functionalities of adapters that are more often changed during deployment, and it is wise to incorporate APIs and extendable designs for them. The goal should be to shorten the customization cycle by building flexible architectures and designs rather than reinventing the wheel by building custom adapters every time.

Object-oriented programming has benefited a lot from the use of design patterns. Programmers are familiar with the more common patterns, such as Model View Controller (MVC), Factory, Singleton, Command, Proxy, and others. Adapter developers should use these patterns to build the adapters and simplify the task of adapter customization in the future.

When evaluating or comparing adapter designs, the capability to customize must take precedence over other features. For resource adapters, the capability to function on different J2EE application servers may be great, but the capability to take advantage of the unique features of an application server is equally important. Hence, the internal architecture of the adapter is important, and consequently the availability of APIs for the different customization domains explored in the chapter is also important. Lack of customization features will hurt the effectiveness of the adapter in the long term, and the effectiveness of the integrated applications will also suffer.

**14**

# Developing Integration-Ready Applications

**IN THIS CHAPTER**

- Importance of Integration Readiness

- Characteristics of Integration-Ready Applications

- Refactoring Legacy Applications

- Designing New Integration-Ready Applications

- Rating Integration Readiness

*"We work day after day, not to finish things, but to make the future better because we will spend the rest of our lives there."*

—Charles F. Kettering

With increasing focus on application integration and the fast pace of technology innovations, future integration will be much simpler. But have we learned our lessons, or do we continue to make the same mistakes and ignore application integration as a fundamental requirement of all software development activities? Are we applying our increasing knowledge about application integration to the new systems under development today? After all, we are building tomorrow's legacy systems today. How good are these applications in terms of integration readiness?

The primary focus of application integration today is indeed on finding the most efficient and cost-effective way to integrate legacy applications that were not designed to easily integrate with new applications. But it is equally important to design the new applications with the proper integration features. This chapter defines the characteristics of integration-ready applications, and focuses on the best practices for developing integration-ready applications.

## Importance of Integration Readiness

Unless software developers change their programming habits and learn to include integration readiness in all software designs, we will be faced with a constant problem of integrating closed applications that are not integration-ready. The term "closed" does not apply only to legacy applications and architectures. It is very easy to build closed applications using the latest software platforms including J2EE. Closed applications do not integrate with other applications or make it very hard for applications to integrate and exchange information. An integration-ready application, on the other hand, has a more open architecture and has built-in capabilities to support integration with applications running on different infrastructures and platforms, running in different locales, developed in different programming languages, and having different core architectures.

The best practices for developing integration-ready applications are derived from real-life project experiences involving many different applications—including legacy and new applications, proprietary and packaged applications, and small and large distributed systems. It is quite possible to build JCA-compatible resource adapters without incorporating any of the best practices highlighted in this chapter, but the result will most likely be a resource adapter that is less flexible and subject to constant modifications and changes—and not delivering any significant business benefits in terms of integrating business processes, functions, and data.

The basic principle of this chapter is that existing (legacy) applications need to change to become truly integration-ready. Many EAI technologies are sold under the banner of "no coding required" to integrate legacy applications. There is a big difference between not changing the functionality of the legacy application during the process of integration and not changing any code of the application to achieve integration. The former is a necessity unless there is a real business reason to change functionality. The latter is very hard to achieve, even with the best EAI, code generation, and business modeling tools.

In the real world, business applications mirror the business processes of the company and as such, business applications vary from company to company. Even the most expensive and flexible ERP and CRM packages need to be customized for automating the unique business processes of a company. In the initial days of ERP, implementation package vendors were trying to encourage companies to change their business processes to match the ERP packages. Over the years, ERP vendors and companies have realized that generally the packages need to be fine-tuned to match the business processes, and not the other way around. This is mainly due to the fact that business processes are driven by market forces and not by technologies. This is an important factor to consider when integrating applications because the solution should be to make legacy applications more flexible and support easy integration (or in other words, applications should be integration-ready).

Most business applications need some code changes to make them integration-ready. These code changes can be few and easy or extensive and complicated. The degree of difficulty depends on the existing architecture and design. A lot depends on the knowledge of the application by its programmers.

We begin the process of building integration-ready applications by defining the characteristics or properties of an integration-ready application. These properties provide important guidelines when developing resource adapters, which extend the integration capabilities of business applications. The best practices of developing integration-ready applications are grouped into two categories: one for legacy applications and one for new applications. Following the best practices, this chapter also includes guidelines on rating integration readiness. This rating model helps measure the integration readiness of individual applications and assesses their capabilities to support different deployment domains (departmental, enterprise, and e-Business domains).

# Characteristics of Integration-Ready Applications

What differentiates one application from another in terms of being integration-ready? Why are some applications easier to integrate with than others? Does the incorporation of open standards in application architecture and design guarantee integration readiness? These are indeed some of the basic questions haunting most developers and IT decision makers. It is harder to find the answers as the technical landscape keeps changing. What was considered the next technology revolution quickly becomes a legacy technology that did not live up to its promise. Nonetheless, there are some core properties or characteristics that all applications should demonstrate to be considered integration-ready.

## Distinct Points of Integration (PIN)

A *point of integration (PIN)* is defined by a business application, and is a gateway or channel to its internal business logic, data, and rules that will be accessible by other business applications. Clearly, the ideal scenario is to have one PIN for each business object exposed by the application. The term *business object* is used as a generic concept encapsulating data, functions, and rules of an application, and is in no way restricted to only object-oriented software artifacts.

Any internal business logic can be exposed by a well-defined PIN. However, having more than one PIN for the same business object is not a good practice because keeping them in sync with each other is almost impossible, or is very costly. A business application can have several PINs that collectively define the integration capabilities of the application.

Defining a PIN depends on the applications architecture and the context or platform on which it runs. So, for a database-centric application, a specific RDBMS table or a specific stored procedure could be a PIN. For a message-centric application, a specific message type will be a PIN. For a J2EE-based application, the resource adapter encapsulates all the PINs, and is accessible by its CCI-compatible API.

The important thing to remember is that the objective is to have a clear definition of all the PINs and to ensure that there is only one PIN for each business object exposed to other applications. So if there is a stored procedure that updates the account object (table), and there is a message type that is capable of performing the same task, it is important to choose one of the two as the PIN. In the long run, it is better to refactor and consolidate all the different PINs.

## Isolated and Localized Integration Logic

Although having well-defined PINs results in a consistent and managed access to business objects, it is important to ensure that similar consistency is preserved in the business objects inside the application. Otherwise, the objective and benefits of defining PINs are lost due to duplicate and redundant code for the same business objects of an application.

Integration logic that includes one or more business objects in the application must be isolated and localized. Isolating integration logic means defining and/or identifying the business rules and functionality required to fulfill specific integration, in the form of a distinctly separate piece of code. It is important to isolate integration code so that future changes to the business application do not easily break its integration capabilities. Localization of integration logic means that there is only one physical copy of the code in the application. One of the challenges is that although the process of isolation of integration logic may be easy, the process of physical localization can be much harder. This will be harder to achieve in legacy applications, and code changes will be inevitable. In many instances, a major redesign of the business application is required to localize the integration logic and associated business objects. The work is not focused as much on changes to the functionality of the application as it is on restructuring the legacy application code structure—a process also known as *refactoring*. A smarter approach to refactoring is the use of design patterns to either encapsulate or wrap legacy business objects and code, or to create new access channels to legacy programs.

## Secured Access Support

As applications become integrated with one another within the corporate network and between corporate networks, secured access to applications is a basic requirement. Security in general, and especially security of application data, is a fundamental requirement. There are too many instances of security breaches resulting in millions of dollars of losses.

Traditionally, application security was restricted to granting access to its direct users. It was relatively easy to identify the potential users and their roles, and assign appropriate privileges. Security in an integrated environment is much more complex. Applications will be accessed (via PIN) by many more users who were not in the original list of users. A common example is that of a departmental application that is integrated with applications from other departments. Not only are there more direct users as a result of the integration, but there is also a need for more granular control of access to appropriate business objects.

Eventually, a single sign-on process is required, in which an employee or a partner can get access to different applications and data as required, without having to sign-on more than once. This requires all applications to support secured access to its business objects using a common security infrastructure or a common security standard.

## Transaction-Enabled

In the context of application integration, transaction-enabled means support for distributed transactions and XA compliance. This may sound like an overhead when dealing with low volumes of transactions, especially in a smaller integration environment with few applications. By definition, any enterprise scale transaction will be distributed because it will involve multiple applications on different platforms. Without proper support for two-phase commit and rollback, transaction integrity could be compromised.

The underlying application may not support distributed transactions, but it does not mean that the adapter cannot fill the obvious holes. In fact, an adapter must complement the application's deficiencies, and enhance its integration capabilities as much as possible. The JCA specifications allow for local transactions that are not managed by an external transaction managers, as well as XA-compliant transaction resources. Adapter developers must become familiar with the XA standard, and enable resource adapter deployment tools to switch between local and XA transaction support when required. Some legacy applications and even some of the new applications may not support transactions (distributed or local). In this case, the choices are few: Either the adapter must implement transaction support and the application should be enhanced to support transactions as well, or the adapter and application do not support transactions at all. If the application is performing a mission-critical application, then it makes sense to spend the time and resources to include transaction support. Sometimes, the application cannot be enhanced to include transaction support. Under such circumstances, the adapter will have to interface with the legacy systems database directly, and replicate the business rules and support transactions. In other words, the adapter will have to do what the application should have done in the first place.

## Customization API

Even the best resource adapters need customization to match business requirements. Many adapters externalize most of their parameters as Java properties. But properties cannot change the behavior of adapters; they also can select one of the prebuilt behaviors. Customization can be made much more simple by clever designing of Java interfaces. When analyzing adapter designs, the first thing I look for is the interface definitions. If there are none, or if the interfaces are not well-designed, then the usefulness of the adapter drops over time.

Chapter 4, "Adapter Reference Model," identifies some key APIs that every adapter should consider implementing. These APIs enable adapters to work in different environments (integration platforms), as well as easily extend the adapters' functionality without impacting existing functions. One use of adapter customization APIs is to handle the customization of business applications or packages. For example, an SAP system may have been customized by its customer to satisfy its unique business requirements. When selecting an SAP adapter, a key decision factor should be the following: How soon can the SAP resource adapter be customized to integrate with the customized SAP system?

## Based on Open Standards

Adapters should support open standards wherever possible. Failure to do so adds to the customization effort during implementation time. Even with resource adapters, the use of XML to define data structures exchanged between the J2EE application and the legacy application is more preferable than any other proprietary document model.

Standards may not be available for every piece of technology that an adapter may have to handle, but when available, standards-based adapters allow for more flexibility in general. This is not to say that proprietary technologies are not flexible or are not as good as open standards. In fact, many innovations start as proprietary technologies before being widely accepted as a standard. Because standards are usually supported by more than one vendor, it is easier to buy products (adapters) from more than one vendor, knowing that they will work together. With the JCA specification, resource adapters from different vendors should work on J2EE-compliant application servers from different vendors. There can be differences between adapters from different vendors, but their common JCA-based interfaces will make interoperability between adapters and application servers much simpler and easier.

Compliance with open standards does not necessarily add any specific integration feature that would make an application integration-ready by itself. But supporting open standards does make the application more flexible, which is one of the main objectives of integration, and hence is important for integration readiness in general.

## Support for I18N and L10N

Internationalization (I18N) may seem an exotic feature not really needed, especially in North America. Yes, there are different languages that an application may have to support (Spanish, French), but the list is short. However, from the perspective of integration, especially in the global context when supply chain automation or other EDI processes need integration, I18N is extremely important.

What is more important is the fact that I18N takes up lot of time if not handled from the start. Converting an application to support I18N requires all text messages, legends, error messages, and pop-up windows to be externalized so that more than one language can be supported without changing the application code. If we extend the I18N issue to include non-Latin languages, we need to handle double-byte character sets (DBCS).

Failure to support I18N invariably results in delayed and sometimes cancelled integration projects, especially in global organizations or integration between global trading partners. Adapter developers must incorporate I18N in the basic design of all adapters, ensuring quick adaptation to different locals, also known as *localization* (L10N).

## Refactoring Legacy Applications

The task of refactoring is never easy because it requires knowledge of the internal architecture and design of the application. Over time, many applications become enormously difficult to maintain, let alone restructure. Even fixing small frustrating bugs becomes a huge task. Integrating these types of applications is extremely difficult. A better approach might be to redesign the integration logic, and implement it as a physically separate component (adapter). An example is a resource adapter for a CICS-based COBOL application. Instead of changing that application, it is better to build a resource adapter, and localize the integration logic in it. One side effect is the potential duplication of some business rules and logic that exist in the COBOL application as well as the adapter. Developers have to keep the duplicate code in sync all the time or risk inconsistent results.

Unfortunately, there is no easy solution to refactoring legacy applications for integration readiness. This is the reason why you must be careful when building new applications today—so that you don't fall in the same trap twice. It is okay to make mistakes, as long as you learn from them and make sincere efforts to not repeat the same mistakes. If the legacy application is one of the mission-critical systems, then it might be worth spending time, money, and resources to restructure the application, isolate the integration logic, and build an adapter for the application. In the long run, this will prove to be the right decision because the application will be able to support complex integration scenarios much more quickly.

The bottom line is you can avoid making changes to legacy applications, to an extent. Perhaps Level I integration readiness (described later in this chapter) can be achieved without changing the internal structure of the legacy application. But getting to Level II and Level III ratings does require code changes in most instances. Refactoring is one of the good principles of software development, and should be used regardless of integration requirements. A few years ago, I initiated a major refactoring of an automated customer service application. The application was very old, based on DOS and developed using Pascal. Its main feature was that customers could dial up from remote locations, and use the automated services quickly and easily. The refactoring project was mainly to enable bidirectional communication between the remote sites and the corporate hub, as well as adding more sophisticated services. It was clear very early in the development process that a major restructuring of the application code was also required. One of the first steps, and perhaps the most important, was to create a comprehensive test plan to ensure that the features and functionality of the application weren't broken after refactoring. The test plan turned out to be the biggest document of the entire project.

Changing existing code (especially code developed by someone else, who may not be working for the company any more) is not a very exciting task. Hence, the task of integrating legacy applications should not be underestimated, even when off-the-shelf adapters are available. It is not unusual for customization of adapters to become a task that is lengthier than estimated. In some instances, it will be impossible to achieve a higher level of integration readiness for legacy applications in the required time frame. This is especially true with Level II and Level III integration, which require integration with workflow and process automation tools. Generally, legacy applications achieve Level I integration readiness by providing direct access to their databases via an adapter. The end result is less than ideal, but helps in keeping the raw data synchronized. Reusing any stored procedures and other SQL procedures can speed up the development of adapters for legacy applications.

In summary, converting a legacy application to an integration-ready application requires the following macro steps:

1. Restructure or refactor existing code.

2. Reuse existing business logic wherever possible.

3. Create a comprehensive test plan to ensure that existing functionality isn't broken.

Each of these steps needs to be expanded further on a case-by-case basis to suit individual legacy applications and integration objectives. Other steps may also be necessary, but the three steps outlined previously are the basic steps required during most legacy integration projects.

# Designing New Integration-Ready Applications

A fundamental assumption for all new applications should be that integration with other applications is inevitable. Hence, every new application must include an adapter with a minimum set of functionalities such as data uploads and downloads, shared procedures, and so on. New applications must be ready with basic integration capabilities from the beginning.

Readers of this book are obviously developing new J2EE applications. But just because you may be using leading-edge technologies does not mean the software will be better. Bad programming practices transcend all technologies, including J2EE and Java. However, the J2EE programming model does enforce a more component-based development model. J2EE application models are more granular, with the application functionality distributed between EJB, Web components, and data components. The addition of resource adapters to this component architecture makes the architecture of J2EE applications more flexible.

One possible exception to the use of resource adapters is when querying JDBC-compliant databases. It is quite natural to search databases directly by using JDBC instead of a resource adapter. Ideally, a resource adapter will define all the points of integration, including database queries. But the overhead of wrapping JDBC calls may sound like extra work for simple queries. However, for the sake of consistency and connection pooling, it may still be a better idea to use a resource adapter for database queries.

Although implementing CCI-based API for a resource adapter is optional according to the JCA specification, it is a good practice to always have an API to access the resource adapter. The CCI standard is very thin in JCA version 1.0, and needs to support remote execution over RMI, IIOP, and other protocols to be really useful. The important thing is to start developing the new application with integration readiness as one of the core objectives.

## Architecture Centric Application Design

When you're developing new applications, starting the design process from an architecture reference model always proves to be cost-effective over the long term. The lack of reference models with legacy applications is one of the challenges of integrating older applications. You should avoid this situation from arising with new applications. Chapter 4 defines an architecture reference model that can be used as a starting point for all adapter development projects. It is important to incorporate concepts such as separation of error handling from the rest of the application, I18N of all error messages, and separation of integration logic from the application as core principles of the application architecture.

A logical architecture reference model, free from any physical constraints such as a specific application server and API, results in a more robust design that is capable of withstanding future changes more easily.

## Component-Based Application Development

J2EE and other component-based application environments such as .NET enable developers to decompose application requirements into smaller components that are capable of higher reuse potential. In fact, resource adapters—especially generic resource adapters such as LDAP resource adapters—can be used by components of many different applications.

A side effect of component-based designs is better manageability of application features. Developers are not faced with the difficult task of understanding big chunks of code as in the legacy applications. It is much easier to understand the code of an EJB (even if it's badly designed and not documented) because it is very likely that there isn't a whole lot of code to analyze in the first place. To that effect, localizing integration logic in a resource adapter will help simplify future enhancements to the integration capabilities. There will be instances in which resource adapters are accessed in a non-managed environment by standalone Java applications or two-tier Java applications. But the real benefit of component-based design is appreciated when a resource adapter needs to access a small piece of business logic encapsulated in an EJB. Having business logic implemented as small components (EJB) helps share the logic much more quickly and precisely between resource adapters.

## XML-Based Document Models

A common solution to exchanging data before XML was the definition of proprietary data structures or document models. The problem with this approach was obvious as the number of application increased and as the data structures became more complex. Barring instances in which proprietary data models cannot be avoided, all other new data exchanges should be based on XML and its derivatives, such as ebXML, WML, and so on.

Even resource adapters for legacy applications can convert legacy data into XML documents before handling the XML document instance to the calling component. The resource adapter may have to do the extra work of mapping native legacy data types and structures to XML elements and attributes, but the result will be increased integration capabilities.

In summary, when you're developing new applications, the following macro steps should be taken to ensure integration readiness:

1. Start with an architecture reference model.

2. Always implement an API to access the integration components (resource adapters).

3. Enforce component-based development, resulting in a more granular, flexible application that's easy to integrate with.

4. Use open standards such as XML for defining data-exchange documents. This allows for greater consistency and cross-platform integration capabilities.

## Rating Integration Readiness

Applications achieve integration readiness at a cost, usually in the form of time and effort. For these and other reasons, a phased approach is often preferred, enabling applications to progress from a basic integration capability to full-blown integration readiness over time. Without a formal rating or measuring scheme for integration readiness, the task of judging the integration capabilities of different applications becomes very subjective. Figure 14.1 shows a scheme that can be used to judge the integration readiness of applications based on the concepts and principles described throughout this book.

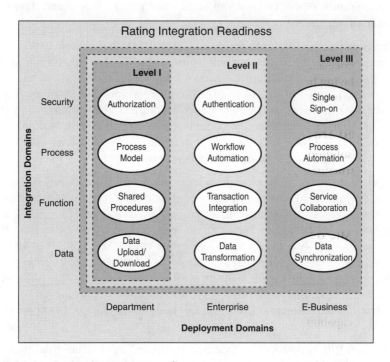

**FIGURE 14.1**    Rating integration readiness.

There are three levels of integration readiness:

- Level I includes the basic integration features and functions that all applications must have to achieve minimal meaningful integration. Usually, Level I integration readiness is good enough for departmental application integration.

- Level II is the enterprise scale integration readiness.

- Level III represents the integration readiness that applications must achieve for participating in e-Business.

Each level has four major integration domains: data, function, process, and security. These four domains represent the features that should be present in any resource adapter. The depth of the functionality implemented in each feature determines the level of integration readiness.

Thus, for any application to be considered for a Level I rating, its resource adapter must support data upload and download, and must use shared procedures or functions, which must be derived from an end-to-end process model and have basic user authorization mechanisms.

To achieve enterprise-level integration readiness (Level II) it is essential to support data transformation because there will be more applications involved, and some of them will need data in different formats. A higher level of security in terms of user authentication is needed to ensure consistent access across applications. Transaction integration features such as XA compliance and distributed transaction support are essential to maintain the integrity of the integrated systems. For workflow-intensive environments, in which job allocation is dynamic (such as customer service), integration with workflow automation tools is very useful.

To support e-Business, all participating applications must get a Level III integration readiness rating. This is the most advanced state of application integration yet, and is not easy to achieve. Significant time, money, and resources are required; but the potential ROI is equally high. For example, applications with a Level III rating must support service collaboration. This is easier now with SOAP-based Web Services. Integration with process-automation tools (both internal processes and external B2B processes) is essential to enable e-Business. Single sign-on and other advanced security features such as digital certificates are also required to prevent hackers and loss of revenues. Data (business objects) need to be synchronized across applications at all times.

The end goal is to get all applications to a consistent level rather than have a mixture of different levels of integration readiness. Often, the application with the lowest level of integration readiness affects the overall effectiveness of all integrated applications. To maintain a certain level of consistency in performance and expectations, it might be better to have all applications get to a particular level. However, the reality may be different, and indeed most companies may end up with different levels of integration readiness. In these situations, integration readiness can be handled within the context of end-to-end integration scenarios. All applications that are part of an integration scenario must have a rating level equal to or higher than other applications. This will help in extracting the maximum benefits from the integration project.

The rating scheme for integration readiness may also be useful when evaluating resource adapters from different vendors. It is important to know at what level the resource adapter will fit before making buying decisions. In some cases, a Level I resource adapter may be enough to satisfy the integration requirements. In other instances, a Level III resource adapter may be needed. Users must insist on getting a roadmap for the resource adapters from the vendors because it will help determine how soon the resource adapter can be rated as Level III.

## Summary

This chapter presented some of the criteria of an integration-ready application. It should be the goal of every resource adapter to make the task of satisfying these criteria simple and easy. The value-add of a resource adapter is not only defined by its depth of functionality, but also by the breadth of its features. Having a comprehensive security feature is not much use if the resource adapter does not include comprehensive support for distributed transactions, I18N, and so on. It is important to maintain the right balance between features and associated functionality in the resource adapters. The section on rating integration readiness helps achieve this goal using a phased approach. The end goal should be to get a Level III rating for all features of resource adapters.

# 15

# Trends in Adapter Technology

It is abundantly clear that adapters are an important part of integration solutions. But the real value of adapters and the surrounding integration technologies can be appreciated more when applied in conjunction with mainstream software development. The trend to formalize and standardize integration will continue and result in integration-ready applications. Chapter 14, "Developing Integration-Ready Applications," takes a closer look at the characteristics of integration-ready applications. This chapter will outline some of the market trends related to adapter technology. The intention is to get an idea of where and how the adapter technology will be used and deployed in the short term and in the future.

## Beyond JCA Resource Adapters

The availability of adapters alone is not enough to promise rapid application integration. Adapters are useful for quantifying the integration solution, but the actual implementation requires many other integration-related artifacts and components. We have also learned that adapter development and implementation is not a one-time exercise, but requires sustainable planned efforts. Some of the emerging technology trends are more disruptive to adapters than others.

## IN THIS CHAPTER

- Beyond JCA Resource Adapters
- Adapters Integrated with IDE and Operating Systems
- Adapter Certification Centers
- Adapter Vendors Will Be the Preferred Source for Adapters
- Standardization of Adapter Platform and Technology
- Tools for Adapter Customization
- Impact of Web Services
- Adapter Patterns Will Emerge
- Proprietary Adapters Will Be Displaced

For example, Chapter 6, "Introduction to Web Services," discusses the emerging Web Service trend and supporting technologies. The impact of Web services on adapters in general is not fully known yet, but it is quite possible that Web services could become the integration platform for inter-enterprise (B2B) collaborations. If this happens, then integration platforms will become fragmented into different integration contexts with one platform for B2B integration, another for EAI integration, and a different platform for e-Commerce and mobile commerce application integration. This leads us to believe that an application will have to integrate with many different integration platforms and standards, in addition to operating systems and business applications. Each integration platform will be specialized and designed to solve a specific integration context. For example, JCA resource adapters are supposed to solve integration from a J2EE application perspective. Web services are expected to solve dynamic collaboration between application services. Other XML-based standards such as cXML, ebXML,and so on are designed to facilitate industry specific collaborations.

J2EE programmers should not expect that JCA resource adapters will solve all integration problems. Programmers need to base the adapter features and functionality on the broader end-to-end integration requirements, which will transcend all the previous integration contexts, standards, and technologies. The integration technologies are not yet mature, and perhaps will always be in a state of flux because technology innovations happen faster each time. Eventually, some of the trends identified in this chapter won't materialize, and others may be truer. Only time will determine which technologies prevail, and developers will determine the overall success of integration standards and tools.

## Adapters Integrated with IDE and Operating Systems

Because the effort required to build adapters is quite extensive, and the realization among IT professionals that the majority of the adapters needed will have to be developed in-house, there will be increasing focus on IDEs (Integrated Development Environments) and their capability to support adapter development. Even the existence of standards such as JCA specifications does not replace the need for better adapter development tools. The capability to look up adapters from a central catalogue, exploring the adapters interfaces and API, and debugging resource adapters using common component interface (CCI)-based test clients are some of the features J2EE developers should expect from Java IDE vendors.

The objective of IDE should be to simplify adapter development and speed up the testing cycles. It will be harder for IDE vendors that do not support development of integration components (transformers, filters, and so on) and adapters to compete in the increasing integration-conscious development community. Support for XML and specific dialects of XML including SOAP, ebXML, and others will prove to be equally essential. After all, without these standards being part of the developer tools it will be hard to motivate the developers to build standards-based integration components and adapters.

Having said this, standards that enable IDE vendors to incorporate adapters into their tools are not defined yet. The JCA's CCI is an attempt to define such a standard for J2EE tool developers. But the CCI specifications need more meat on them. Resource adapters are components, such as GUI components, and developers should have the tools to build new applications using component-based development techniques. It makes no sense to build new applications using the J2EE platform without using existing resource adapters. Similarly, all new applications must have a resource adapter to enable integration with other applications. Managing adapters as integration components in an IDE will go a long way toward ensuring the better reuse of adapters. But we are long way from that; in the meantime, developers will have to do most of these management tasks, including version control, manually and by using self-discipline. (*Version control*, in this sense, means not just controlling source code, but maintaining different versions of the adapters.)

Programming language compatibility has been an historical issue, and continues to get worse. Microsoft will not support Java on its platforms and development environments, and likewise J2EE doesn't support other programming languages. This does limit the programming language choice from an integration perspective, and it is quite possible that in the future (when application integration is as common as database management today), the programming language choice could be limited to Java and C#. Already, more new applications are built using Java than C++ or Visual Basic. These ongoing problems with programming languages and platforms will mean that technologies such as XML will become even more critical to integration and application development in general.

Most adapters will be for business applications, but some adapters will manage integration between protocols and middleware. These adapters will eventually become part of the vendors' operating systems and servers. It may not be too farfetched to think that Oracle database servers may soon have prepackaged Oracle JCA resource adapters. After all, who would know the internals of Oracle database and the database server better than the Oracle Corporation itself? Similarly, package vendors big and small will include standards-based adapters as part of their software. This trend is discussed in more detail in the section "Adapter Vendors Will Be the Preferred Source of Adapters," in which the arguments for adapter vendors are explored.

As adapters continue to mature and become indispensable, developers and system administrators will realize the importance of integrating adapters with system management tools and platforms. This is one area that is weak, no matter what application platform we evaluate and select. A lot of work needs to be done in defining the interface between adapters and system management tools. The more traditional Simple Network Management Protocol (SNMP)-based tools can be useful for managing adapters as long as adapters implement the SNMP interfaces. It is important from a system administration perspective to have visibility on the end-to-end scenario, not just individual adapters and other integration components.

## Adapter Certification Centers

One common problem faced by adapter developers and IT decision-makers involved in selecting integration software is how to evaluate similar adapters from different adapter vendors. How do you determine which SAP adapter is better when you have a choice of 20 SAP adapters for the same platform that supports the features you need? One deciding factor could be certification of the adapter by SAP. Another could be certification from the platform vendor. Even with the respective certifications, there are other factors you must consider before choosing an adapter: extensibility of the adapter, performance, integration with system management tools, capability to work in different hardware and software platforms, and so on. All these factors effect the adapter's long term-value to an organization.

Today, there is very little information in terms of formal certification available for adapters. All adapter vendors claim they have tested their adapters extensively, but very few will actually share their test plans to prove their level of QA.

Independent certification centers do not exist today, but may be established in the future. One of the challenges these centers will face will be to establish the partnerships with adapter vendors, platform vendors, IDE vendors, package vendors, and so on. Without the right partnerships, the certification center may not have the required credibility in the market. But the benefits of certification centers go beyond just compliance testing. These centers can establish performance benchmarks, such as those in the database world, in which we can compare the transaction processing power of different databases using a standard set of tests. As the integration platforms are more standardized, certification centers will be easier to build.

## Adapter Vendors Will Be the Preferred Source for Adapters

This could be one of the most controversial trends presented in this chapter. Some of the package vendors do provide adapters today. For example, SAP will soon provide its own version of JCA-compliant resource adapters. Although a handful of package vendors continue to have a similar strategy, most of the other package vendors will prefer not to. The reason is fragmentation of the application infrastructure technology.

Even today, you must deal with J2EE-compliant application servers on different Windows and UNIX platforms—and then there is the emerging .NET platform from Microsoft, mainframe operating systems, and other proprietary platforms. It will be very hard for package vendors to provide adapters to their software on all these platforms. It is expensive and requires a long-term strategy to generate a decent ROI and sustain the adapter offering. Things get more complicated with adapters for wireless applications in which even the platforms are not very stable yet.

Customers will need many adapters besides just the package adapters. Some of the adapters will be for their proprietary applications. Hence, consistency in architecture, uniformity in implementation, and administration support by common adapter tools will be considered higher priority than the source of adapters. These factors will mean customers will prefer to source their adapters and adapter tools from adapter vendors, not necessarily package vendors. The difficulty for adapter vendors is the certification of their adapters by the package vendors. Nonetheless, between vendor certification and consistency in architecture and implementation, most customers may prefer the latter.

The challenge to adapter vendors is to form long-term relationships with package, platform, and other software and hardware vendors. Many vendors would like to see their packages and platforms getting preference from the adapter vendor. Most likely, adapter vendors will choose specific industries as their core competency and establish partnerships with software vendors focused in the particular industry. This trend is already visible in the ASP market, in which service providers that have a niche are better at providing focused services than the more generic ASPs. Perhaps a similar trend will emerge in adapter providers over the long term.

## Standardization of Adapter Platform and Technology

The JCA specifications is the first attempt by a vendor to define a standard platform for adapters. JCA is not a complete adapter platform yet. It is more of a component interface for J2EE applications especially designed for adapters. J2EE has become the de facto standard for application servers. This is a good launching platform for JCA to follow in those steps.

Serious holes in the JCA specification need to be addressed before it becomes a decent adapter platform standard that is capable of supporting complex integration scenarios, however. Some of the glaring deficiencies in JCA are being handled in the next version of the specifications. Among these include the lack of asynchronous interfaces to other adapters and messaging engines, the capability of XML-based meta-data processing, and so on. But more importantly, JCA solves integration only from the J2EE application's perspective. In other words, JCA assumes that the integration is initiated by a J2EE application. What about a legacy application that needs to integrate with a J2EE application and invoke one of its EJBs? Can a COBOL program running on a mainframe machine call an EJB hosted by a J2EE application server? These types of integration scenarios are not easily supported by JCA. This will be one area in which the specifications need to be expanded with significant new features.

If JCA is to become a meaningful standard over the long term, it needs to address the issues of administration tools and integration with system maintenance platforms. Those of you who are familiar with MQSeries will recall the different tools available to manage and administer the queues and queue managers, and so on. Those tools are proprietary to the tool vendor, so it is very hard to integrate applications that use MQSeries with the tools. The tool vendors typically provide proprietary API, if any at all. JCA will have to tackle this issue for resource adapters very soon, and enable system administrators to manage the resource adapters from different vendors without problems due to incompatibility.

The standardization of adapter platforms and tool frameworks will provide greater flexibility to adapter vendors and customers. Although this is highly desirable, it probably can't be achieved any time soon. Major system management software vendors such as IBM could take the lead and work within the Java community process to establish standards for resource adapter administration tools.

XML is fast emerging as the de facto document model standard. Given the increasing support for complex data models and the various implementations derived from XML—such as ebXML, cXML, and so on—it will be harder to argue against using XML as the common document model for application integration. It will take time to replace existing proprietary document models, but any new document models will most likely be based on some form of XML.

## Tools for Adapter Customization

Adapter customization is a highly manual task at the moment. Most adapters require some customization to fit the specific business processes and business patterns of an organization. Business processes and patterns are unique, and therefore the underlying applications are also unique.

One of the problems of ERP and CRM package implementations was the heavy customization required to make them work as required. ERP vendors tried to change the business processes, but that turned out to be the wrong approach. After all, if all companies use a common set of business processes, there is no differentiation between companies, and that goes against the basic principles of business innovation.

Adapters will have to support quick and easy customization driven by the business processes and the applications. As business process integration becomes a more mature and complete technology, adapters will integrate with process automation tools. This means that changes to the business processes made by the process automation tools need to ripple to the adapters. This is largely uncharted territory today, but likely to change in the future. Business process integration and automation is still an elusive goal, and adapters will be the key middleware to achieve integration between business processes and applications.

## Impact of Web Services

Even if this book is focused on resource adapters and J2EE, we cannot ignore the .NET phenomenon—and especially its Web service capabilities. Microsoft .NET supports SOAP and UDDI based Web services. Chapter 6 provides an overview of Web services, and especially SOAP and UDDI.

If all goes well for Web services, the role of resource adapters will be very different. Web services advocate a service-based architecture and approach to application integration. JCA promotes a component-based approach to integration. The difference is that with SOAP and UDDI, Web services are not tied to any specific platform. JCA, on the other hand, is dependent on the J2EE platform. As a result, the appeal of Web services is understandably more.

The initial focus of Web services is dynamic collaboration between enterprises or B2B transactions. This is mainly because the applications and platforms between companies will most likely be different. At some point, the Web services will have to interact with J2EE applications, and the resource adapters may be useful in these scenarios.

The bottom line is that it may not be enough to just have JCA-compliant resource adapters for legacy applications. SOAP- and UDDI-based Web services will be equally important. In fact, in a non-J2EE environment, Web services will be the preferred option.

## Adapter Patterns Will Emerge

Design patterns have changed software development in the last few years. Support for design patterns in modeling tools and IDE is getting very common, and programmers are now more familiar with terms such as *singleton, MVC, factory pattern,* and so on. A few years ago, these terms did not mean much to most programmers. Today, many developers understand their benefits, and apply design patterns to their software designs on a regular basis. One of the contributing factors to the popularity of the design patterns is the familiarity with the problems it solves. Software architects, designers, and programmers have encountered similar problems that the patterns solve, and hence accept the pattern concept and solutions.

A similar common and widespread understanding of the integration-related problems will lead to integration and adapter patterns in the future. These patterns could be categorized by different integration contexts (data integration, Web services, process automation, and so on), and their solutions will result in better adapters.

## Proprietary Adapters Will Be Displaced

With all the current activity in establishing adapter standards, it is anybody's guess whether proprietary adapters will be displaced in the near future. EAI vendors and other integration platform vendors will have to redesign their adapters. A very common approach to JCA compliance is wrapping proprietary adapters with JCA-compliant resource adapters. Although this strategy results in faster product delivery, it adds a lot of unnecessary code to the resource adapters. Given the choice between a proprietary SAP adapter wrapped by a resource adapter and a native SAP resource adapter, we can safely assume that customers will prefer the native resource adapter. Existing adapter vendors with proprietary architectures will have to quickly redesign their adapters and replace proprietary code with JCA specifications wherever applicable.

Another possibility is resulting changes to adapter prices. Proprietary code is generally more expensive when compared with open standards-based code. This is because of the additional time required to define the interfaces, which are readily available in open standards. With more competition between adapter vendors (especially for JCA resource adapters), adapter prices will be lower in the future. Alternately, adapters will have to offer more functionality for the same price charged today. Either way, adapter customers will be better off in the near future.

## Summary

There are numerous factors affecting adapter technology, and it is anybody's guess as to how the adapter industry will shape up over the next few years. Will Web services wipe out resource adapters? Will resource adapters become a standard for adapters across platforms? Many of these questions can only be answered in time. However, the trends identified in this chapter and the potential outcome of these trends may indicate what to expect in the near future.

Adapter developers must constantly evaluate their adapter strategies, adapter architecture, and design with the emerging trends in mind. It doesn't take long for technology to become obsolete. Just recently, XML was the be-all and end-all. Today, many XML-based software companies are finding that the market adoption of XML is much slower than expected. XML-based business exchanges and other commerce initiatives are equally suffering from lack of commitment by end-users. Older legacy systems, including EDI and mainframe applications, are still driving mission-critical business applications and revenues. However, the need to integrate these old applications with new Web-based applications and J2EE-based applications is increasing every day. Much of the debate is over how the integration should be achieved; not whether integration is required.

# 16

# Components of Integration Technology

"Skeptical scrutiny is the means, in both science and religion, by which deep insights can be winnowed from deep nonsense."

—Carl Sagan

The task of integrating applications does not end with adapters, but merely begins a lengthy, sometimes complex integration process. There are several other components besides adapters that are required to achieve meaningful integration. A standalone resource adapter capable of supporting point-to-point interactions with other adapters is not a very scalable integration solution. Point-to-point adapters do the integration job well in a small integration scenario or scenarios in which the number of points of integration (connections) between adapters is relatively small. As the number of applications in the integration scenario increases, or as the number of points of integration increases, a more sophisticated integration platform is required. This chapter presents some of the fundamental components of integration technology besides adapters that are required to enable true application integration.

The classic EAI products typically include a component called an *integration broker*. An integration broker is a software component that centralizes the management of other integration components, and provides essential services such as message routing, transformation, filters, and so on. An integration broker is essential to manage the integration of distributed applications.

Not all EAI products are alike. Some take a bottom-up approach to solve the integration problem. These products have a messaging engine, transformation capabilities, and lately have a fair selection of adapters. Other products take a top-down approach, and begin with a business process view of the organization before drilling down into actual integration.

Regardless of the type of EAI product you select, the need for adapters is universal. Hence, it is important to understand the type of services and environment adapters usually encountered in an EAI environment. This chapter covers some of the important components of integration technology other than adapters, and outlines their interactions with adapters.

## Integration Platform

The notion of what constitutes an integration platform is not very clear. Some vendors refer to integration brokers as integration platforms; others point to a combination of middleware (messaging engine, object broker, transaction process monitor). Even portal servers, application servers, and in some cases a set of transformation tools are sold as integration platforms.

For the purpose of this book, our definition of *integration platform* is very broad: It includes the operating system, different types of middleware, an integration hub including an integration broker, and administration tools. Without them, application integration quickly becomes patchy and cumbersome to manage. Even with all the different pieces of an integration platform in place, real integration is not easy to achieve; however, the task becomes a little bit simpler and easier.

## Operating Systems

A key part of what any integration platform is the operating system and the system services provided by it. The basic system services are usually similar, but the support and performance for Java will be different. A major consideration in selecting an operating system for the integration platform should be its system administration support. As integration scenarios become complex, and as performance demands increase, the capability to scale a hardware platform depends on the ability of the operating system. After all, adding more memory, more disk space, or more CPU will not result in expected performance improvements if the operating system does not manage the hardware properly.

Most of the time, the operating system is selected by default rather than based on an analysis of the long-term integration requirements and the operating system's capability to effectively support the requirements.

## Middleware

Integration platforms typically have more than one type of middleware technologies. In fact, it is entirely reasonable to find middleware products from multiple vendors bolted together in the integration platform. Even with the J2EE-compliant application servers, different vendors package different types of additional middleware. IBM WebSphere application server, for example, comes with the IBM MQSeries messaging engine. The BEA WebLogic application server includes Tuxedo transaction monitor. SUN's iPlanet application server has a director server and a portal server, among other middleware.

The challenge is to piece together the necessary middleware technologies from different potential vendors. This challenge becomes more difficult if the customer has some middleware as part of its legacy system. Although there are many middleware technologies available, some of them serve basic integration requirements, whereas others are required for specific integration scenarios.

### Application Server

It is a well-established fact that Web applications are hosted by application servers. J2EE is clearly the standard for application servers, but there are still quite a few proprietary application servers, especially in niche technology markets such as wireless applications.

The main function of an application server is to provide a hosting environment for the various types of components that constitute a business application, including adapters. Applications have indeed existed with application servers for a long time, and it is not entirely critical that all applications be hosted by a J2EE-compliant server. Most enterprises are moving to a Web-based application model, and the application server is an essential piece of middleware. The leading application server vendors, such as IBM and BEA, include many complementary technologies—such as transaction monitors, messaging engines, and databases—with the application server.

### Messaging Engine

Before application servers became necessary for Web applications, messaging engines played a direct role in application integration. More often than not, applications were interfacing directly with messaging engines to exchange data. Since application servers became the preferred hosting platform, applications no longer interact with messaging engines directly. Communication with messaging engines is managed by the application server, which exposes a higher-level API for application developers. This significantly reduces the complexity of the applications, and prevents redundant code between applications. It is good for you to be aware of some of the basic features of messaging engines because you may need to use such an engine to facilitate complex integration scenarios.

### Asynchronous Messaging

One of the benefits of using a messaging engine is its capability to transform synchronous, single-task applications to asynchronous, multitasking applications. This is usually achieved by developing an adapter capable of managing multiple requests on behalf of the application. There are significant challenges in bridging the gap between a synchronous application and an asynchronous messaging engine. Adapters can use asynchronous messaging to support parallel transaction processing and other complex integration patterns. However, the challenge is that you have to deal with lower-level APIs to accomplish this.

### Distributed Transaction Management

One problem that often troubles adapter developers is transaction management. This is because not all participating applications in an integration scenario are transaction-enabled. As a result, distributed transaction management is very difficult or almost impossible unless adapters support two-phase commit and rollback features. Although distributed transaction management is not strictly a messaging engine job, it is definitely tied to it. Transaction monitors usually require a messaging engine to manage transactions, and you should plan ahead of time when to interface with a TPM (Transaction Processing Monitor) and when to interface with a messaging engine. Straightforward data exchanges can be achieved by messaging engines, but any state management or transaction management requirements need a transaction engine or a TPM.

### Synchronous Messaging

Although asynchronous messaging is more powerful in its capabilities to support different types of message exchange sessions, a very specific case is synchronous messaging. There are some business services that are fundamentally synchronous (for example, depositing money at a bank ATM machine). The ATM user will not walk away from the ATM without a confirmation that the money was received and credited to the correct account. In such instances, adapters have to support synchronous messaging to enable the appropriate business services. It is much easier to implement synchronous messaging over asynchronous messaging engine than the other way around.

All this requires additional work on the part of adapter developers, and it is usually one of the underestimated efforts of adapter development. If you're keen on learning new lower-level APIs, you'll soon learn that a lot of work needs to be done to support simple business services.

## Integration Hub

An *integration hub* is usually the centerpiece of an integration solution. There are other topologies, such as peer-to-peer integration, but one of the most common topologies is the hub-and-spoke topology. The integration hub includes a broker that coordinates several types of integration components, such as transformers, messaging engines, routing engines, and so on. The integration spokes include components such as adapters and gateways that connect business applications, databases, and so on with the integration hub.

## Broker

A *broker* is an intermediary component capable of integrating loosely coupled applications. One of the biggest benefits of a broker is that it simplifies connectivity between applications. With a broker, adapters need not manage 1:$N$ connections (one application to $N$ applications), resulting in simpler adapter design and connectivity management. It is true that brokers can be overkill in simple integration scenarios, but anything complex in terms of number of applications or distributed environments requires a broker to manage the complexities.

A broker typically also hosts other integration components and services such as routing and transformation. Adapters integrating with a broker are also more easily scalable. There is no standard for an integration broker yet, but there are emerging standards for some other components such as transformers (XSLT) and messaging engines (JMS). Until there is a broker API standard, you have to manage with proprietary broker API. Nonetheless, brokers streamline connections between adapters, and that in itself is a huge benefit, both during adapter development and at run-time in a production environment.

## Transformation Engine

One of the most important tasks of application integration is data or message transformation. The basic need for integration arises from incompatible applications, so transformation capabilities are at the heart of any integration solution. There are different types of transformation services that can be effective in application integration. Not all integration platforms or transformation engines can provide these services. Some integration platforms have specialized transformation capabilities, whereas others are more generic. For example, an XSLT-based transformer (an instance of a transformation engine) is capable of transforming any XML document with an associated XML style sheet. The rules for transformation, in this case, are defined by the stylesheet, and the transformer interprets these rules and applies them to the XML document. But transformation capability is required by other non-XML data and documents as well. Some of the basic transformation services that a good transformation engine should provide are described in the next section.

## Structure Transformation Service

This service is used to change the structure of a data object, document, or message. The actual data is not changed, nor is the metadata describing the data. Structural transformation is important when the same data is required in different order (structure) by different applications. For example, two RDBMS databases have different table structures for the customer table. The fields have similar attributes, but the order is different, or (more likely) the keys are different. In such cases, a structural transformation service acts as a lightweight transformer capable of moving individual fields around to change the data structure.

Although the structure transformation service does not change the data, it can apply business rules for validation. Business applications tend to apply different business rules to the same or similar data. What could be acceptable to one business application in one context may be unacceptable to another application in a different context. Hence, the better transformers supply an option to apply validation rules after the structural transformation is complete. This is an important feature that helps maintain data integrity during data exchanges.

### Format Transformation Service

A format transformation service changes the actual metadata of a data object, message, or a document. So an incoming XML document can be changed to an HTML document or an MQSeries message. To achieve this type of transformation, the transformation engine requires more knowledge and access to metadata information in different contexts. The engine must also have the capability to read and parse different formats of data. Generally, this is the most common transformation service found in integration platforms and transformation tools. You can frequently find transformation tools claiming the capability of transforming legacy data (typically, a dump of RDBMS table) to XML or EDI formats.

The challenge in using this service is the availability of all the metadata definitions for each format. Many times, metadata information does not exist (especially for legacy applications), making it very difficult to apply the format transformation services. A good transformation engine must have a very flexible formatting service.

### Object Transformation Service

The term *object* refers to data, a document, a message, or any other software artifact with state information. The *object transformation service* enables a complete transformation of one object type to another. For example, a purchase order could be placed for many different types of items. Some of the items ordered may need to be procured from a supplier, or perhaps need some special additional paperwork before fulfilling the purchase order. In these scenarios, the purchase order actually initiates the creation of other objects.

Another scenario is where a customer object in the CRM application needs to be converted (transformed) into an account object in the accounting package. An account object possibly has similar data attributes, but the object type and object ID are different. An object transformation service is capable of creating new objects and carrying forward the same data as the original object.

Sometimes, in doing object transformation, the transformation engine may need to fetch more data from other applications. This could mean interacting with the application directly or, more appropriately, by interacting with the application's adapters. The capability to fetch data when required is essential in many instances, especially when transforming object types.

### End-to-End Transformation Service

Many times, transformations are not a one-step process. A sequence of steps and a combination of different transformation services is required to achieve end-to-end transformations. An *end-to-end transformation* is driven by the end-to-end integration scenario. Therefore, it involves many applications, each requiring varying degrees of transformed data. Most transformers and transformation tools do not provide end-to-end transformation services. These kinds of services require state management capabilities in the transformer and the capability to chain or link different transformation services as one unit. In some cases, the end-to-end transformation capability is distributed across the integration components, with some work done by adapters, some by the integration platform, and most by the transformation engine.

### Routing Engine

A *routing engine's* primary function is to facilitate the movement of data or messages based on different criteria. There are various methods of routing implemented by integration vendors, but some of the most common and fundamental routing services include content-based routing and fail-over routing.

The intention of using a routing engine is to relieve adapters from the responsibility of deciding how to send a message from point A to point B. Unless two adapters are communicating in a point-to-point model, and there are no other adapters involved in the integration scenario, routing can be a very complex issue. Adapters that perform data routing are extremely hard to maintain, especially when new adapters participate in integration scenarios. Externalizing the job of routing in a routing engine ensures that the routing rules can be changed without changing adapters.

### Content-Based Routing

As the name suggests, *content-based routing* means that the routing engine is capable of reading the data structures or messages, and making routing decisions based on business rules associated with the contents of the data structure or messages. These business rules are maintained in a separate repository, and can be changed without affecting the adapter, data, or message. Complex business rules can affect the overall performance of the integration, but the resulting flexibility outweighs the performance issues most of the time.

### Fail-Over Routing

Although content-based routing is useful for implementing intelligent data routing mechanisms, an often-overlooked part of data routing is *fail-over routing*. Fail-over routing doesn't decide the data route based only on its content or business rules; it also makes the decision based on the characteristics of the supporting hardware.

The objective of fail-over routing is to ensure that data reaches its final destination, using alternate routes if the primary route has failed for software or hardware reasons. Not all data requires such fail-over routing support, but critical business data or highly sensitive data may need to take alternate routes for reasons not obvious from the contents of the data. Perhaps the primary network is down, in which case an alternate network is required to carry the data. Ideally, you need not worry about these issues. Good routing engines are capable of encapsulating fail-over routing schemes.

## Administration Tools

One of the most important aspects of managing integration platforms at run-time is the availability of good administration tools. Often, the realities of application integration are different and somewhat unexpected despite the best analysis. Transaction load can be higher than expected, or the hardware and middleware performance may not be as anticipated. Adjusting to these situations as fast as possible is the only way to support the business. Without administration tools, it is almost impossible to isolate problems in a production environment, or even fix known problems. Two types of administration tools are usually considered essential components of an integration platform: a deployment management tool and a platform monitoring tool.

### Deployment Management Tools

Deployment tools are usually tightly coupled with specific platforms. It is not easy to develop a multiplatform deployment tool because the operating systems do not have a standard for deployment management functions. Perhaps in the future, such a standard will emerge. Until then, deployment is a platform-specific issue.

Adapters must not be tied to a specific deployment environment. Ideally, an adapter can function across different integration platforms. This is a lot harder to achieve without a comprehensive adapter framework that supports more than one integration platform.

Note that an integration platform is not just the operating system, but includes all components presented in this chapter. Nevertheless, adapters may need to implement a specific API to facilitate easier and better deployment. The deployment descriptor is a step in the right direction for resource adapters in a J2EE environment, and adapter developers must take the maximum advantage of this feature in J2EE.

### Monitoring Tools

Monitoring tools have traditionally been a weakness in all platforms. Especially during application integration, such tools are almost nonexistent. Some vendors do provide tools to view log files and so on, but it is very rare to find a real-time integration monitoring tool.

If you have access to such a tool, there may be a need to generate statistics or even post events as adapter functions execute. Typically, monitoring capabilities at a system level are found more often in large distributed environments. SNMP- (Simple Network Monitoring Protocol)-compatible tools provide APIs that adapters can use to integrate with the tool.

### High Availability Repository

A common problem with systems is too many points of failure. This means that a failure in one of the system components results in the total failure of the system. These days, mission-critical systems are often installed on fault-tolerant hardware capable of running many processors, dual power supplies, and other redundant features. Similarly, a distributed software system needs to provide some redundancy to its critical components. One such critical component of most integration solutions is usually the repository, which holds all types of data required to ensure the smooth operation of the integrated platform.

The failure of repositories or data corruption in the repositories affects the overall performance of the integration platform. Access to backup repositories can solve some of the problems, but a better solution is to use a high-availability database to store integration configurations, process state, and other critical information.

Externalizing adapter configurations and storing them in a high-availability data store ensures a consistent state of the overall integration platform. There is nothing more disastrous than not knowing the exact state and reasons for failure. Without knowing where things have gone wrong and having the capability to recover from the failed state, it is very difficult to deploy integration solutions involving mission-critical applications.

Adapters should ideally use a central repository to store configuration and state information. Most Java developers will argue about using serialized objects, which is a much simpler and perhaps easier method of storage. However, if the adapter is integrating critical data or functions, and its availability is important to business, then a high-availability repository such as a high RDBMS must be used instead.

## Adapter Interactions with Integration Components

With so many components in a typical integration solution, there are times when interactions and collaboration between the integration components becomes a challenge. Without careful planning and proper architecture and design, adapters may not work with different parsers, integration brokers, or transformers. In fact, it is quite common for integration product vendors to constrain adapter developers by providing proprietary APIs that will work only with a limited set of integration components and technologies.

You need to pay extra attention to these potentially show-stopping problems. The best solution is to build or select a set of adapters that are not tied to any specific set of integration platforms, tools, and solutions. This gives you the freedom to concentrate on solving the business application integration problem, and allows IT specialists to focus on selecting the best set of integration platforms and tools.

Regardless of the type of integration components in use, a general pattern of how these components interact with each other is identified in Figure 16.1. The figure shows a snapshot of the most common integration components and their interactions. Adapters are merely the tip of the integration iceberg. There are many things happening inside the integration platform that facilitate application integration. Knowing the individual roles of these integration components stops you from building duplicate or redundant functionality, and helps you define a cleaner adapter architecture and design.

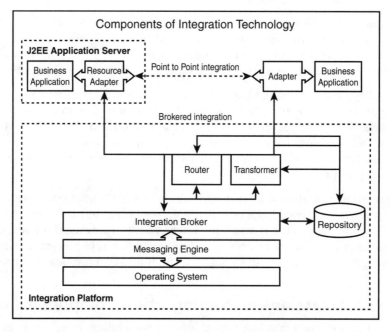

*FIGURE 16.1*    Different Types of Integration Components.

The figure clearly shows the difference between a point-to-point integration between adapters and broker-based integration. The advantages of having a broker are added flexibility and scalability. Even in the case of an application server hosting the adapters, the role of an integration broker does not change. An application server only hosts the application components and the adapters. Integration brokers provide functionality not covered by application servers.

## Summary

Application integration requires a lot more than just adapters and an application server. A typical integration solution involves more than one vendor, and is more complex than most IT teams expect it to be. Adapter developers need to understand the different roles of these integration components. One of the best design principles is to know what to avoid. An understanding of the responsibilities of transformation components, routing components, and so on enables you to not overdevelop the adapters and assign the right responsibilities to all integration components including adapters.

Over time, the complexity of integration technology will reduce, and architectures will become simpler. Until then, you must confront many different types of technologies and concepts. This chapter was a brief overview of these technologies, which are an important part of any application integration solution.

# 17

# Source Code for ASCII File J2EE Adapter

IN THIS CHAPTER

- Environment for the ASCII File J2EE Adapter
- Access Layer Source Code
- Engine Layer Source Code
- Shared Service Layer Source Code
- Test Harness

"When you come to the edge of all the light you know, and are about to step off into the darkness of the unknown, faith is knowing one of two things will happen: There will be something solid to stand on, or you will be taught how to fly."

— Barbara J. Winter

This chapter has listings of all source programs of the J2EE adapter. The source programs are grouped into two Java packages: `com.iconexio.asciiFileAdapter` and `com.iconexio.jca.asciiFileRA`. The first package contains all non-JCA classes that collectively provide the adapter's functionality. The second package has JCA classes that implement the JCA system contracts and invoke the non-JCA classes, as required.

The `com.iconexio.asciiFileAdapter` package classes are listed in the following order:

- Access layer classes
- Engine layer classes
- Shared service layer classes

There is also a standalone test harness class that uses all the classes in the `com.iconexio.asciiFileAdapter` package to parse the test files `METADATA.DAT` and `CUSTDATA.DAT`. The intention of this test harness is to provide readers with a simple testing tool, and to serve as an example of how a standalone Java application can be changed into a resource adapter. The associated test data and deployment descriptor for the J2EE reference implementation is also included. Chapter 11, "Developing J2EE Resource Adapters," has the source code listings of JCA classes that use the application-level classes listed in this chapter.

The source for all programs listed in this book can be downloaded from the
www.samspublishing.com Web site. This Web site will have the latest bug fixes and
further information on any system configurations (application server configurations)
that may be added in the future.

## Environment for the ASCII File J2EE Adapter

The resource adapter was developed on a Windows platform. All unit tests were
performed on the Windows platform by first using the testHarness class as the
testing tool. System tests were performed on the SuSE Linux platform with the J2EE
reference implementation for Linux. Both the development machine and the test
server had 256K of RAM and a minimum of 8GB of disk space.

The testing environment had the following data files:

- METADATA.DAT (valid metadata file):

    ```
    <METADATATYPE>Control</METADATATYPE>
    <FIELD_DELIM>,</FIELD_DELIM>
    <MAX_NO_DATAREC>100</MAX_NO_DATAREC>
    <DEFAULT_DATAFILENAME>\com\iconexio\CUSTDATA.DAT</DEFAULT_DATAFILENAME>
    <METADATATYPE>Layout</METADATATYPE>
    <CUSTOMER_ID>String</CUSTOMER_ID>
    <CUSTOMER_NAME>String</CUSTOMER_NAME>
    <DATAACTION_IND>char</DATAACTION_IND>
    <CUSTOMER_ADDRESS>String</CUSTOMER_ADDRESS>
    <ACCOUNT_STATUS>String|Active,Dormant</ACCOUNT_STATUS>
    <OUTSTANDING_BAL>float</OUTSTANDING_BAL>
    ```

- ER1MDATA.DAT (metadata file with non-existent customer data filename):

    ```
    <METADATATYPE>Control</METADATATYPE>
    <FIELD_DELIM>,</FIELD_DELIM>
    <MAX_NO_DATAREC>100</MAX_NO_DATAREC>
    <DEFAULT_DATAFILENAME>\com\iconexio\CUST.DAT</DEFAULT_DATAFILENAME>
    <METADATATYPE>Layout</METADATATYPE>
    <CUSTOMER_ID>String</CUSTOMER_ID>
    <CUSTOMER_NAME>String</CUSTOMER_NAME>
    <DATAACTION_IND>char</DATAACTION_IND>
    <CUSTOMER_ADDRESS>String</CUSTOMER_ADDRESS>
    <ACCOUNT_STATUS>String|Active,Dormant</ACCOUNT_STATUS>
    <OUTSTANDING_BAL>float</OUTSTANDING_BAL>
    ```

- CUSTDATA.DAT (valid customer data file):

  12345,ATUL,A,CANADA,Active,1000.00

  94959,ARATI,C,CANADA,Dormant,20000.00
  66565,Victoria,A,CANADA,Active,3030.00
  88484,Fern,C,USA,Active,1020.00
  11345,Norman,A,CANADA,Active,1000.00
  92959,Vijay,C,CANADA,Dormant,20000.00
  63565,Sachin,A,CANADA,Active,300.30
  84484,Rick,C,USA,Active,1020.00
  15345,Kate,A,CANADA,Active,1000.00
  96959,Venkat,C,CANADA,Dormant,20000.00
  67565,Sally,A,CANADA,Active,3030.00
  89484,Dick,C,USA,Active,1020.00
  80222,Harry,D,USA,Dormant,9399.99

- ER1CDATA.DAT  (invalid customer data file):

  12345,ATUL,A,CANADA,Active,1000.00

  94959,ARATI,C,CANADA,Dormant,20000.00
  66565,Victoria,A,CANADA,Active,3030.00
  88484,Fern,C,USA,Active,1020.00
  11345,Norman,A,CANADA,Active,1000.00
  92959,Vijay,C,CANADA,Dormant
  63565,Sachin,A,CANADA,Active,300.30
  84484,Rick,C,USA,Active,1020.00
  15345,Kate,A,CANADA,Active,1000.00
  96959,Venkat,C,CANADA,Dormant,20000.00
  67565,Sally,A,CANADA,Active,3030.00
  89484,Dick,C,USA,Active,1020.00
  80222,Harry,D,USA,Dormant,9399.99

## Access Layer Source Code

The access layer classes include interfaces for three APIs (ClientAPI, ConfigAPI, and AdminAPI) and their respective implementations. The ClientAPI is used by adapter clients (standalone Java applications or JCA clients). The ConfigAPI and AdminAPI are for administration and deployment tools.

Listings 17.1 and 17.2 are the interface and implementation of the highest-level API (ClientAPI). Listings 17.3 and 17.4 contain the interface and implementation of a simple configuration API. In actual production environment this API can retrieve data from property files, system environment, or other configuration repositories. Listings 17.5 and 17.6 contain the interface and implementation of a simple administration API. Production environment will require more sophisticated APIs that gather statistics in real time and help the system administrator to determine the points of failure and their causes, as well as track successful transactions.

*LISTING 17.1*    ClientAPI.java

```
/** * Title:        ASCII File Adapter<p>
 * Description:  This package contains all non-JCA classes of the
 * ASCII file adapter.<p>
 * Copyright:    Copyright (c) Atul Apte<p>
 * Company:      iConexio Technologies Inc.<p>
 * @author Atul Apte
 * @version 1.0
 */
package com.iconexio.asciiFileAdapter;

import java.util.Vector;

/*
 * This is the API for all client services offered by the ASCII File
 * resource adapter. Since the contents of the ASCII file can change
 * their structure the adapter services accept metadata
 * information in a different file.
 * All customer objects created as a result of the
 * process are stored in a Vector instance.
 */

public interface ClientAPI
{

    // This API uses the default metadata filename set by the configuration
    // interface. If there is no default metaData filename then this API
    // returns an exception. The metadata file contains the filename of the
    // customer data ASCII file
    // Pre-condition: The calling method must check for the files existence
    // The implementation of this method assumes the file is accessible and
    // readable
```

**LISTING 17.1**  Continued

```
public void extractRecords() throws Exception;
// This API requires the invoking method to define a specific metadata
// and customer data filename
// Pre-condition: The calling method must check for the files existence and
//                and if its readable
public void extractRecords(String dataFileName, String metadataFileName)
                                          throws Exception;
// This API returns the Vector holding the parsed customer record objects.
// objects.
// Pre-condition: Either one of the processASCIIFile methods has been
//                successfully executed.
public Vector getCustomerRecordList();
// This API checks the validity of the customer record
public boolean isCustomerRecordValid(CustomerRec aRec);
}
```

**LISTING 17.2**  ClientAPIImpl.java

```
/**
 * Title:        ASCII File Adapter<p>
 * Description:  This package contains all non-JCA classes of the
 * ASCII file adapter.<p>
 * Copyright:    Copyright (c) Atul Apte<p>
 * Company:      iConexio Technologies Inc.<p>
 * @author Atul Apte
 * @version 1.0
 */
package com.iconexio.asciiFileAdapter;

import java.util.Vector;

public class ClientAPIImpl implements ClientAPI
{

  public ClientAPIImpl()
  {
    custService = new CustomerDataServiceAPIImpl();
  }
```

*LISTING 17.2*   Continued

```
public void extractRecords() throws Exception
{
  ConfigAPIImpl c = new ConfigAPIImpl();
  try
  {
    custService.loadCustomerRecords(c.getDefaultMetadataFileName());
  }
  catch(Exception e)
  {
    throw e;
  }
}


public void extractRecords(String dataFileName, String metadataFileName)
                                    throws Exception
{
  try
  {
    custService.loadCustomerRecords(metadataFileName, dataFileName);
  }
  catch(Exception e)
  {
    throw e;
  }
}


public Vector getCustomerRecordList()
{
  return(custService.getCustomerRecordTable());
}


public boolean isCustomerRecordValid(CustomerRec aRec)
{
  return(custService.isCustomerRecordValid(aRec));
}


private CustomerDataServiceAPIImpl custService;


}
```

**LISTING 17.3** ConfigAPI.java

```
/**
 * Title:        ASCII File Adapter<p>
 * Description:  This package contains all non-JCA classes of the
 * ASCII file adapter.<p>
 * Copyright:    Copyright (c) Atul Apte<p>
 * Company:      iConexio Technologies Inc.<p>
 * @author Atul Apte
 * @version 1.0
 */
package com.iconexio.asciiFileAdapter;

/*
 * This is the API for all configuration services offered by the
 * ASCII File resource adapter. This interface can be implemented by an EJB
 *  or any other Java class besides the resource adapter.
 * However in the example adapter
 * this interface will be implemented by a simple Java class which
 * is used by
 * other classes to get and set the default metaData filename.
 */

public interface ConfigAPI
{
  // This API sets the default metaData filename.
  // Pre-condition: None
  public void setDefaultMetadataFileName(String metadataFileName);
  // This API returns the default metaData filename
  public String getDefaultMetadataFileName();
}
```

**LISTING 17.4** ConfigAPIImpl.java

```
/**
 * Title:        ASCII File Adapter<p>
 * Description:  This package contains all non-JCA classes of the
 * ASCII file adapter.<p>
 * Copyright:    Copyright (c) Atul Apte<p>
 * Company:      iConexio Technologies Inc.<p>
 * @author Atul Apte
```

**LISTING 17.4**   Continued

```
 * @version 1.0
 */
package com.iconexio.asciiFileAdapter;

public class ConfigAPIImpl implements ConfigAPI
{

  public ConfigAPIImpl()
  {
    defaultFileName = new String("METADATA.DAT");
  }

  public void setDefaultMetadataFileName(String fileName)
  {
    defaultFileName = new String(fileName);
  }

  public String getDefaultMetadataFileName()
  {
    return(defaultFileName);
  }

  private String defaultFileName;
}
```

**LISTING 17.5**   AdminAPI.java

```
/**
 * Title:       ASCII File Adapter<p>
 * Description: This package contains all non-JCA classes of the
 * ASCII file adapter.<p>
 * Copyright:   Copyright (c) Atul Apte<p>
 * Company:     iConexio Technologies Inc.<p>
 * @author Atul Apte
 * @version 1.0
 */
package com.iconexio.asciiFileAdapter;

/*
 * This is the API for all administration services offered by the
```

*LISTING 17.5*   Continued

```
* ASCII File resource adapter. This interface can be implemented by an EJB
* or even integrated with a system management tool. However in the
* example adapter this interface will be implemented by a simple Java class
*/

public interface AdminAPI
{
  // This API returns the total number of records parsed by
  // the resource adapter
  // since it was instantiated. The implementation can be serial
  // ized to store
  // the statistics if required.
  // Pre-condition: None
  public int getNoOfRecordsProcessed() throws Exception;
  // This API returns the total number of bad records parsed by
  //  the resource
  // adapter since it was instantiated. The implementation can
  // be serialized
  // to store the statistics if required.
  // Pre-condition: None
  public int getNoOfBadRecords();
}
```

*LISTING 17.6*   AdminAPIImpl.java

```
/**
 * Title:        ASCII File Adapter<p>
 * Description:  This package contains all non-JCA classes of the
 * ASCII file adapter.<p>
 * Copyright:    Copyright (c) Atul Apte<p>
 * Company:      iConexio Technologies Inc.<p>
 * @author Atul Apte
 * @version 1.0
 */
package com.iconexio.asciiFileAdapter;

import java.io.FileInputStream;
import java.io.IOException;
public class AdminAPIImpl implements AdminAPI
{
```

*LISTING 17.6*    Continued

```java
public AdminAPIImpl()
{
}
public int getNoOfRecordsProcessed() throws Exception
{
  FileInputStream fis;
  byte[] rec;
  int n, r;

  fis = new FileInputStream("PSTATS.DAT");
  try
  {
    n = fis.available();
    if (n <= 0)
    {
      Exception e = new Exception("Empty PSTATS.DAT file");
      throw e;
    }
    if (n > 0)
    {
      rec = new byte[n];
      r = fis.read(rec);
      if (r > 0)
      {
        String s = new String(rec);
        String s1 = s.substring(0,s.indexOf(10));
        Integer n1 = new Integer(s1);
        return(n1.intValue());
      }
    } // End of n > 0
  } catch (IOException e) { throw e; }
  fis.close();
  return(0);
}

public int getNoOfBadRecords()
{
  return(0);
}
}
```

# Engine Layer Source Code

The engine layer classes include implementations for the two parsers (one for meta-data file, and the other for the customer data file), as well as an API for extracting customer records from the ASCII file. This API is used by the ClientAPIImpl class in the access layer. Listings 17.7 and 17.8 contain the code for the API and its implementation.

**LISTING 17.7**    CustomerDataServiceAPI.java

```
/**
 * Title:       ASCII File Adapter<p>
 * Description:  This package contains all non-JCA classes of the
 * ASCII file adapter.<p>
 * Copyright:   Copyright (c) Atul Apte<p>
 * Company:     iConexio Technologies Inc.<p>
 * @author Atul Apte
 * @version 1.0
 */
package com.iconexio.asciiFileAdapter;

// The customerDataServiceAPI interface defines the methods representing
// the services offered by sync-service module of the engine layer.
// These services enable the client to load customer records from an
// ASCII file whose structure is defined by a metaData file.

import java.util.Vector;
import java.io.IOException;

public interface CustomerDataServiceAPI
{
  // This method parses and loads the customer data from the data filename
  // stated in the metaData file. The structure of the customer data file is
  // also defined in metaData file.
  public void loadCustomerRecords(String metaDataFileName) throws Exception,
                ParserException, IOException;

  // This method does the same function as above except the data filename is
  // explicit.
  public void loadCustomerRecords(String metaDataFileName, String dataFileName)
                throws Exception, ParserException, IOException;
```

*LISTING 17.7*    Continued

```
    // This method allows client to verify if the customer record is valid
    public boolean isCustomerRecordValid(CustomerRec aRec);

    // This method returns the Vector instance holding all the
    // customer records
    public Vector getCustomerRecordTable();

    // This method returns a specific customer record with matching ID
    public CustomerRec getCustomerRecord(String ID);
}
```

*LISTING 17.8*    CustomerDataServiceAPIImpl.java

```
/**
 * Title:        ASCII File Adapter<p>
 * Description:  This package contains all non-JCA classes of the
 * ASCII file adapter.<p>
 * Copyright:    Copyright (c) Atul Apte<p>
 * Company:      iConexio Technologies Inc.<p>
 * @author Atul Apte
 * @version 1.0
 */
package com.iconexio.asciiFileAdapter;

import java.util.Vector;
import java.io.IOException;

public class CustomerDataServiceAPIImpl implements CustomerDataServiceAPI
{

  public CustomerDataServiceAPIImpl()
  {
    customerRecs = null;
    metadataRecs = null;
  }

  public void loadCustomerRecords(String metaDataFileName, String dataFileName)
                      throws Exception, IOException, ParserException
  {
    ASCIIDataFileParser dfp;
```

## LISTING 17.8  Continued

```java
TagValueParser tvp;
TagValueParserEngine tvpEngine;

int sFlag;

// Create an instance of tag value parser engine. We only do this so that
// we can assign our own metadata record container and pass it to the
// engine.
tvpEngine = new TagValueParserEngine();
// Creat a new instance of MetadataRec
metadataRecs = new MetadataRec();
// Assign it to the tag value parser engine
tvpEngine.setMetadataRec(metadataRecs);
// Associate the engine with the tag value parser
tvp = new TagValueParser(tvpEngine);

// Create an instance of ASCII file parser
dfp = new ASCIIDataFileParser();
customerRecs = dfp.getRecordContainer(); // We can extract
                                         // individual records later

sFlag = 0;

try
{
  // Since the metadata definition file is in a tag value format
  // The tag value parser is used to parse the file and store the
  // the data in Java objects
  tvp.processFile(metaDataFileName);
}
catch (Exception e)
{
  // Exceptions thrown indicating errors in the parsing cycles
  sFlag = 1;
  throw e;
}

if (sFlag == 0)
{
  // No errors during parsing the metadata definition file
```

*LISTING 17.8*    Continued

```
   // Retrieve the control fields FIELD_DELIM and DEFAULT_DATAFILENAME
   // The FIELD_DELIM record indicates the field delimiter used in the
   // customer data file and the DEFAULT_DATAFILENAME record indicates
   // the name of the default customer data filename
   String s = tvp.getControlRecord("FIELD_DELIM");
   byte [] b = s.getBytes();
   // Set the appropriate field delimiter
   dfp.setFieldDelimiter(b[0]);

   try
   {
     // Parse the customer data file using the ASCII data file parser
     dfp.processFile(dataFileName);
   }
   catch (Exception e)
   {
     throw e;
   }
 }
 return;
}

public void loadCustomerRecords(String metaDataFileName) throws Exception,
                      ParserException, IOException
{
  ASCIIDataFileParser dfp;
  TagValueParser tvp;
  TagValueParserEngine tvpEngine;

  int sFlag;

  // Create an instance of tag value parser engine. We only do this so that
  // we can assign our own metadata record container and pass it to the
  // engine.
  tvpEngine = new TagValueParserEngine();
  // Creat a new instance of MetadataRec
  metadataRecs = new MetadataRec();
  // Assign it to the tag value parser engine
  tvpEngine.setMetadataRec(metadataRecs);
  // Associate the engine with the tag value parser
  tvp = new TagValueParser(tvpEngine);
```

**LISTING 17.8**  Continued

```java
// Create an instance of ASCII file parser
dfp = new ASCIIDataFileParser();
customerRecs = dfp.getRecordContainer(); // We can extract
                                         // individual records later


sFlag = 0;

try
{
  // Since the metadata definition file is in a tag value format
  // The tag value parser is used to parse the file and store the
  // the data in Java objects
  tvp.processFile(metaDataFileName);
}
catch(Exception e)
{
  // Exceptions thrown indicating errors in the parsing cycles
  sFlag = 1;
  throw e;
}

if (sFlag == 0)
{
  // No errors during parsing the metadata definition file

  // Retrieve the control fields FIELD_DELIM and DEFAULT_DATAFILENAME
  // The FIELD_DELIM record indicates the field delimiter used in the
  // customer data file and the DEFAULT_DATAFILENAME record indicates
  // the name of the default customer data filename
  String s = tvp.getControlRecord("FIELD_DELIM");
  byte [] b = s.getBytes();
  // Set the appropriate field delimiter
  dfp.setFieldDelimiter(b[0]);

  String f = tvp.getControlRecord("DEFAULT_DATAFILENAME");
  try
  {
    // Parse the customer data file using the ASCII data file parser
    dfp.processFile(f);
  }
```

**LISTING 17.8**    Continued

```
      catch(Exception e)
      {
        throw e;
      }
    }
    return;
  }

  public boolean isCustomerRecordValid(CustomerRec aRec)
  {
    if (aRec.getID() == null)
      return(false);
    if (aRec.getName() == null)
      return(false);
    if (aRec.getRecAction() == 0x00)
      return(false);
    if (aRec.getAddress() == null)
      return(false);
    if (aRec.getStatus() == null)
      return(false);
    if (aRec.getOutstandingBal() < (float)0.00)
      return(false);

    return(true);
  }

  public Vector getCustomerRecordTable()
  {
    return(customerRecs);
  }

  public CustomerRec getCustomerRecord(String ID)
  {
    if (customerRecs == null)
      return(null);
    int n = customerRecs.size();
    CustomerRec crec;
    String cID;
```

**LISTING 17.8**   Continued

```java
    for (int i = 0; i < n; i++)
    {
      crec = (CustomerRec) customerRecs.get(i);
      cID = crec.getID();
      if (cID.equalsIgnoreCase(ID) == true)
        return(crec);
    }
    return(null);
  }


  // Member variables
  private Vector customerRecs;
  private MetadataRec metadataRecs;
}
```

Listings 17.9 and 17.10 contain the interfaces for the parsers. The source for the two parsers, ASCII data file parser and metadata parser (implemented as Tag Value parser), is contained in source code Listings 17.11 to 17.17.

**LISTING 17.9**   FileParser.java

```java
/**
 * Title:        ASCII File Adapter<p>
 * Description:  This package contains all non-JCA classes of the
 * ASCII file adapter.<p>
 * Copyright:    Copyright (c) Atul Apte<p>
 * Company:      iConexio Technologies Inc.<p>
 * @author Atul Apte
 * @version 1.0
 */
package com.iconexio.asciiFileAdapter;

import java.io.IOException;

public interface FileParser
{
    public void processFile(String fileName) throws IOException, Exception;
}
```

*LISTING 17.10*    ParserEngine.java

```java
/**
 * Title:       ASCII File Adapter<p>
 * Description: This package contains all non-JCA classes of the
 * ASCII file adapter.<p>
 * Copyright:   Copyright (c) Atul Apte<p>
 * Company:     iConexio Technologies Inc.<p>
 * @author Atul Apte
 * @version 1.0
 */
package com.iconexio.asciiFileAdapter;


public interface ParserEngine
{
    public void parseBuffer(byte[] buff, int buffLen) throws ParserException;
}
```

*LISTING 17.11*    TagValueParser.java

```java
/**
 * Title:       ASCII File Adapter<p>
 * Description: This package contains all non-JCA classes of the
 * ASCII file adapter.<p>
 * Copyright:   Copyright (c) Atul Apte<p>
 * Company:     iConexio Technologies Inc.<p>
 * @author Atul Apte
 * @version 1.0
 */
package com.iconexio.asciiFileAdapter;


import java.lang.String;
import java.io.IOException;
import java.io.FileInputStream;


public class TagValueParser extends Object implements FileParser
{

  public TagValueParser()
  {
    pEngine = new TagValueParserEngine(); // Default tag value parser engine
  }
```

*LISTING 17.11*    Continued

```
TagValueParser(ParserEngine aEngine)
{
  pEngine = (TagValueParserEngine)aEngine; // Custom engine
}


public void processFile(String fileName) throws IOException, Exception,
                        ParserException
{
  FileInputStream fis;
  byte[] rec;
  int n, r;

  fis = new FileInputStream(fileName);
  try {
    while (true) {
      n = fis.available();
      if (n <= 0)
        break;
      if (n > 10241)
      {
        Exception e = new Exception("File too big.. > 10K");
        throw e;
      }
      if (n > 0)
      {
        // There is data to be read, create a byte array to hold the data
        rec = new byte[n+1];
        r = fis.read(rec);
        if (r == -1)
          break; // break out of the while loop
        try
        {
          pEngine.parseBuffer(rec,n); // This buffer contains all the data
                                      // in the ascii file
        }
        catch (ParserException e)
        {
            throw e;
        }
      }
    }
```

*LISTING 17.11*    Continued

```
    } catch (IOException e) { throw e; }
  }

  public String getControlRecord(String tag)
  {
    MetadataControl m;
    m = pEngine.getControlRecord(tag);
    return(m.getValue());
  }

  public String getLayoutRecord(String tag)
  {
    MetadataLayout l;
    l = pEngine.getLayoutRecord(tag);
    return(l.getType());
  }
  // Associated TagValueParserEngine instance
  private TagValueParserEngine pEngine;
}
```

*LISTING 17.12*    TagValueParserEngine.java

```
/**
 * Title:        ASCII File Adapter<p>
 * Description:  This package contains all non-JCA classes of the
 * ASCII file adapter.<p>
 * Copyright:    Copyright (c) Atul Apte<p>
 * Company:      iConexio Technologies Inc.<p>
 * @author Atul Apte
 * @version 1.0
 */

 /*
  * This parser engine transforms text strings into metadata control and
  * layout objects
  */
 */

package com.iconexio.asciiFileAdapter;

import java.util.Hashtable;
```

## LISTING 17.12   Continued

```java
public class TagValueParserEngine extends Object implements ParserEngine
{

  public TagValueParserEngine()
  {
    // This is the default state machine for the engine
    psMachine = new TagValueParserStateMachine();
  }

  public void parseBuffer(byte[] buff, int len) throws ParserException
  {
    String startTag;
    String endTag;
    String tagValue;
    String v, d;
    int sFlag = 0;
    int fid = 1;
    int recType; // Control = 0 or Layout = 1

    psMachine.resetParser();
    startTag = null;
    endTag = null;
    tagValue = null;
    recType = 0;

    for (int i = 0; i < len; i++)
    {
      if (sFlag == 1) // Previous error detected do not continue
        break;
      try
      {
        // Call the parser state machine to process the data
        psMachine.processByte(buff[i]);
      } catch(ParserException e) { throw e; }

      if (psMachine.startTagDetected() == true)
      {
        // Start tag has been detected and is stored in the parserEngine
        // Get the tag name stored in the state engine
        startTag = psMachine.getData();
```

*LISTING 17.12*    Continued

```
      psMachine.resetDataBuffer();
   } // Start tag detected

   if (psMachine.endTagDetected() == true)
   {
     endTag = psMachine.getData();
     // Validate if the element tags are the same before adding the tag
     // value pair to the Hashtable
     if (startTag.equalsIgnoreCase(endTag) == true)
     {
       if (startTag.equalsIgnoreCase("METADATATYPE") == true)
       {
         // This element defines the metadata type - control or layout
         if (tagValue.equalsIgnoreCase("Layout") == true)
         {
           recType = 1;
           psMachine.resetDataBuffer();
           continue;
         }
         else if (tagValue.equalsIgnoreCase("Control") == true)
         {
           recType = 0;
           psMachine.resetDataBuffer();
           continue;
         }
         else
         {
           recType = -1;
           sFlag = 1;
           ParserException e = new
                       ParserException("Invalid meta data type");
           throw e;
         }
       }
       if (recType == 0)
       {
         // This metadata record has control information
         MetadataControl m = new MetadataControl(fid,startTag,tagValue);
         mRec.addControlRecord(m);
         fid++;
       }
```

**LISTING 17.12**   Continued

```
            else if (recType == 1)
            {
                // This metadata record has layout information
                // If there are any domain values extract them from the tagValue
                int j = tagValue.indexOf((int)'|');
                if (j == -1)
                {
                    d = new String("NO_DOMAIN_DEFINED");
                    MetadataLayout m = new MetadataLayout(fid,startTag,tagValue,d);
                    mRec.addLayoutRecord(m);
                    fid++;
                }
                else
                {
                    d = tagValue.substring(j);
                    v = tagValue.substring(0,j);
                    MetadataLayout m = new MetadataLayout(fid,startTag,v,d);
                    mRec.addLayoutRecord(m);
                    fid++;
                }
            }
        }
        else
        {
            // Log data to error log
            sFlag = 1;
            ParserException e = new
                        ParserException("Start Tag " + startTag +
                                        " and End Tag " + endTag +
                                        " do not match");

            throw e;
        } // Start tag and End tag do not match
        psMachine.resetDataBuffer();
    } // End of tag detected
    if (psMachine.tagValueDetected() == true)
    {
        tagValue = psMachine.getData();
        psMachine.resetDataBuffer();
    } // An element value detected
```

**LISTING 17.12**    Continued

```
   } // End of for
 } // End of method

 public MetadataControl getControlRecord(String tagName)
 {
   return(mRec.getControlRecord(tagName));
 }

 public MetadataLayout getLayoutRecord(String tagName)
 {
   return(mRec.getLayoutRecord(tagName));
 }
 public void setMetadataRec(MetadataRec aRec)
 {
   this.mRec = aRec;
 }
 // Member variables
 private TagValueParserStateMachine psMachine;
 private MetadataRec mRec;
}
```

**LISTING 17.13**    TagValueParserStateMachine.java

```
/**
 * Title:       ASCII File Adapter<p>
 * Description: This package contains all non-JCA classes of the
 * ASCII file adapter.<p>
 * Copyright:   Copyright (c) Atul Apte<p>
 * Company:     iConexio Technologies Inc.<p>
 * @author Atul Apte
 * @version 1.0
 */

package com.iconexio.asciiFileAdapter;

public class TagValueParserStateMachine
{
 // The default constructor of this class resets the parser state
 public TagValueParserStateMachine()
 {
```

**LISTING 17.13**   Continued

```
        resetParser();
}


// This method returns true if the tag represents start of an element
public boolean startTagDetected()
{
  if (currentState == endTag && tagType == prefixTag)
    return(true);
  return(false);
}
// This method returns true if the tag represents end of an element
public boolean endTagDetected()
{
  if (currentState == endTag && tagType == suffixTag)
    return(true);
  return(false);
}
// This method returns true if the parsing of element value is complete
public boolean tagValueDetected()
{
  if (currentState == processingDataComplete)
    return(true);
  return(false);
}
// This method just resets the data buffer
public void resetDataBuffer()
{
  dataIterator = 0;
}
// This method returns the string representing the parsed data
public String getData()
{
  String s;
  if (dataIterator == 0)
    return((String)null); // No data has been parsed or the statemachine
                          // has been reset.
  s = new String(parsedData,0,dataIterator);
  return(s);
}
```

*LISTING 17.13*    Continued

```
public void processByte(byte a) throws ParserException {
  switch (currentState)
  {
    case idleState:
      if (a == tagSDelim) // Start of an element tag is detected
        currentState = startTag; // Change state
      // Else ignore all bytes until start of tag is detected
      break;

    case startTag:
      if (a == tagEDelim) // Tag end delimiter detected
      {
        currentState = endTag; // End of tag is detected
        break;
      }
      else
      {
        // Store the bytes as tag name
        if (dataIterator >= 32)
        {
          // Tag cannot be bigger than 32 bytes long
          ParserException e = new
                       ParserException("Tag name cannot exceed 32 bytes");
          throw(e);
        }
        if (a == '/' && dataIterator == 0)
          tagType = suffixTag; // Do not store the byte
        else
        {
          // Store the byte as data
          parsedData[dataIterator] = a;
          dataIterator++;
        }
      }
    break;

    case endTag:
        if (a == tagSDelim) {
          currentState = startTag;
          break;
        }
```

**LISTING 17.13**   Continued

```
            if (a == EOR) // This indicates end of a record in the buffer
            {
                currentState = idleState;
                tagType = prefixTag;
                break;
            }
            parsedData[dataIterator] = a;
            dataIterator++;
            currentState = processingData;
        break;

        case processingData:

          if (a == tagSDelim)
          {
            // Start of end tag detected
            currentState = processingDataComplete;
          }
          else
          {
            parsedData[dataIterator] = a;
            dataIterator++;
          }

        break;

        case processingDataComplete:

          if (a == tagEDelim) {
            // Null tag name detected throw exception
            ParserException e = new
                ParserException("End Tag naming error expecting /");
            throw e;
          }
          else {
            if (a == '/')
                currentState = startTag;
                tagType = suffixTag;
          }
        break;
    }
```

*LISTING 17.13*    Continued

```
    return;
  }

// This method resets the entire parser state including allocating a new
// buffer. The maximum data size is set to 1K
public void resetParser()
{
    currentState = idleState;
    parsedData = new byte[1025];
    for (int i = 0; i <= 1024; i++)
        parsedData[i] = 0;
    tagType = prefixTag;
    dataIterator = 0;
    setTagSDelim((byte)'<');
    setTagEDelim((byte)'>');
}

public void setTagSDelim(byte a) {
      tagSDelim = a;
}
public void setTagEDelim(byte a) {
      tagEDelim = a;
}
public byte getTagEDelim() {
      return(tagEDelim);
}
public byte getTagSDelim() {
      return(tagSDelim);
}

  // Parser state engine member variables

  private byte[] parsedData;
  private int dataIterator;

  private byte tagSDelim;
  private byte tagEDelim;

  private int currentState;
  private int tagType; // prefixTag, suffixTag
```

## LISTING 17.13   Continued

```
    // Parser states
    private final static int idleState = 0;
    private final static int startTag = 1;
    private final static int endTag = 2;
    private final static int processingData = 3;
    private final static int processingDataComplete = 4;
    private final static byte EOR = 13;

    // Tag types
    private final static int prefixTag = 1;
    private final static int suffixTag = 2;
}
```

## LISTING 17.14   ASCIIDataFileParser.java

```
/**
 * Title:        ASCII File Adapter<p>
 * Description:  This package contains all non-JCA classes of the
 * ASCII file adapter.<p>
 * Copyright:    Copyright (c) Atul Apte<p>
 * Company:      iConexio Technologies Inc.<p>
 * @author Atul Apte
 * @version 1.0
 */
package com.iconexio.asciiFileAdapter;

import java.io.FileInputStream;
import java.io.IOException;
import java.util.Vector;

public class ASCIIDataFileParser extends Object implements FileParser
{

  public ASCIIDataFileParser()
  {
    this.pEngine = new ASCIIDataFileParserEngine();
  }

  public ASCIIDataFileParser(ASCIIDataFileParserEngine theEngine)
  {
```

**LISTING 17.14**    Continued

```
  this.pEngine = theEngine;
}

public void setFieldDelimiter(byte fieldDelim)
{
  this.pEngine.setFieldDelimiter(fieldDelim);
}

public void processFile(String fileName) throws IOException, ParserException,
                                                Exception
{
  FileInputStream fis;
  byte[] rec;
  int n, r;

  fis = new FileInputStream(fileName);
  try
  {
    while (true)
    {
      n = fis.available();
      if (n <= 0)
        break;
      if (n > 10241)
      {
        Exception e = new Exception("File too big.. > 10K");
        throw e;
      }
      if (n > 0)
      {
        // There is data to be read, create a byte array to hold the data
        rec = new byte[n];
        r = fis.read(rec);
        if (r == -1)
          break; // break out of the while loop
        try
        {
          pEngine.parseBuffer(rec,n);
        }
        catch (ParserException e)
        {
```

**LISTING 17.14**   Continued

```
            throw e;
        }
      } // End of if n > 0
    } // End of while loop
  } catch (IOException e) { throw e; }
}


public Vector getRecordContainer()
{
  // Call the ASCIIDataFileParserEngine.getRecordContainer
  return(pEngine.getRecordContainer());
}
// Member variables
private ASCIIDataFileParserEngine pEngine;
}
```

**LISTING 17.15**   ASCIIDataFileParserEngine.java

```
/**
 * Title:        ASCII File Adapter<p>
 * Description:  This package contains all non-JCA classes of the
 * ASCII file adapter.<p>
 * Copyright:    Copyright (c) Atul Apte<p>
 * Company:      iConexio Technologies Inc.<p>
 * @author Atul Apte
 * @version 1.0
 */
package com.iconexio.asciiFileAdapter;

import java.util.Vector;

public class ASCIIDataFileParserEngine implements ParserEngine
{

  public ASCIIDataFileParserEngine()
  {
    psMachine = new ASCIIDataFileParserStateMachine();
    recordContainer = new Vector();
  }
```

**LISTING 17.15**    Continued

```java
public void setFieldDelimiter(byte fieldDelim)
{
  psMachine.setFieldDelim(fieldDelim);
}

public void parseBuffer(byte[] buff, int len) throws ParserException
{
  String f1,f2,f3,f4,f5,f6;
  CustomerRec cRec;
  int f;

  f1 = f2 = f3 = f4 = f5 = f6 = null;
  psMachine.resetParser();
  f = 1;

  for (int i = 0; i < len; i++)
  {
    try
    {
      psMachine.processByte(buff[i]);
    } catch (ParserException e) { throw e; }

    if (psMachine.fieldDetected() == true)
    {
      // A new field delimiter was detected. Store the data as a field
      // and assign it to the right customer record field
      if (f == 1)
      {
        f1 = psMachine.getData();
        f++;
      }
      else if (f == 2)
      {
        f2 = psMachine.getData();
        f++;
      }
      else if (f == 3)
      {
        f3 = psMachine.getData();
        f++;
      }
```

### LISTING 17.15  Continued

```
      else if (f == 4)
      {
        f4 = psMachine.getData();
        f++;
      }
      else if (f == 5)
      {
        f5 = psMachine.getData();
        f++;
      }
      psMachine.resetDataBuffer();
    }
    if (psMachine.EORDetected() == true)
    {
      if (f <= 5)
      {
        // We have fewer than anticipated fields
        ParserException e = new
          ParserException(f1+","+f2+","+f3+","+f4+","+f5+
                             " Missing field detected");
        psMachine.resetDataBuffer();
        f = 1;
        throw e;
      }
      else
      {
        // Get the last field
        f6 = psMachine.getData();
        cRec = new CustomerRec(f1,f2,f3,f4,f5,f6);
        recordContainer.add(cRec);
        psMachine.resetDataBuffer();
        f = 1;
      }
    }
  }
}

public Vector getRecordContainer()
{
```

***LISTING 17.15***    Continued

```
    return(recordContainer);
  }

  private ASCIIDataFileParserStateMachine psMachine;
  private Vector recordContainer; // Each record in this container is an
                                  // instance of CustomerRec
}
```

***LISTING 17.16***    `ASCIIDataFileParserStateMachine.java`

```
/**
 * Title:        ASCII File Adapter<p>
 * Description:  This package contains all non-JCA classes of the
 * ASCII file adapter.<p>
 * Copyright:    Copyright (c) Atul Apte<p>
 * Company:      iConexio Technologies Inc.<p>
 * @author Atul Apte
 * @version 1.0
 */
package com.iconexio.asciiFileAdapter;

public class ASCIIDataFileParserStateMachine
{

  public ASCIIDataFileParserStateMachine()
  {
    resetParser();
  }

  public boolean fieldDetected()
  {
    if (currentState == endOfField)
      return(true);
    return(false);
  }

  public boolean EORDetected()
  {
    if (currentState == endOfRecord)
      return(true);
```

## LISTING 17.16     Continued

```java
      return(false);
  }

  public void resetParser()
  {
    currentState = idleState;
    dataIterator = 0;
    parsedData = new byte[10240+1];
  }

  public String getData()
  {
    String s;
    if (dataIterator == 0)
      return((String)null); // No data has been parsed or the statemachine
                            // has been reset.
    s = new String(parsedData,0,dataIterator);
    resetDataBuffer();
    return(s);
  }

  public void resetDataBuffer()
  {
    dataIterator = 0;
  }

  public void processByte(byte a) throws ParserException {
    switch (currentState)
    {
      case idleState:
        if (a == fieldDelim) // Start of an element tag is detected
        {
          currentState = endOfField; // Change state
          break;
        }
        if (a == EOR)
        {
          currentState = endOfRecord;
        }
        else
        {
```

*LISTING 17.16*   Continued

```
      // Store into parsedData
      parsedData[dataIterator] = a;
      dataIterator++;
      if (dataIterator > 10240)
      {
        ParserException e = new ParserException("Data field too long");
        throw e;
      }
    }
  break;

  case endOfField:
    if (a == EOR) // Tag end delimiter detected
    {
      currentState = endOfRecord; // End of tag is detected
      dataIterator = 0;
      break;
    }
    else
    {
      // Store data in parsedData
      parsedData[dataIterator] = a;
      dataIterator++;
      currentState = idleState;
      if (dataIterator > 10240)
      {
        ParserException e = new ParserException("Data field too long");
        throw e;
      }
    }
  break;

  case endOfRecord:
    parsedData[dataIterator] = a;
    dataIterator++;
    currentState = idleState;
    if (dataIterator > 10240)
    {
      ParserException e = new ParserException("Data field too long");
      throw e;
    }
```

*LISTING 17.16*   Continued

```
      break;
    }
    return;
  }

  public void setFieldDelim(byte a)
  {
    fieldDelim = a;
  }
  public byte getFieldDelim()
  {
    return(fieldDelim);
  }

  // private member variables

  private static final int idleState = 0;
  private static final int endOfField = 1;
  private static final int endOfRecord = 2;
  private static final byte EOR = 13;
  private byte fieldDelim;
  private byte[] parsedData;
  private int dataIterator;
  private int currentState;
}
```

*LISTING 17.17*   ParserException.java

```
/**
 * Title:        ASCII File Adapter<p>
 * Description:  This package contains all non-JCA classes of the
 * ASCII file adapter.<p>
 * Copyright:    Copyright (c) Atul Apte<p>
 * Company:      iConexio Technologies Inc.<p>
 * @author Atul Apte
 * @version 1.0
 */

package com.iconexio.asciiFileAdapter;
```

*LISTING 17.17*    Continued

```
public class ParserException extends Exception
{

  public ParserException(String s)
  {
    super(s);
  }
}
```

## Shared Service Layer Source Code

The source code in this layer contains all data objects (customer and metadata), as well as the log manager. Listings 17.18 to 17.21 contain source code for the data objects, and Listings 17.22 to 17.28 contain the log manager-related source code.

*LISTING 17.18*    CustomerRec.java

```
/**
 * Title:        ASCII File Adapter<p>
 * Description:  This package contains all non-JCA classes of the
 * ASCII file adapter.<p>
 * Copyright:    Copyright (c) Atul Apte<p>
 * Company:      iConexio Technologies Inc.<p>
 * @author Atul Apte
 * @version 1.0
 */
package com.iconexio.asciiFileAdapter;

// Objects of CustomerRec class hold the parsed customer data information
// Each customer record has a unique ID. There can be more than one record
// with the same ID as there can be multiple actions performed on a record
// including add, update, delete

public class CustomerRec
{
  public CustomerRec()
  {
    ID = null;
    name = null;
    actionID = 0x00;
```

## LISTING 17.18    Continued

```java
    address = null;
    status = null;
    outstandingBal = (float)0.00;
}


// Since this customer record is supposed to be read-only all the setters are
// declared as private methods accessible from the constructor

public CustomerRec(String ID, String name, String actionID, String address,
                   String status, String balance) {
    setID(ID);
    setName(name);
    setRecAction(actionID.charAt(0));
    setAddress(address);
    setStatus(status);
    Float x = new Float(1.00);
    x.parseFloat(balance);
    setOutstandingBal(x.parseFloat(balance));
}
public String getID() {
    return(ID);
}
private void setID(String theID) {
    ID = new String(theID);
}
public String getName() {
    return(name);
}
private void setName(String theName) {
    name = new String(theName);
}
public char getRecAction() {
    return(actionID);
}
private void setRecAction(char theAction) {
    actionID = theAction;
}
public String getAddress() {
    return(address);
}
private void setAddress(String theAddress) {
```

**LISTING 17.18**    Continued

```java
      address = new String(theAddress);
    }
    public float getOutstandingBal() {
      return(outstandingBal);
    }
    private void setOutstandingBal(float theBal) {
      outstandingBal = theBal;
    }
    private void setStatus(String theStatus) {
      status = new String(theStatus);
    }
    public String getStatus() {
      return(status);
    }
    public boolean isCustomerAccountActive() {
      if (status.equalsIgnoreCase("Active") == true)
        return(true);
      return(false);
    }

    private String ID;
    private String name;
    private char actionID; // A = Add, U = Update, D = Delete
    private String address;
    private float outstandingBal; // Default = 0.00
    private String status; // Active, Dormant, Bad Account
}
```

**LISTING 17.19**    MetadataRec.java

```java
/**
 * Title:       ASCII File Adapter<p>
 * Description: This package contains all non-JCA classes of the
 * ASCII file adapter.<p>
 * Copyright:   Copyright (c) Atul Apte<p>
 * Company:     iConexio Technologies Inc.<p>
 * @author Atul Apte
 * @version 1.0
```

**LISTING 17.19**   Continued

```
    */
package com.iconexio.asciiFileAdapter;

import java.util.Hashtable;

public class MetadataRec
{

    public MetadataRec()
    {
      controlRec = new Hashtable();
      layoutRec = new Hashtable();
    }
    public MetadataControl getControlRecord(String tag)
    {
      return((MetadataControl)controlRec.get(tag));
    }
    public void addControlRecord (MetadataControl cRec)
    {
      controlRec.put(cRec.getName(), cRec);
    }
    public void addLayoutRecord (MetadataLayout lRec)
    {
      layoutRec.put(lRec.getName(),lRec);
    }
    public MetadataLayout getLayoutRecord(String tag)
    {
      return((MetadataLayout)layoutRec.get(tag));
    }
    private Hashtable controlRec;
    private Hashtable layoutRec;
}
```

**LISTING 17.20**   MetadataControl.java

```
/**
 * Title:        ASCII File Adapter<p>
 * Description:  This package contains all non-JCA classes of the
 * ASCII file adapter.<p>
 * Copyright:    Copyright (c) Atul Apte<p>
```

***LISTING 17.20***    Continued

```
 * Company:       iConexio Technologies Inc.<p>
 * @author Atul Apte
 * @version 1.0
 */
package com.iconexio.asciiFileAdapter;

// This class contains the basic control data required to parse any ASCII
// file namely the field delimiter. This class can be extended for more complex
// control data.

public class MetadataControl extends Object
{
  public MetadataControl()
  {
  }
  public MetadataControl(int afID, String fName, String fValue)
  {
    fID = afID;
    fname = new String(fName);
    fvalue = new String(fValue);
  }
  public int getID()
  {
    return(fID);
  }
  public String getName()
  {
    return(fname);
  }
  public String getValue()
  {
    return(fvalue);
  }
  private int fID;
  private String fname;
  private String fvalue;
}
```

## LISTING 17.21   MetadataLayout.java

```java
/**
 * Title:        ASCII File Adapter<p>
 * Description:  This package contains all non-JCA classes of the
 * ASCII file adapter.<p>
 * Copyright:    Copyright (c) Atul Apte<p>
 * Company:      iConexio Technologies Inc.<p>
 * @author Atul Apte
 * @version 1.0
 */
package com.iconexio.asciiFileAdapter;

// This class defines the structure of a field including its name, type, and
// the actual value. An example of MetaDataLayout instance is:
// fID = 1
// fName = ACCOUNT_STATUS
// fType = String
// fDomain = ACTIVE,DORMANT (values that define the domain of this field.)
// The domain parameter is optional and can be used by the parser to validate
// any values assigned to the field.

public class MetadataLayout
{

  public MetadataLayout()
  {
  }
  public MetadataLayout(int afID, String fName, String fType, String fDomain) {
    fID = afID;
    fname = new String(fName);
    ftype = new String(fType);
    fdomain = new String(fDomain);
  }
  public int getID() {
    return(fID);
  }
  public String getName() {
    return(fname);
  }
  public String getDomainValue() {
    return(fdomain);
  }
```

**LISTING 17.21**    Continued

```
  public String getType() {
    return(ftype);
  }
  private int fID;
  private String fname;
  private String ftype;
  private String fdomain;
}
```

**LISTING 17.22**    LogManager.java

```
/* Generated by Together */

package com.iconexio.asciiFileAdapter;

/**
 * A log manager is a generic interface to different types of audit
 * trails that track different aspects of the resource adapter.
 * Some of the audit trail will be managed local to the resource
 * adapter (on the same J2EE application server) while other audit
 * trails will be remote to the adapter. For example if a resource
 * adapter is integrating a CICS COBOL application then it may well
 * be necessary to maintain a log in the CICS environment as well as
 * the application server environment.
 *
 * Designing a log manager independent of the actual location and
 * implementation is an important part of adapter customization and
 * flexibility. In more advanced IT centers a NMS (Network Monitoring
 * System) based log manager may be needed.
 *
 * An adapter may have to open more than one log at the same time.
 * One of the customization could be to I18N one or more of the log
 * files. This will ensure that geographically distributed centers
 * and users get messages in local languages.
 *
 * @author Atul Apte
 * @version 1.0
 */
import java.io.*;

public interface LogManager {
```

*LISTING 17.22*   Continued

```
    /* The LogManager implementation can open and manage more than one
     * log of different types including transaction logs, system logs,
     * exception logs,and performance logs. Mode can be WRITE or APPEND
     */
    public void openLog(String logName, String mode) throws Exception;

    /* Some logs may need a secured access especially if the log file is
     * maintaining details of a business transaction and not just system
     * information. MODE can be WRITE or APPEND
     */
    public void
      openLog(String logName, String mode, String userID, String password)
            throws Exception;

    public void closeLog(String logName) throws IOException;
    public void logMessage(String logName, String logMessage)
            throws Exception;

    public void setTimestamp(String logName) throws Exception;
}
```

*LISTING 17.23*   LogFileManager.java

```
/* Generated by Together */
/* The LogFileManager provides a class for managing file based logs
 * This class must be extended to manage specific types of log files
 *
 * @author Atul Apte
 * @version 1.0
 */

package com.iconexio.asciiFileAdapter;

import java.io.*;
import java.util.*;
import java.lang.*;

abstract public class LogFileManager extends Object implements LogManager {
    public LogFileManager() {
        // The default constructor allows for only one log file
```

**LISTING 17.23**    Continued

```java
        // to be open at any given time
        _noOfLogFilesOpen = 0;
        _maxLogFilesOpen = 2;
        logFileTable = new Hashtable();
    }
    public LogFileManager(int maxNoOfLogFiles) {
        // If you need more than one log file open at the same
        // time use this constructor. The actual maximum files open
        // in any environment is defined by the system kernel.
        _maxLogFilesOpen = maxNoOfLogFiles;
        _noOfLogFilesOpen = 0;
        logFileTable = new Hashtable();
    }

    // mode can be a string with the value WRITE or APPEND
    public void openLog(String theLogFileName, String mode) throws
        TooManyLogFilesOpenException, Exception {
        // Check to see if there is any room to open more files
        if (getNoOfLogFilesOpen() >=  getMaxNoOfLogFiles()) {
            TooManyLogFilesOpenException e = new
                TooManyLogFilesOpenException("Cannot open " +
                    theLogFileName + "Too many log files open");
          throw e;
        }
            // Open a log file and store the handle in a hash table

            File logFile = new File(theLogFileName);
            FileOutputStream logFileStream;
            if (mode.equalsIgnoreCase("WRITE") == true) {
             try {
                // Open file in write mode
                logFileStream = new
                        FileOutputStream(theLogFileName);
             } catch (Exception e) {
                throw e;
                }
             logFileTable.put(theLogFileName, logFileStream);
                    incrementNoOfFilesOpen();
             }
            else if (mode.equalsIgnoreCase("APPEND") == true) {
              try {
```

**LISTING 17.23**  Continued

```
                        // Open file in append mode
                        logFileStream = new
                             FileOutputStream(theLogFileName, true);
                    } catch (Exception e) {
                        throw e;
                    }
            logFileTable.put(theLogFileName, logFileStream);
               incrementNoOfFilesOpen();
                }
            else {
                // Throw an exception
                TooManyLogFilesOpenException e = new
                    TooManyLogFilesOpenException("File " +
                          theLogFileName +
                          " exists. Cannot open in WRITE mode");
                throw e;
            }
        }


    public void openLog(String theLogFileName, String mode,
            String userID, String password)
            throws TooManyLogFilesOpenException, Exception {
        openLog(theLogFileName,mode);
    }


    public void closeLog(String theFileName) throws IOException {
        Object logFileStream = (Object)logFileTable.remove(theFileName);
        if (logFileStream != null) {
            Class logClass = logFileStream.getClass();
                String className = logClass.getName();
                if (className.equalsIgnoreCase("FileOutputStream") == true) {
                    FileOutputStream theStream = (FileOutputStream)logFileStream;
                    try {
                    theStream.close();
                    } catch (IOException e) {
                      throw e;
                    }
                }
        }
    }
}
```

*LISTING 17.23*    Continued

```java
public void logMessage(String logName, String logMsg) throws Exception {
    // Retrieve the correct file stream object matching the log name
    FileOutputStream theFileStream;
    theFileStream = (FileOutputStream)logFileTable.get(logName);
    if (theFileStream == null) {
        NullPointerException e = new
            NullPointerException("Cannot find matching file stream for "
                + logName);
        throw e;
    }
    byte[] msgInBytes = logMsg.getBytes();
    theFileStream.write(msgInBytes);
    theFileStream.write((int)10);
    theFileStream.write((int)13);
}

public int getNoOfLogFilesOpen() {
    return(_noOfLogFilesOpen);
}

public int getMaxNoOfLogFiles() {
    return(_maxLogFilesOpen);
}

public void incrementNoOfFilesOpen() {
    _noOfLogFilesOpen++;
}

public void decrementNoOfFilesOpen() {
    _noOfLogFilesOpen--;
}

private int _noOfLogFilesOpen;
private int _maxLogFilesOpen;
private Hashtable logFileTable;
private final char nl = '\n';
}
```

**LISTING 17.24**   `AdapterDefaultLogManager.java`

```
/* Generated by Together */
/* The AdapterDefaultLogManager extends LogFileManager class
 * The example resource adapter in this book uses this
 * as the default log manager.
 *
 * @author Atul Apte
 * @version 1.0
 */


package com.iconexio.asciiFileAdapter;

import java.util.*;
import java.text.*;

public class AdapterDefaultLogManager extends LogFileManager {
    public AdapterDefaultLogManager() {
        super(1); // Only one default log manager
    }
    public void setTimestamp(String logName) throws Exception {
        Date now = new Date();
        DateFormat fmt = DateFormat.getDateTimeInstance();
        String timeStamp = fmt.format(now);
        try {
           logMessage(logName, timeStamp);
        } catch (Exception e) {
            throw e;
        }
    }
}
```

**LISTING 17.25**   `AdapterExceptionLogManager.java`

```
/* Generated by Together */
/* The AdapterExceptionLogManager extends LogFileManager class
 * The example resource adapter in this book uses this
 * as the exception log manager.
 * Notice the logException method has been extended to support
 * severity of the exception
 *
```

**LISTING 17.25**   Continued

```java
 * @author Atul Apte
 * @version 1.0
 */

package com.iconexio.asciiFileAdapter;

import java.lang.*;
import java.util.*;
import java.text.*;

public class AdapterExceptionLogManager extends LogFileManager {
    public AdapterExceptionLogManager() {
        // set max number of files that can be opened to 3
        super(3);
    }
    public void setTimestamp(String logName) throws Exception {
        Date now = new Date();
        DateFormat fmt = DateFormat.getDateTimeInstance();
        String timeStamp = fmt.format(now);
        try {
          logMessage(logName, timeStamp);
        } catch (Exception e) {
            throw e;
        }
    }
    public void logException(String logName, String msg,
            String severity) throws Exception {
        try {
          logMessage(logName,severity);
        } catch (Exception e) {
            throw e;
        }
        try {
          logMessage(logName,msg);
        } catch (Exception e) {
            throw e;
        }
    }
}
```

**LISTING 17.26**   LogManagerFactoryIF.java

```java
/* Generated by Together */
/* This factory interface creates a log manager depending
 * on the key defined by the parameter logType
 * The benefits of having a factory create instances of
 * log managers is that the decision to associate a specific
 * key or log type to appropriate class is localized in
 * this class and easier to change in the future without
 * affecting the other classes.
 *
 * @author Atul Apte
 * @version 1.0
 */

package com.iconexio.asciiFileAdapter;

public interface LogManagerFactoryIF {
    public LogManager createLogManager(String logType);
}
```

**LISTING 17.27**   LogManagerFactory.java

```java
/* Generated by Together */
/* This is the implemenation of the log manager factory
 * interface
 * If the logType is == Adapter Exception Log then
 * an instance of the exception log manager is created.
 * Otherwise the default log manager is created
 * If the exceptions need to be directed to the system
 * admin by an email, the AdapterExceptionLogManager can
 * be extended to send an email using SMTP or other mail
 * protocols
 *
 * @author Atul Apte
 * @version 1.0
 */

package com.iconexio.asciiFileAdapter;

public class LogManagerFactory implements LogManagerFactoryIF {
    public LogManagerFactory() {
    }
```

*LISTING 17.27*    Continued

```
    public LogManager createLogManager(String logType) {
        LogManager aNewManager;
        if (logType.equalsIgnoreCase("EXCEPTION") == true)
            aNewManager = new AdapterExceptionLogManager();
        else
            aNewManager = new AdapterDefaultLogManager();
        return(aNewManager);
    }
}
```

*LISTING 17.28*    TooManyLogFilesOpenException.java

```
/* Generated by Together */
/* This is the exception throw when too many log files are
 * open at the same time.
 *
 * @author Atul Apte
 * @version 1.0
 */

package com.iconexio.asciiFileAdapter;

public class TooManyLogFilesOpenException extends Exception {
    public TooManyLogFilesOpenException() {
        super("Too many log files open");
    }
    public TooManyLogFilesOpenException(String s) {
        super(s);
    }
}
```

# Test Harness

Every adapter must have a test harness capable of testing the adapter classes in a non-JCA environment. This simplifies the unit testing of the adapter classes. Listing 17.29 contains a test harness for the ASCII file adapter.

**LISTING 17.29**   testHarness.java

```java
/**
 * Title:        ASCII File Adapter<p>
 * Description:  This package contains all non-JCA classes of the
 * ASCII file adapter.<p>
 * Copyright:    Copyright (c) Atul Apte<p>
 * Company:      iConexio Technologies Inc.<p>
 * @author Atul Apte
 * @version 1.0
 */
package com.iconexio.asciiFileAdapter;

/**
 * The test harness is a standalone Java program that uses the ASCII file
 * parser classes to parse the customer data file and display the contents
 * to the standard output.
 */
import java.util.Vector;
import java.lang.Integer;
import java.io.File;

public class testHarness
{
  public testHarness()
  {
    LogManager lm;
    LogManagerFactory lmf;
    int badRec;
    badRec = 0;

    // Create a log manager for exception log files
    lmf = new LogManagerFactory();
    lm = lmf.createLogManager("EXCEPTION");

    try
    {
      lm.openLog("BADREC.DAT","APPEND");
    } catch(Exception e)
    {
```

*LISTING 17.29*    Continued

```
    System.err.println(e.getMessage());
  }
  try
  {
    lm.setTimestamp("BADREC.DAT");
  } catch(Exception e)
  {
    System.err.println(e.getMessage());
  }

  ClientAPIImpl cAPI = new ClientAPIImpl();
  try
  {
    cAPI.extractRecords();
  } catch(Exception e)
  {
    // Log the exception in a log file
    try
    {
      lm.logMessage("BADREC.DAT",e.getMessage());
    } catch(Exception e1)
    {
      System.err.println(e1.getMessage());
    }
  }

  // Open the statistics log file
  try
  {
    lm.openLog("PSTATS.DAT","WRITE");
  } catch(Exception e)
  {
    System.err.println(e.getMessage());
  }

  Vector custRecs;
  custRecs = cAPI.getCustomerRecordList();
  CustomerRec cRec;
  int z;
  z = custRecs.size();
```

## LISTING 17.29   Continued

```java
for (int i = 0; i < z; i++)
{
  cRec = (CustomerRec)custRecs.get(i);
  if (cAPI.isCustomerRecordValid(cRec) == true)
  {
    System.out.println(cRec.getID());
    System.out.println(cRec.getName());
    System.out.println(cRec.getRecAction());
    System.out.println(cRec.getAddress());
    System.out.println(cRec.getStatus());
    System.out.println(cRec.getOutstandingBal());
  }
  else
    badRec++; // Keep a counter for recording number of invalid records
}

// Log statistics before closing the log files
Integer zz = new Integer(z);
Integer yy = new Integer(badRec);
// Write this information to the PSTATS.DAT log file
try
{
  lm.logMessage("PSTATS.DAT",zz.toString());
  lm.logMessage("PSTATS.DAT",yy.toString());
} catch(Exception e1)
{
  System.err.println(e1.getMessage());
}

try
{
  lm.closeLog("BADREC.DAT");
  lm.closeLog("PSTATS.DAT");
} catch(Exception e)
{
  System.err.println(e.getMessage());
}
}


/** The parameter metaDataFileName references the metadata definitions
 *  and the parameter customerDataFileName references the actual customer
```

**LISTING 17.29**   Continued

```
 *   data filename
 */
public testHarness(String metaDataFileName, String customerDataFileName)
{
  // Since we are testing the same data files the pstats.log file is not
  // present in this method
  LogManager lm;
  LogManagerFactory lmf = new LogManagerFactory();
  lm = lmf.createLogManager("EXCEPTION");
  try
  {
    lm.openLog("BADREC.DAT","APPEND");
  } catch(Exception e)
  {
    System.err.println(e.getMessage());
  }
  try
  {
    lm.setTimestamp("BADREC.DAT");
  }
  catch(Exception e)
  {
    System.err.println(e.getMessage());
  }

  ClientAPIImpl cAPI = new ClientAPIImpl();

  try
  {
    cAPI.extractRecords(customerDataFileName,metaDataFileName);
  }
  catch(Exception e)
  {
    // Log the error in a log file
    try
    {
      lm.logMessage("BADREC.DAT",e.getMessage());
    }
    catch(Exception e1)
    {
```

*LISTING 17.29*    Continued

```
      System.err.println(e1.getMessage());
  }
}


  Vector custRecs;
  custRecs = cAPI.getCustomerRecordList();


  CustomerRec cRec;
  int z;
  z = custRecs.size();
  for (int i = 0; i < z; i++)
  {
    cRec = (CustomerRec)custRecs.get(i);
    if (cAPI.isCustomerRecordValid(cRec) == true)
    {
      System.out.println(cRec.getID());
      System.out.println(cRec.getName());
      System.out.println(cRec.getRecAction());
      System.out.println(cRec.getAddress());
      System.out.println(cRec.getStatus());
      System.out.println(cRec.getOutstandingBal());
    }
  }
  try
  {
    lm.closeLog("BADREC.DAT");
  }
  catch(Exception e)
  {
    System.err.println(e.getMessage());
  }
}

public static void main(String[] args)
{
  if (args.length == 0)
  {
    // First parse the default customer data file as defined in the
    // default metadata definition file METADATA.DAT
    testHarness testHarness1 = new testHarness();
    // Print the total number of records processed
```

*LISTING 17.29*    Continued

```java
AdminAPIImpl a = new AdminAPIImpl();
try
{
  System.out.println("No of record processed = " +
            a.getNoOfRecordsProcessed());
} catch(Exception e)
{
  System.err.println(e.getMessage());
}
return;
}
if (args.length == 2)
{
  // Next parse the customer data file and metadata file passed to this
  // program as arguments
  File testArg;
  testArg = new File(args[0]);
  if (testArg.exists() == false)
  {
    System.out.println("File name specified in args[0] " + args[0] +
        " Does not exist");
    return;
  }
  testArg = new File(args[1]);
  if (testArg.exists() == false)
  {
    System.out.println("File name specified in args[0] " + args[1] +
        " Does not exist");
    return;
  }

  testHarness testHarness2 = new testHarness(args[0], args[1]);
  return;
}
if (args.length > 2 || args.length == 1)
{
  System.out.println(
        "Usage 1: java com.iconexio.asciiFileAdapter.testHarness");
  System.out.println(
        "Usage 2: java com.iconexio.asciiFileAdapter.testHarness " +
        "<Meta data filename> <Cutomer data filename>");
```

*LISTING 17.29*   Continued

```
        return;
    }
  }
}
```

## Summary

The source code listed in this chapter is the complete set of classes providing the core functionality of the resource adapter. Together with the classes presented in Chapter 11 (which contains the JCA-related classes), the source represents a complete J2EE resource adapter. The test harness and the test data presented in the earlier sections of this chapter will be useful in unit and system testing of the adapter.

# A

# Glossary

**abstraction**   A representation in terms of presumed essentials, with a corresponding suppression of the non-essential.

**ACID (Atomicity, Consistency, Isolation, Durability) Properties**   Hallmark properties of OLTP systems.

**AIA (Application Integration Adapter)**   A software component whose sole objective is to integrate two business applications in a point-to-point or brokered environment.

**API (Application Programming Interface)**   An application-specific interface that enables different programs to interact with each other.

**architecting**   The process of creating and building architectures. Depending on your perspective, architecting may or may not be seen as a separable part of engineering. These aspects of system development are most concerned with conceptualization, objective definition, and certification for use.

**architecture**   The structure (components, connections, and constraints) of a product, process, or element. The architecture of a particular application is defined by the classes and the interrelation of the classes. At another level, the architecture of a system is determined by the arrangement of the hardware and software components. The terms *logical architecture* and *physical architecture* are often used to emphasize this distinction.

**asynchronous request**   A request where the client does not pause to wait for results.

**atomicity**   One of the ACID properties; all or none of the transaction must occur. If all parts of the transaction cannot occur successfully, all effects of the transaction must be undone or "rolled back."

**B2B**   Business to Business connectivity over the Internet, especially in the context of supply chain automation. B2B exchanges could be private exchanges between trading partners or public exchanges with a wider set of members.

**CCI (Common Connector Interface)**   The specification defining an API for accessing Java Connector Architecture-compliant resource adapters. It is not mandatory to implement a CCI-compliant API for each resource adapter; however, it is advisable to do so for the sake of consistency.

**commit**   The declaration or process of making a transaction's updates and messages visible to other transactions. When a transaction commits, all its effects become public and durable. After commitment, the effects of a transaction cannot be reversed automatically.

**complexity**   A measure of the numbers and types of interrelationships among system elements. Generally speaking, the more complex a system, the more difficult it is to design, build, and use.

**composite object**   An object that is composed of objects, and delegates defined responsibilities to those objects. The validity of the composite object depends on the continued connection with its component objects. The composite object is defined by its parts; the termination of a component object would require the termination or declassification of the composite object.

**consistency**   One of the ACID properties; a transaction's results must be reproducible and predictable, even when the processing is distributed across different platforms.

**constraint**   A condition or proposition that must be maintained as true. Constraints are typically applied to the permissible states of an object or the extension of one or more types.

**delegation**   The notion that an object can issue a request to another object in response to a request. The first object, therefore, delegates the responsibility to the second object. Delegation can be used as an alternative to inheritance.

**design pattern**   A recurring structure or approach to a solution.

**distributed computing**   The distribution of process among computing components that are within the same computer or different computers on a shared network.

**domain**   A recognized field of activity and expertise, or of specialized theory and application.

**durability**   One of the ACID properties; a transaction's results must be permanent. The transaction must also have robustness; transactions must be able to survive application errors and rollbacks for resubmission to the application.

**EAI (Enterprise Application Integration)**   A set of technologies that allows the movement and exchange of information between different applications and business processes with and between organizations.

**EDI (Electronic Data Interchange)**   A standard for sharing information (data) between trading partners in the context of interorganization process integration. EDI has been in use, both in commercial environments as well as government departments.

**EJB (Enterprise Java Bean)**   A component model for J2EE servers. There are three types of EJB in the latest version of the EJB specifications, version 2.0: entity beans, session beans, and message driven beans.

**factory**   An entity that provides a service for creating objects.

**IDE (Integrated Development Environment)**   A development tool usually considered as a comprehensive environment supporting the full development lifecycle, from design to coding to testing and deployment.

**integration pattern**   A design pattern defined in the domain and context of application integration. An integration pattern connects to incompatible software or application artifacts.

**interface table**   A data table in a relational database intended to be a staging area for data external to the application. Interface tables are used to hold external data before transforming and validating the data into application-compatible formats, and committing the transformed and validated data to the application's production tables.

**isolation**   One of the ACID properties; a transaction must be distinguishable as discrete from other transactions. No executing transaction can interfere with another concurrently existing transaction.

**J2EE (Java 2 Enterprise Edition)**   An enterprise-scale Java platform capable of supporting EJB, JCA, and other specifications. J2EE is the ideal platform for Internet-based, component-oriented, enterprise applications.

**J2SE (Java 2 Standard Edition)**   The standard edition of Java used to develop two-tier, standalone business applications.

**JCA (Java Connector Architecture)**   A specification for extending the integration capabilities of a J2EE-compatible server. JCA specifications define specific system contracts for developing resource adapters that integrate J2EE applications with legacy systems.

**LAN (Local Area Network)**   A departmental network inside the corporate firewall. LAN environments are still useful for isolating internal integration environments from external interactions.

**legacy system**   A production system that was designed for technology assumptions that are no longer valid or expected to become invalid in the foreseeable future.

**lifecycle services**   Operations that manage object creation, deletion, copy, and equivalence.

**message routing/content based routing**   A super-application process in which messages are routed to applications based on business rules. A particular message may be directed based on its subject or actual content.

**methodology**   A process for the production of software using a collection of predefined techniques and notational conventions.

**module**   A collection of objects, methods, and classes that collaborate to provide a subset of the functionality of an application. Modules can retain their own state, and share information and behavior with the rest of the application.

**n-tier client/server**   An application development approach that partitions application logic across three or more environments: the desktop computer, one or more application servers, and a database server. The main advantage of the n-tier client/server is that it extends the benefits of client/server to the enterprise level. Other advantages include added manageability, scalability, security, and higher performance.

**open system**   A system whose architecture permits components developed by independent organizations or vendors to be combined.

**On-Line Transaction Processing (OLTP)**   The area of business computing that involves mission-critical business transactions that are processed in real time. These systems require high volume throughput and rapid response times.

**persistent object**   An object that can survive the process that created it. A persistent object exists until it is explicitly deleted.

**Points Of Integration (PIN)**   The program code of an application that is invoked by an external entity. User interfaces of an application are an example of points of integration used by end-users of the application. Other application functions and database tables form points of integration for external systems.

**post-condition**   A constraint that must be satisfied after the termination of an operation.

**precondition**   A constraint that must be satisfied for the invocation of an operation.

**referential integrity**   The assurance that an object handle identifies a single object.

**Remote Procedure Call (RPC)**   A local procedure call that is executed in a non-local program or address space. Enables application logic to be split between a client and a server in the way that best uses available resources.

**role**   A job type defined in terms of a set of responsibilities.

**rollback**   Terminates a transaction so that all resources updated within a transaction revert to the original state before the transaction started.

**SOAP (Simple Object Access Protocol)**   An XML-based protocol for invoking remote procedures. SOAP has become one of the cornerstones of Web services, and has been accepted as a standard by all major vendors including Microsoft, SUN, IBM, and others.

**synchronous request**   A request where the client pauses to wait for completion of the request.

**two-phase commit**   A mechanism to synchronize updates on different machines or platforms, so that they all fall or all succeed together. The decision to commit is centralized, but each participant has the right to veto. This is a key process in real-time, transaction-based environments.

**TPM (Transaction Processing Monitor)**   Based on the premise of a transaction. A *transaction* is a unit of work with a beginning and an end. The reasoning is that if an application's logic is encapsulated within a transaction, then the transaction either completes or is rolled back completely. If the transaction has been updating remote resources, such as databases and queues, then they too will be rolled back if a problem occurs.

**transient object**   An object whose existence is limited to that of the process that created it.

**transaction**   A logical construct through which applications perform work on shared resources (for example, databases). The work done on behalf of the transaction conforms to the four ACID properties: Atomicity, Consistency, Isolation, and Durability.

**UDDI (Universal Description, Discovery and Integration)**   A standard API for accessing Web service registries. UDDI simplifies discovering Web services over the Internet before accessing them using SOAP. UDDI-compliant Web service registries are expected to become the preferred mechanism of publishing and locating Web services.

**WSDL (Web Services Description Language)**   The de facto standard for describing Web services. WSDL is derived from XML, and is a platform-independent language useful for defining the specific interfaces and other properties of a Web service.

**XML (Extensible Markup Language)**   One of the major technology break-throughs, XML is a platform-independent and extendable language used to exchange self-describing data and data models.

**XSL (Extensible Style Sheet Language)**   This language has two parts: XSLT or XSL transformations, and XSL-FO or XSL formatting objects. The objective of XSL is to simplify transforming an XML document from one format to another without requiring specific transformation code.

**XSLT (XML Style Sheet Language Transformation)**   An XSLT stylesheet is an XML document that contains templates. An XSLT processor compares the elements in an input XML document to the templates in a stylesheet. When a matching stylesheet is found, the template's contents is written to an output tree.

# B

# References

This appendix contains references to books and informative sites on various technologies covered in this book. Some of these resources are online and subject to change.

## Books

Fowler, Martin. *Refactoring: Improving the Design of Existing Code*. Addison-Wesley, 1999.

Grand, Mark. *Patterns in Java*. John Wiley and Sons, 1998.

Harold, Elliotte Rusty. *JAVA IO*. O'Reilly, 1999.

Harold, Elliotte Rusty, and W. Scott Means. *XML in a Nutshell: A Desktop Quick Reference*. O'Reilly, 2001.

Horton, Ivor. *Beginning Java 2*. Wrox, 1999.

Jacobson, Ivar, Grady Booch, and James Rumbaugh. *The Unified Software Development Process*. Addison-Wesley, 1999.

Linthicum, David S. *Enterprise Application Integration*. Addison-Wesley, 1999.

———. *Guide to Client/Server and Intranet Development*. Wiley Computer Publishing, 1997.

Monson-Haefel, Richard. *Enterprise Java Beans*. O'Reilly, 2001.

Nichols, Randall K., Daniel J. Ryan, and Julie J. C. H. Ryan. *Defending Your Digital Assets Against Hackers, Crackers, Spies, and Thieves*. McGraw-Hill Professional Publishing, 2000.

Rechtin, Eberhardt, and Mark W. Maier. *The Art of Systems Architecting*. CRC Press, 1997.

Rumbaugh, James, Ivar Jacobson, and Grady Booch. *The Unified Modeling Language Reference Manual*. Addison-Wesley, 1998.

Yee, Andre, and Atul Apte. *Integrating Your e-Business Enterprise*. Sams, 2001.

## Resources on the Web

eAI Journal: http://www.eaijournal.com

EJB Specifications: http://java.sun.com/products/ejb

Integration Portal: http://www.ebizq.net

IBM Developer Works: http://www-106.ibm.com/developerworks

IBM's XML Zone: http://www-106.ibm.com/developerworks/xml

J2EE Tutorial: (online): http://java.sun.com/j2ee/tutorial/1_3-fcs/index.html

J2EE Tutorial (downloadable):
http://developer.java.sun.com/developer/earlyAccess/j2ee/tutorial.html

JCA Specifications: http://java.sun.com/j2ee/connector

Object Management Group: http://www.omg.org

TogetherSoft: http://www.togethersoft.com

UDDI: http://www.uddi.org

W3C: http://www.w3c.org

W3C Recommendations: http://www.w3.org/TR/#Recommendations

Workflow Management Coalition: http://www.wfmc.org

XML 1.0 (Second Edition): http://www.w3.org/TR/REC-xml

# Index

## Symbols

## A

# J - K

# T

# X - Y - Z

# Other Related Titles

# Hey, you've got enough worries.

## Don't let IT training be one of them.

Get on the fast track to IT training at InformIT,
your total Information Technology training network.

 | **www.informit.com** | **SAMS**

■ Hundreds of timely articles on dozens of topics ■ Discounts on IT books from all our publishing partners, including Sams Publishing ■ Free, unabridged books from the InformIT Free Library ■ "Expert Q&A"—our live, online chat with IT experts ■ Faster, easier certification and training from our Web- or classroom-based training programs ■ Current IT news ■ Software downloads ■ Career-enhancing resources